The European Community External Cooperation Programmes

Policies, Management and Distribution

Aidan Cox
Jenny Chapman

Overseas Development Institute
London
1999

The authors accept sole responsibility for this book, drawn up on behalf of the Commission of the European Communities. This book does not necessarily reflect the views of the Commission.

Published by the European Commission
Rue de la Loi 200, B-1049 Brussels, Belgium

Top and middle cover photos © Panos Pictures, bottom cover photo owned by the Information and Communication Unit, DG Development, European Commission.

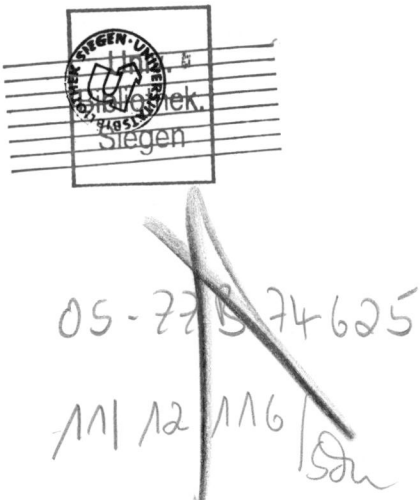

A great deal of additional information on the European Union is available on the Internet. It can be accessed through the Europa server (http://europa.eu.int).

Cataloguing data can be found at the end of this publication.

Luxembourg: Office for Official Publications of the European Communities, 2000

ISBN 92-828-8666-2

© European Communities, 2000
Reproduction is authorised provided the source is acknowledged.

Printed in Belgium

Contents

Acknowledgements ix
Preface x
Acronyms xii
Executive Summary... xiii

Chapter 1: The Nature of the European Community External Cooperation Programmes 1

    EC External Cooperation Today.. 1

    Main Trends in Size and Distribution 2

    The Political Context 5

    Evolution of the Main EC Cooperation Programmes................................... 9
        Cooperation with the ACP Countries 9
        Cooperation with the Mediterranean Countries................................. 9
        Cooperation with Asia and Latin America 10
        Cooperation with Central and Eastern European Countries............. 11
        Cooperation with the New Independent States................................ 12
        EC Support for Regional Economic Integration 13

    Sources of EC Cooperation.. 14

    Forms of EC Cooperation 16
        Official Development Assistance and Official Aid 16
        EC External Cooperation in Loan Form 17

    The Management of EC External Cooperation 19
        Management Structure... 19
        Staffing 20
        Administrative Costs... 22
        Decision-making... 22
        Project Design, Appraisal and Evaluation 26

Chapter 2: How is EC External Cooperation Spent? 27

    Categorising EC External Cooperation 27

    Overview of the Main Instruments and Sectors of EC Cooperation......... 29

    EC External Cooperation through Instruments 32
        Programme Aid 32
        Food Aid 33
        Humanitarian Assistance.. 34
        Aid to NGO's... 37

    Project Aid... 39
        Natural Resources Productive Sector 40
        Other Productive Sectors 42

Economic Infrastructure and Services	43
Social infrastructure and Services	44
Cross-cutting Issues	45

Loans 48

Chapter 3: EC External Cooperation with African, Caribbean and Pacific Countries 49

Trends and Distribution of EC External Cooperation with the ACP Countries 49

Recipients of EC Cooperation with the ACP..51

Sectoral Distribution of EC Cooperation the ACP..52

Sources of EC Cooperation with the ACP...54

The European Development Fund 55
    Policies and Objectives of the Lomé Convention...55
    Financial and Technical Cooperation 57
    Trade Cooperation 58
    Mid-term Review of Lomé IV 59
    Post Lomé Negotiations 59

Financial and Technical Cooperation Instruments 61
    Support for Structural Adjustment 61
    Stabex 62
    Sysmin 63
    Humanitarian Aid and Aid for Refugees 64
    Food Aid 65
    Aid to NGOs 65
    Project Aid by sub-region 65
    Cross-cutting issues 68

Risk Capital and Loans from the EIB's Own Resources 69

Assistance to South Africa...71

Chapter 4: EC External Cooperation with the Mediterranean and Middle East................73

Trends and Distribution 73

Recipients of EC Cooperation with the Mediterranean 74

Sectoral Distribution of EC Cooperation with the Mediterranean 75

Sources of EC Cooperation with the Mediterranean 79
    Grants...79
    Loans..80

Policy and Objectives..80
    Evolution of EC Cooperation with the Med and Middle East 80
    Euro-Mediterranean Partnership and the Barcelona Conference..........................82
    The MEDA Budget Line...83
    Trade Cooperation 84

Chapter 5: EC External Cooperation with Asia and Latin America...................................87

Trends and Distribution 87

Recipients of EC Cooperation with Asia and Latin America................................88

Sectoral Distribution of EC Cooperation with Asia and
Latin America 90

Loans 93

Policy and Objectives 96
Evolution of EC Cooperation with Asia and Latin America 96

Cooperation Instruments 97
Programme Aid 97
Project Aid 98
Cross-cutting issues 99
Trade Cooperation 100

Chapter 6:   EC External Cooperation with Central and Eastern Europe 101

Trends and Distribution of EC Cooperation with the CEECs 101

Recipients of EC Cooperation with the CEECs 101

EC Cooperation with the CEECs 102

ion with the CEECs 106

.... 107
.... 107
are, ISPA and SAPARD 108

.... 109

ation with the New Independent States 111

of EC Cooperation with the NIS 111

ation with the NIS 112

EC Cooperation the NIS 112

Sources of EC Cooperation with the NIS 114

Policy and Objectives 116

Cooperation Instruments 117

Chapter 8:   A Decade of EC External Cooperation in a Global Context 119

Global Trends 119

EC External Cooperation Relative to Other Major Donors 121

The European Community as a Multilateral Donor 121

The Main Recipients of OECD Aid 124

Recipients of EC External Cooperation by Level of Income 125

Sectoral Distribution of EC and Other OECD ODA 126

Appendices

1. The Major Recipients of EC External Cooperation 129
2. Distribution of EC External Cooperation by DAC Region, 1970–97 133
3. EC Cooperation by DAC Region 1986–98 134
4. Recipients of EC External Cooperation Grouped by EC Region and by Level of Income 135
5. Major European Community External Cooperation Budget lines 136

List of Tables, Figures and Boxes

Figures

1.1	OECD Aid in 1997	1
1.2	Distribution EC External Cooperation by DAC Region	2
1.3	Regional Distribution of EC External Cooperation	6
1.4	Sources of EC External Cooperation	14
2.1	Main Instruments of EC External Cooperation	29
2.2	Sectoral Allocation of EC Cooperation to all Regions	30
2.3	Sectoral Allocation of Loans managed by the EIB	48
3.1	Regional Distribution of EC Cooperation with the ACP	50
3.2	Sectoral Distribution of EC Cooperation with the ACP	54
3.3	Trend in Sources of EC Cooperation with the ACP	55
3.4	Programme Aid	63
3.5	EIB-managed Loans from 'Own Resources' and Risk Capital to ACP Countries	70
3.6	Sectoral Allocation of EC Aid to South Africa	72
4.1	Regional Distribution of EC Cooperation with the Med & Mid East	73
4.2	Sectoral Allocation of allocable EC Cooperation with Med & Mid East	76
4.3	EIB-managed Loans from Own Resources & Risk Capital to Med & Mid East	79
5.1	EC Cooperation with Asia and Latin America	87
5.2	Sectoral Allocation of allocable EC Cooperation with Asia	92
5.3	Sectoral Allocation of allocable EC Cooperation with Latin America	92
6.1	EC Cooperation with the CEECs	101
6.2	Sectoral Allocation of EC Cooperation with the CEECs	106
7.1	EC Cooperation with the NIS	111
7.2	Sectoral Allocation of EC Cooperation with the NIS	115
8.1	Total Aid by Donor	120
8.2	Average Aid	122
8.3	Share of Total OECD Aid	122
8.4	Share of Total Multilateral ODA	123
8.5	Regional Distribution of Aid	124
8.6	Total OECD ODA and EC ODA by Sector	127

Tables

1.1	Major Recipients of EC External Cooperation	3
1.2	Regional Distribution of EC External Cooperation	4
1.3	EU Member States' Shares of Budget Aid and EDF	15
1.4	Regional Distribution of Official Development Assistance and Official Aid	16
1.5	Concessional Loans to Developing Countries managed by the European Investment Bank	17
1.6	Macro-financial Assistance to Third Countries	18
1.7	Staffing of the European Community External Cooperation Programmes	21
1.8	Comparative Analysis of External Relations Group: financial responsibilities and staffing levels	23
2.1	Sectoral Allocation of all EC Cooperation	31
2.2	Main Recipients of Developmental Food Aid	35
2.3	Sources of Humanitarian Assistance	36
2.4	Regional & Country Distribution of EC Humanitarian Aid	38
2.5	ECIP Facilities	42
3.1	Regional Distribution of EC External Cooperation with the ACP	51
3.2	Top 15 Recipients of EC Cooperation – ACP	52
3.3	Sectoral Allocation of EC Cooperation with the ACP	53
3.4	Evolution of the EDF and EIB Own Resources	56
3.5	EIB-managed Loans from 'Own Resources' and Risk Capital (from the EDF) to the ACP	70
4.1	Regional Distribution of EC Cooperation with the Med & Middle East	74
4.2	Top 10 Recipients of EC Cooperation – Med & Mid East	75
4.3	Sectoral Allocation of EC Cooperation with Med & Mid East	77
4.4	Association and Cooperation Agreements between EC and Mediterranean Countries	81
4.5	Progress of Negotiations on Euro-Mediterranean Association Agreements	84
5.1	Regional Distribution of EC Cooperation with Asia and Latin America	88
5.2	Top 10 Recipients of EC Cooperation – Asia & Latin America	89
5.3	Sectoral Distribution of EC Cooperation with Asia	94
5.4	Sectoral Distribution of EC Cooperation with Latin America	95
6.1	Top 10 Recipients of EC Cooperation with the CEECs	102
6.2	Regional Distribution of EC Cooperation with CEECs	102
6.3	Sectoral Allocation of Phare Programme	103
6.4	Sectoral Allocation of EC Cooperation with CEECs	104
6.5	Sources of EC Cooperation with the CEECs	107
7.1	Regional Distribution of EC Cooperation with the NIS	112
7.2	Top 10 Recipients of EC Cooperation with the NIS	112
7.3	Sectoral Allocation of EC Cooperation with the NIS	114
7.4	Sources of EC External Cooperation with the NIS	115
8.1	Ranking of Major Donors	121
8.2	Proportion of Total Multilateral ODA	123
8.3	Regional Distribution of Aid by Major Donors	125
8.4	Share of Bilateral OECD and EC aid to recipients by Level of Income	126
8.5	Total OECD ODA and EC ODA by Sector	127

Boxes

1.1	The Maastricht Treaty and External Cooperation	8
1.2	The Essen Strategy	12
1.3	The Edinburgh Summit	15
1.4	European Legislation	24
1.5	The Amsterdam Treaty and External Cooperation	24
1.6	Deconcentration and Decentralisation in the Phare Programme	25
2.1	Objectives of Food Aid and Operations in Support of Food Security	33
2.2	European Community Humanitarian Office (ECHO)	36
2.3	NGO co-financing	39
2.4	European Community Investment Partners Scheme (ECIP)	42
2.5	Micro-finance	43
2.6	HIV/AIDS	44
2.7	Decentralised cooperation	46
3.1	Institutional Framework of Lomé Convention	55
3.2	EC–ACP Regional Cooperation	57
3.3	The Centre for the Development of Industry (CDI)	59
3.4	Counterpart Funds Generated by Structural Adjustment Assistance	62
4.1	The MEDA Programme	76
4.2	MEDA-Democracy	82
4.3	Relaunch of Decentralised cooperation programmes in the Mediterranean	83
5.1	EC–Latin America Regional Cooperation	96
5.2	AL-invest	98
5.3	Energy aid in Latin America (ALURE)	99
6.1	Special Preparatory Programme	108
6.2	Twinning	109
7.1	Regional Transport Programmes	117
7.2	Tempus	118

Acknowledgements

This edition builds on the original inventory, *Understanding European Community Aid* by Aidan Cox and Antonique Koning, with Adrian Hewitt, John Howell and Ana Marr.[1] The authors of the current addition recognise the essential role played by those responsible for the original edition, without which it would have been impossible to complete *The European Community's External Cooperation Programmes*.

The authors would like to express thanks to the many individuals who have made it possible to write this book. We have greatly valued the encouragement and advice received from Mr Sean Doyle and Mr Pieter van Steekelenburg of the Evaluation Unit of the SCR. Many others within the SCR have also assisted us, especially Mr Bruno Kruijer, who gave very generously of his time, and Mr Roland Fox.

In DG Development Mr Cyril Ludwigczak and Ms Jean-Colette Plunkett were particularly helpful, while Mr Quince, Mr Mikos, Mr Strom and Mr Ruyssen also provided us with important information. In the External Relations DG and the Enlargement Service we received the cooperation of many individuals, especially Ms Bagge, Ms Barre, Ms Lefèvre and Ms Notarangelo. Mr Roe supplied information on the European Community Investment Partners Scheme, Mr Mulcahy helped us with data on EC aid flows managed by the European Investment Bank. Mr Barfod and Mr Billing assisted us with information on the policies and aid managed by ECHO and Mr Mestre-Sanchez and Mr Pierre Baut provided information on Community macro-financial assistance. Data on commitments and sectors was also supplied by Ms Bourdy, Mr Cladakis, Ms Dias, Ms Garcia, Ms Hebberecht, Mr Johanen, Mr Padilla, Mr Pangratis, Ms Perez, and Mr Van der Linden, among others. Madame Chadel has facilitated the publication process, while Mr Leysen provided the photograph for the front cover.

Very many officials gave generously of their time in interview. Those not already mentioned include Mr Muller, Mr Ponette, Mr Michael Green, Mr Bataller, Mr Rashbash, Mr John Winter, among others. We benefited greatly from the constructive and helpful comments received on the first draft from these individuals and many others.

In preparing Chapter 8 on the global context we received valuable guidance and information from Mr Simon Scott, Mr Rudolphe Petras and Ms Aimée Nicols of the Development Cooperation Directorate of the OECD.

Finally, we are especially grateful for the dedicated support of staff here at ODI, especially Ms Lucy Morris, whose professionalism and patience knew no limits. Dr Henri-Bernard Solignac Lecomte lent his expertise on Community trade and development policies to great effect. Mr Adrian Hewitt, who contributed to the original edition, again provided insightful comments and suggestions for improvement. Ms Clare Lockhart and Ms Clare Ireland were invaluable members of the ODI team, and conducted extensive research on Community policy and aid flows. Mr Anand Madhvani refined the original database and eased our lives considerably. Dr Peter Gee and Ms Pippa Leask assisted the authors with preparing the document to publication standard, while Mr Daniel Demie provided effective information technology support.

Aidan Cox
Jenny Chapman
ODI, London, 21 December, 1999

---

1 Aidan Cox and Antonique Koning, 1997, Understanding European Community Aid: Aid Policies, Management and Distribution Explained. Overseas Development Institute/European Commission: London.

Preface

This revised inventory of European Community external cooperation programmes is published at a time when the overall framework for EC external cooperation is being refocused and clarified. The Commission opened up to broad debate its current and future cooperation policies by publishing a Green Paper on future EU-ACP relations in November 1996. EU policy-makers actively sought empirically-based findings and advice from all quarters of 'civil society' – business, academia, the press and media, non-governmental organisations, back-bench politicians and others – with a stress on reforming European policies so that they would prove more effective in addressing development needs in a rapidly changing world.

This process has continued through the broader process of the ongoing reform of European external cooperation and its associated administration. This publication is part of the research base designed to inform this process of reform. Its origins lie in the decision, in June 1995, of the EU Council of Development Ministers to launch a major evaluation of European Community development aid. ODI was invited to establish the detailed inventory of the entire (and often disparate) external cooperation programme. The inventory provided a baseline for the evaluations of EC aid to the Africa, Caribbean, and Pacific countries (ACP), Asia and Latin America (ALA), and the Mediterranean and Middle East (MED) which have recently been carried out. This second edition brings the original book up-to-date, and is designed to serve as a public information document in its own right.

The recent evaluations of European Community external cooperation underlined that:

- the Commission's aid system is too complex and fragmented in terms of objectives, instruments, procedures and institutional mechanisms;
- the Commission has insufficient human resources to handle the huge and growing volume of external cooperation managed.

With the recent reorganisation of external relations' responsibilities under the new Commission there is now one single external cooperation. This presents an opportunity to address past difficulties, to ensure consistency in the implementation of external cooperation policy, and to tackle coherence issues. The latter include promoting increased coherence between Community external cooperation policy on the one hand, and other Community policies on the other (eg, foreign policy (CFSP), trade policy, agricultural policy, environmental policy). The new Commission has stated its determination to ensure that European Community aid is centred on poverty reduction, and that cooperation is managed with increased focus and effectiveness.

This publication aims to provide an accurate and comprehensive information base upon to inform the ongoing process of reform. Both this and the original edition were funded by the Evaluation Unit of the Common Service for External Relations of the European Commission. It follows terms of reference drawn up by the Heads of Evaluation Services of the Commission and the Member States. The book describes the institutions, policies and legal basis of EC aid, together with a detailed inventory which analyses all EC aid flows on a sectoral as well as a geographical basis.

The term 'European Community external cooperation' refers to that portion of European Union aid that is managed by the European Commission and the European Investment Bank, as distinct from the bilateral aid programmes of the individual Member States. It comprises all concessional public flows to developing countries (Official Development Assistance) and to the transitional economies of Central and Eastern Europe and the New Independent States (Official Aid).

'European Community aid' has existed since the European Economic Community was established in 1957. All six original Member States accepted that measures to develop internal economic integration should be reinforced by a mechanism – initially the European Development Fund (EDF)

– for pooling resources for external assistance, to be managed by the European Commission, while retaining their nationally managed aid programmes. This process of pooling resources has now developed to a point where the European Community's external cooperation programme (both to developing countries and transitional economies) is among the five leading donor programmes in its own right. Aid from the European Union, both from the Member States individually and the portion managed by the European Commission, now accounts for 55% of total world aid.

It has not been a process without controversy, however. The growth in EC aid has been characterised by frequent change, largely associated with the acquisition of new regional commitments, the establishment of new aid instruments and the need to reorganise Commission services in response to shifts in priorities. In the view of its detractors, EC aid has become too disaggregated and too uncoordinated to have the impact on development that it should. To those more sympathetic to EC aid, its growth and diversification are a reflection of the vitality and adaptability of the European Union itself.

Europe's external cooperation policies have always been broad and multifaceted, going well beyond just the supply of financial aid. External trading relationships in coal, steel, agriculture and manufactures were determined from the start at European level. The Community began by giving special trade preferences to selected countries, later offering generalised preferences to the other developing countries as well. Cooperation with developing countries has, moreover, usually been offered as part of a package, often with aid, trade, cultural and political elements.

Our analysis concentrates upon the *aid* policies, institutions and, in expenditure terms, performance of the European Community external cooperation programmes. All the Community's external cooperation programmes are included, covering the ACP states, the Mediterranean and Middle East, Asia and Latin America and the CEECs and NIS. The first chapter provides an overview of the evolution of EC external cooperation, describing the legal and political basis for current assistance programmes, and indicating how these are managed and how decisions are taken on the allocation of funds provided by the Member States. In the second chapter, there is an account of EC external cooperation expenditure which provides a framework for comparing – across regions and countries – different categories of aid delivery and different sectors receiving aid. In the following five chapters, EC external cooperation is described in more detail, through both statistical and institutional analysis, for each of the main recipient 'regions'.

The final chapter places Community aid in a global context, comparing the regional spread and sectoral emphasis of EC external cooperation with those of the major OECD donors. Past debates on European Community aid have often been ill-informed and diminished by an inadequate empirical base of information. The debate is already better focused and clearer, and this publication seeks to contribute further towards this.

Aidan Cox
ODI, London
21 December, 1999

Acronyms

ACP	Africa, Caribbean and the Pacific
ALA	Asia and Latin America
CAP	Common Agricultural Policy
CEECs	Central and Eastern European Countries
CFSP	Common Foreign and Security Policy
DAC	Development Assistance Committee of the OECD
DG	Directorate General
DG IA, IB	External Relations DG
DG II	Economic and Financial Affairs DG
DG VIII	Development DG
EAGGF	European Agricultural Guidance and Guarantee Fund
EC	European Community
ECIP	European Community Investment Programme
ECHO	European Community Humanitarian Office
EDF	European Development Fund
EEC	European Economic Community
EIB	European Investment Bank
EU	European Union
euro	European currency unit, worth approximately US$1.1 (1997)
GATT	General Agreement on Trade and Tariffs
GSP	Generalised System of Preferences
HIPC	Debt initiative for Heavily indebted poor countries
IDA	International Development Association
IRDP	Integrated rural development project
LDCs	Less developed countries
LICs	Low Income Countries
LLDCs	Least developed countries
MED	Mediterranean programme
MFN	Most favoured nation
NGO	Non-governmental organisation
NIP	National Indicative Programme
NIS	New Independent States (of the Former Soviet Union)
OCTs	Overseas Countries and Territories
ODA	Official Development Assistance
OA	Official Aid (to DAC Part II countries; mainly CEECs and NIS)
ODI	Overseas Development Institute
OECD	Organisation for Economic Cooperation and Development
OPEC	Organisation of Petroleum Exporting Countries
PCA	Partnership and Cooperation Agreement (Tacis)
Phare	EC initiative for the CEECs
PNG	Papua New Guinea
RIP	Regional Indicative Programme
Tacis	EC initiative for the New Independent States and Mongolia
SCR	Common Service for External Relations
SME	Small and medium enterprise
Stabex	System for the stabilisation of export earnings from agricultural commodities system
Sysmin	Special financing facility for the mining sector (under the Lomé Convention)
WTO	World Trade Organisation

Executive Summary

The Nature of EC External Cooperation (Chapter 1)

The European Community (EC), as a distinct entity apart from the bilateral aid programmes of the individual Member States, has become the *world's fifth largest aid donor* in the 1990s, providing in 1997 $6.6 billion or 12.2% of all aid disbursed by the OECD countries. This reflects the rapid growth of the Community's aid programme over the past three decades, when it increased steeply in real terms and almost quadrupled as a proportion of total OECD aid. Indeed, taken together European Community and European Union Member States' aid accounted for well over half (55.3%) of world aid in 1997.

Since the 1970s, EC aid has changed not only in volume but also in terms of its regional composition. Currently, EC aid to *sub-Saharan Africa* accounts for aid disbursements of $2.0bn, considerably larger than to any other region. World aid volumes to the region have declined significantly at the end of the 1990s, although EC aid increased over the decade. Nevertheless the region's share of total allocable EC aid has fallen far more sharply, averaging 30% for 1996-97, down from over 70% at the beginning of the 1970s and 60% a decade later. In contrast, the share to a new group of beneficiaries, the *Central and East European Countries (CEECs)* and the *New Independent States (NIS)*, increased rapidly in the 1990s, accounting for almost a fifth of all EC aid disbursements for 1996–97.

Countries in the *Middle East and Southern Europe* were the third largest beneficiaries of EC aid, averaging disbursements of almost $1bn for 1996-97 (or 14% of total EC external assistance). *Asia*, has the fourth largest programme, with over $800m (or 12% of total assistance), representing a sharp decline from a peak of 21% of total aid for 1980-81. *Latin America* is the next largest programme, receiving close to $700m (or 10%), then *Africa north of the Sahara* with nearly $400m (6%) and finally *Oceania* with some $70m (1%).

The changing *regional composition* of European Community aid reflects to a large degree the *political basis for European aid-giving*. The leading recipients in the early 1970s, after India and Bangladesh (major recipients of food aid), were African and francophone, in line with the preponderance of former French and Belgian colonies among the 'associated countries'. More recently, the Russian Federation and the countries of Central and Eastern Europe have loomed large, along with Mediterranean and Middle East countries, Africa north of the Sahara and South Africa (see Chapter 1, Table 1.1). This shift followed the end of the Cold War, democratic elections in South Africa and movements towards peace in the Middle East, as well as conflict in the states of former Yugoslavia.

The *main sources of EC aid* for the 1996–98 period were the *EC Budget*, funding some three-quarters of all European Community external assistance, and the *European Development Fund (EDF)*, which provided almost a fifth of total commitments. The remainder, some 7%, was financed from the 'own resources' of the European Investment Bank (EIB). The relative weight of the EDF has fallen from an average of 57% for 1986–88, when the Budget providing only 36%, and the EIB a further 7%. This shift is largely as a result of the initiatives for the CEECs (Phare) and the New Independent States (Tacis) in the 1990s. The share of EIB resources remained constant over the two time periods.

The vast majority (84%) of EC aid goes to the developing countries and qualifies as *Official Development Assistance (ODA)*. The remaining 16% of commitments has gone to the transitional economies of Central and Eastern Europe and the New Independent States, and is therefore classed as Official Aid (OA). Between 1986 and 1998 some 6.7 bn euro out of a total of 73.1 bn euro of EC external assistance commitments were provided as *concessional loans*. Most of these came from the *European Investment Bank's (EIB) own resources*, with some financed from the EDF, and a small remainder from the EC Budget. This means that over 90% of EC aid, as defined in this exercise, was provided in *grant* form.

EC aid is managed by the European Commission and the EIB. The Commission has three Directorates General with geographical responsibilities for administering European Community external cooperation. In addition, a separate Humanitarian Office (ECHO) deals with humanitarian assistance, and the Common Service (SCR) is responsible for technical, financial and legal aspects of Community external cooperation programmes. Several other Directorates General have smaller roles with respect to external cooperation. The *management of Community* aid is described in detail in Chapter 1, including an examination of staffing levels, together with an analysis of the fora for *decision-making*.

Categorising EC Aid (Chapter 2)

Prior to the publication of *Understanding European Community Aid* in 1997 by the European Commission and ODI, the inadequate or inconsistent categorisation of EC aid did not allow a clear, unified presentation of all the development purposes to which Community aid has been put. The current study, funded by the Evaluation Unit of the Common Service, built on this. It again involved gathering data at a highly disaggregated level and recategorising it according to a standard sectoral classification, and provides comprehensive information on the development purpose of 90% of all EC external cooperation. The system is based on the OECD Development Assistance Committee (DAC) categories.

Five main instruments have been identified, with the fifth – Project Aid – subdivided into six sectors, making a total of 11 distinct sectors:

1. **Programme Aid** (support to structural adjustment, Stabex, Sysmin)
2. **Food aid (developmental)**
3. **Humanitarian Aid**
4. **Aid to NGOs**
5. **Project Aid**
    5.1 Natural Resources Productive Sectors *(agriculture, forestry, fisheries)*
    5.2 Other Productive Sectors *(industry, mining & construction, trade, tourism, investment promotion)*
    5.3 Economic Infrastructure & Services *(transport & communications, energy, banking & business)*
    5.4 Social Infrastructure & Services *(education, health & population, water, other)*
    5.5 Governance & Civil Society
    5.6 Multi-sector/Crosscutting *(environment, women in development, rural development, other)*
6. **Unallocable**

Overview of the Main Instruments and Sectors of EC Aid

Aid to the first four instruments declined significantly as a share of total allocable aid from 46% of total allocable aid for 1986-90, to 43% for 1991-95, and 36% for 1996-98. Project aid, in contrast, increased from 54% of total aid for 1986-90 to 64% for 1996-98.

Overall, the volume of aid through some instruments increased much faster than others, with the result that some instruments increased their share of total aid at the expense of others between the 1986–90, 1991–95 and 1996-98 periods:

- *humanitarian aid* increased enormously, more than doubling as a proportion of total allocable aid to 13% from 1986-90 and again to 14% for 1996-98, partly due to the creation of ECHO and the crises in former Yugoslavia and Rwanda/Burundi;

- *programme aid* declined from 16% of total allocable aid in 1986-90, to 13% (1991-95), and then to 10% (1996-98), due largely to a fall in Stabex, since support to structural adjustment and Sysmin maintained their shares;

- *food aid* declined sharply as a proportion of the total allocable aid, from 21%, to 14% and then to 8%;

- *aid to NGOs* doubled in volume between 1986-90 and 1991-91, keeping pace with the growth in the overall programme and thereby maintaining a constant 2.5% share. It subsequently rose to 3.1% of total allocable aid for 1996-98;

- trends in *project aid* reveal: one group of sectors increased in absolute terms during the three time periods (1989-90, 1991-95 and 1996-98) – industry, mining and construction; tourism and investment promotion; transport and communications; banking, financial and business services; all social sectors; and governance and civil society. The second group of sectors peaked in absolute terms during the 1991-95 period, but has since fallen – agriculture, forestry and fisheries; trade; environment; and energy. The only exception is rural development which declined and then rose slightly.

EC Aid through Instruments

Programme Aid:
Support for structural adjustment is provided as balance of payments support, in kind or in foreign currency, which supports the central budget of recipient countries. Most of these concessional funds went to the ACP countries and were financed from the EDF (see Chapter 3), while a small amount of structural adjustment support has been allocated to Mediterranean countries from the EC budget since 1992.

The category 'programme aid' also includes two distinct commodity compensation schemes – Stabex and Sysmin – for agricultural exports and the mining sector. These are financed from EDF contributions to ACP countries, and are discussed in detail in Chapter 3 (between 1987 and 1991 a 'Stabex-type' facility was also provided to a few non-ACP countries).

Between 1986 and 1998, almost 8.6 bn euro has been committed to programme aid, making this the fourth largest sector after economic infrastructure, food aid and social infrastructure and services. More than half of this (4.4 bn euro) was support for Structural Adjustment, with 41% (3.5 bn euro) through Stabex, and only 0.8% of total allocable aid through Sysmin.

Food Aid:
Food aid was the first instrument to be introduced outside the framework of existing cooperation agreements (introduced in 1967). It was originally managed according to the rules of the Common Agricultural Policy (CAP), but over the years food aid policy was gradually reformed (in 1982, 1986, 1987 and 1996), delinking it from the CAP and integrating it more firmly into

Community development policy. DG Development is responsible for the planning and commitment of food aid, with the Common Service for External Relations responsible, with the Agriculture DG, for procurement and delivery.

- Food aid formed the second largest area of EC aid over the decade 1986–98 (after economic infrastructure and services); commitments totalled 9.1 m euro.

- Food aid has traditionally represented a large proportion of EC aid, accounting for as much as 40 to 50% of EC Budget aid in the late 1980s.

- Recently its share of total aid has declined to around 7% of total allocable aid, partly as more of the budget line has become devoted to food security projects which are not classified under food aid.

- From 1996 the food aid instrument has focused on a small number of priority countries, with very high levels of food insecurity, or very low income, or those in crisis.

Humanitarian Assistance:

European Community humanitarian assistance encompasses a broad range of actions, from providing emergency relief to victims of natural disasters and wars, to disaster prevention and preparedness, to assisting refugees, or to carrying out short-term rehabilitation and reconstruction work. Longer-term rehabilitation and reconstruction is classified, and managed, as part of 'normal' aid via projects, and often through NGOs.

Humanitarian aid commitments totalled 7.6 bn euro for the 1986–98 period, making it the fifth largest sector, accounting for 10.4% of total commitments. The Commission created the European Community Humanitarian Office (ECHO) in 1992, and from 1993 55%, or 3.2 bn euro, of all EC humanitarian aid has been financed through ECHO's budget lines. The EDF has provided over 1.1 bn euro to the ACP countries since 1986, while other budget lines have financed over 3.3 bn euro in the same period. During the 1986–98 period:

- the largest proportion of humanitarian assistance went to Central and Eastern Europe (2.6 bn euro), largely to the states of former Yugoslavia; ACP countries received 2.2 bn euro;

- the largest recipient countries were: the states of former Yugoslavia (which together received 2.2 bn euro between 1992 and 1998); Palestinian Administrative Areas (535 m euro); Rwanda/Burundi (259 m euro); Angola (255 m euro); Afghanistan (244 m euro) and Sudan (207 m euro);

- EC aid for rehabilitation doubled in 1994 and tripled in 1995 (to 300 m euro), following the establishment of the Special Initiative for Africa (covering the Horn and Southern Africa) and has since stabilised at about this level.

Aid to NGOs:

EC aid supports the work of NGOs both by 'contracting' NGOs to provide particular services and through its co-financing scheme (see Box 2.3). EC aid *through* NGOs, where the NGO is contracted to implement Commission-designed projects and programmes, is accounted for under the total of aid to that particular sector (eg agriculture, or humanitarian aid), and cannot currently be quantified separately.

The NGO co-financing scheme provides funds up to a maximum of 500 000 euro for any one project for a maximum of five years, usually up to 50% of the total project cost.

- EC aid to NGOs has increased significantly in recent years, doubling in the 1990s to reach an annual average of about 200 m euro from 1995 onwards, though its share of total aid remains broadly constant (about 2.5%).

- Most aid to NGOs is through the NGO co-financing scheme, which dates back to 1976, and went mainly to the ACP and Latin American countries.

- Central and Eastern European countries received 100 m euro through Phare, while the New Independent States have as yet received very little.
- The largest recipients over the 1986-98 period were Brazil (93 m euro), India (75 m euro), Chile (73 m euro), Peru, Bolivia and Nicaragua (all about 50 m euro), followed by Ethiopia (40 m euro) and Kenya (34m euro).

Project Aid

The distinction between the four instruments and project aid is an imperfect one, since aid through instruments such as structural adjustment, Stabex, Sysmin, NGOs or humanitarian aid may be designed to assist the social and economic infrastructure sectors, natural resources or governance and civil society, among others. Of particular importance is the way in which counterpart funds generated by structural adjustment assistance are used to support the social sectors (health and education in particular) – see Chapter 3, Box 3.4.

Natural Resources Productive Sector:

- EC support to the ***rural development and agriculture*** sectors has traditionally been an important focus of EC aid, accounting for over one-fifth of all aid in the 1980s, but this fell to only 6% for 1991-95, and 3.7% for 1996-98.

- EC support to *forestry* has increased in the 1990s as international concern for tropical forests has grown. Aid increased from an annual average of 12 m euro for 1986-90 to nearly 70 m euro in the 1990s.

- No clear definition exists of ***environment*** projects, but activities funded with environmental conservation as their specific aim saw annual average commitments increase from under 50 m euro for 1986-90 to over 160 m euro for 1991-98, representing an increase from 1.6% of total aid to 2.7% for 1991-95 and 2.4% for 1996-98. In the 1990-98 period most went to the CEECs (40%), followed by the Mediterranean and Middle East (290 m euro or 20%), followed by Asia (240 m euro) and the ACP (150 m euro).

- EC aid to the *fisheries* sector promoted efforts towards greater policy coherence, improved enforcement of regulations, private sector competitiveness, research, and conservation. Aid amounted to over 230 m euro between 1986 and 1998.

Other Productive Sectors:

This encompasses a wide range of activities including industry, mining, construction, trade policy and administration, tourism policy and management and investment promotion.

- The largest sub-sector by far is ***industry, mining and construction***, for which commitments totalled 3.3 bn euro, or nearly 80% of all aid to the sector.

- Most industry, mining and construction aid went to ***ACP countries***, principally Mauritania (185 m euro) and Nigeria (170 m euro), followed by Zambia, Papua New Guinea and Mali, all of which received over 100 m euro. However, ***Egypt*** was the largest recipient overall, benefiting from commitments of 580 m euro, (over 300 m euro were loans from the EIB).

- EC aid for ***investment promotion*** represented the fastest growing subsector, mainly due to the development and success of the European Community Investment Partners *(ECIP)* scheme.

Economic Infrastructure and Services:

With activities ranging from transport and communications, to energy, banking and business services, economic infrastructure and services formed the largest sector of EC aid, with commitments totalling over 8 bn euro, accounting for nearly 17% of total EC aid commitments.

- Aid for economic infrastructure and services was heavily **concentrated (87%) in three regions**: the ACP (45%), CEECs (23%) and the NIS (15%).
- ACP countries received two-thirds of all **transport and communications** aid, and the CEECs received over half of all aid to the banking, financial and business services subsector reflecting the concentration of the Phare programme in this area.
- Nearly half of all **energy** aid went to the ACP and a third to the NIS, due in part to a concentration on nuclear safety in the case of the NIS.

Social Infrastructure and Services:

Commitments to education (3.3 bn euro, and to health and population (1.9 bn euro), accounted for almost 60% of all aid to this sector. In the 1990s Community policies on the health and population sub-sector emphasised the need for greater coordination between Community and Member State aid, and developed strategies for action in areas such as drugs policy and HIV/AIDS. EC aid policy on education and training was clarified in a Council Resolution in 1994 which focused on increasing access to education, reducing the bias against the education of girls and improving quality as the priority areas.

- Aid to **health and population** grew rapidly from an annual average of 35 m euro for 1986-90, to an annual average of 170 m euro for 1991-95, and again to over 270 m euro for 1996-98.
- The **ACP region** received about a third of the 1.9 bn commitments to health and population
- Between 1991 and 1995 the ACP also benefited from an allocation of 370 m euro of **counterpart funds** to health and population generated by structural adjustment financing over the period.
- 30% of aid to the education sector when to the CEECs (Poland being the largest recipient); the ACP received 25%.
- The former Soviet Union and the Russian Federation alone received nearly a fifth of all EC aid to education (1986–95); Nigeria and Uganda were the largest ACP recipients.

Cross-cutting Issues:

- European Community aid has given increasing weight to cross-cutting issues such as governance and civil society, poverty reduction, gender, and environment in the 1990s. This is reflected in new Council Resolutions (eg on governance and human rights issues in 1999, on poverty and human development (1993 and 1996), on forestry (1999), and gender (1995 and a Common Position in 1998) – and in increased aid commitments.
- Support for governance and civil society rose from an annual average of 130 m euro a year for 1991-95 (less than 2% of total EC aid), to almost 550 m euro a year for 1996-98 (over 7%).
- Poverty reduction cannot be discretely identified as an activity, but policy has been strengthened in two Council resolutions.
- EC policy seeks to mainstream gender analysis systematically into the design and implementation of major interventions. In addition, awareness-building measures are financed from a specific budget line.
- A strategy for Community aid was set out in a 1997 Communication, addressing the importance of complementarity between Development and External Affairs DGs and the specific development research programmes of the Research DG.

Main Regional Programmes of European Community Aid

EC Aid to the African, Caribbean and Pacific States (Chapter 3)

The *71[1] African, Caribbean and Pacific states* received 30.0 bn euro between 1986 and 1998, or 43.5% of all EC aid that can be allocated geographically. In 1998 it totalled nearly 2.9 bn euro. More than three-quarters of this was provided through the European Development Fund (EDF) – a five-yearly financial allocation from the EU Member States, 16% of commitments were from the EC Budget and the remaining 7% from concessional European Investment Bank loans. The *Lomé Convention* sets out the principles and objectives of Community cooperation with the ACP. Its distinguishing characteristics include: the partnership principle; the contractual nature of the relationship; the combination of aid and trade aspects; the long-term (five-year) perspective.

- Most ACP aid (78%) went to sub-Saharan Africa; the *main beneficiaries* in 1996-98 were Ethiopia, Malawi, Zambia, Mali and Mozambique.

- The three components of the *programme aid* instrument – structural adjustment assistance, Stabex and Sysmin (the latter two are largely specific to the ACP) – make up just over a quarter of all aid to the group.

- *Stabex,* which provides compensation for losses of export earnings from non-metal commodities, has formed an important component of aid to the ACP, amounting to 3.4 bn euro. The main beneficiaries have been Côte d'Ivoire, Cameroon, Ethiopia, Sudan, Papua New Guinea, Senegal, Kenya and Uganda. The declining size of Stabex flows has resulted in many of these countries slipping down the table of major EC aid recipients.

- *Food aid* remained relatively important for the ACP countries. Ethiopia was by far the largest recipient (640 m euro), followed by Sudan, Mozambique, and Angola. *Humanitarian assistance* rose substantially in recent years due to the crisis in Rwanda and Burundi.

- *Project aid* which accounted for 58% of all EC aid to the ACP went mainly to the transport and communications sector (11%), followed by industry, mining and construction (8%), social infrastructure (7.4%), rural development (6.9%) and agriculture (5.8%).

- *Cross-cutting issues* grew in importance, with gender analysis and environment, for instance, receiving far greater weight in Lomé IV for instance, and poverty reduction being emphasised in the Commission Green paper on the future of EU-ACP relations.

- The more developed ACP countries, such as Nigeria, Zimbabwe, Kenya, Ghana, Jamaica and Papua New Guinea, benefited most from the concessional *loans managed by the EIB*, half of which went to the industry and energy sectors.

- Very broad consultations are in the process of redefining post Lomé IV EU-ACP relations on the basis of a stronger political foundation, regionalised economic partnership agreements, greater incorporation of non-state actors, and streamlined procedures.

- *South Africa*, not included in the Lomé Convention until 1997, has received EC aid from the Budget, largely through a Special Programme for Assisting the Victims of Apartheid; in 1995 this was extended to form the European Programme for Reconstruction and Development. South Africa received commitments of nearly over 950 m euro since 1986, of which over 65% was committed since 1994. This focused on education (33%) and governance and civil society (21%).

---

[1] South Africa was included in the Lomé Convention in 1997. Chapter 3 analyses aid to South Africa in a separate section.

Mediterranean and Middle East (Chapter 4)

The European Community has been committed to support its neighbouring countries in the South since the Treaty of Rome. Agreements were, however, mainly bilateral until the beginning of the 1990s, when a more regional approach was adopted (the *New Mediterranean Policy*). Following the Barcelona Declaration in 1995, the priorities for Euro-Mediterranean relationship were defined as political and security partnership (including human rights and democracy), economic and financial partnership and partnership in social, cultural and human affairs.

- Aid to the Mediterranean and Middle Eastern countries has increased from 400 m euro in 1986 to over 1300 m euro in both 1997 and 1998; most went to East and Southern Mediterranean (the Maghreb and Mashraq countries), and aid to the Palestinian Administrative Areas has also increased.

- *Main recipients* of aid in the region in 1996-98 were Egypt, Morocco, the Palestinian Administrative Areas, Algeria, Turkey and Tunisia.

- *Humanitarian assistance* and *food aid* together accounted for a 14% of all aid to the region, lower than in previous years due to a decline in the food aid instrument.

- *Structural adjustment assistance* grew from zero to over 750 m euro (1992–98 total).

- *Social infrastructure and services* (mainly through support to water and sanitation projects, and latterly education) witnessed a sharp rise in the 1990s, accounting for 22% of all aid over the 1986-98 period. Natural resources saw average annual commitments fall in the 1990s, though it still accounted for over 8% of all aid over the 1986-98 period.

- Concessional *loans* managed by the EIB accounted for over a quarter (27%) of all EC aid to the Mediterranean and Middle East. The East and Southern Mediterranean countries received almost all of this; it was concentrated particularly in the water supply, and industry, mining and construction sub-sectors.

Asia and Latin America (Chapter 5)

Whereas development cooperation between the European Community and the associated colonial and ex-colonial countries (later to become ACP countries) dates back to the Treaty of Rome in 1957, the Community's aid relationship with Asia and Latin America (ALA) is more recent. A programme of financial and technical cooperation with the ALA countries was formally established in 1976, though limited, mainly trade, cooperation, through the Generalised System of Preferences, had occurred before that. The establishment of a new legal basis in 1992 and the development of so-called *'third generation' agreements* (with Latin American countries) strengthened EC-ALA relations, provided for five-year programming and enhanced the profile of economic cooperation.

- Annual average commitments to Asia more than doubled between 1986-90 and 1996-98, while those to Latin America have nearly tripled. As a proportion of total EC aid, ALA's share has risen slightly from 13.2% in 1986-90 to 14.6% in 1996-98. Commitments to Asia for 1986-98 totalled 5.6 bn euro and those to Latin America, 4.3 bn euro.

- The largest Asian recipients in 1996-98 period were *India* (total commitments of nearly 300 m euro), *Bangladesh* (nearly 220 m euro), followed by China, Afghanistan, North Korea and Vietnam.

- The main Latin American recipients in the 1996-98 period were *Peru* (160 m euro), *Nicaragua and Bolivia* (each about 150 m euro), followed by Guatemala and Brazil.

- Latin American countries received far more *aid per capita* than Asian countries.

- Both regions were major beneficiaries of aid through three instruments: food aid; humanitarian assistance; and aid to NGOs. South Asia alone received food aid commitments worth nearly 600 m euro between 1986-88, but while food aid to Latin America was also substantial (totalling over 450 m euro), it has fallen dramatically since 1996, partly because funds from the budget line concerned are now spent on activities broader than developmental food aid. ***Humanitarian aid*** to both regions was only slightly lower, and in contrast to food aid is increasing. Aid to NGOs has been consistently high in Latin America (12% of total aid), and has nearly doubled in Asia as a proportion of allocable aid from 7% in 1986-90 to 7% in 1996-98.

CEECs (Chapter 6)

Although there were occasional and small flows to a number of Central and East European countries (CEECs) in the 1980s, the commencement of the ***Phare*** programme in 1990 marks the beginning of significant EC cooperation with the region. Flows through Phare were augmented from 1990 by food aid funded through the ***European Agricultural Guidance and Guarantee Fund*** (EAGGF), and from 1993 by large flows of ***humanitarian aid*** managed by ECHO. Total commitments to the CEECs reached 1.6 bn ecu in 1998.

- Aid was heavily concentrated in a limited number of countries, the top recipients of aid to the ***CEECs*** were Yugoslavia (with 14%, much in the form of humanitarian aid), Poland (13%), Bosnia-Herzogovina (with 11%) and Romania, Hungary and Bulgaria with less than 10% each.
- ***Economic infrastructure*** received the greatest amount of priority representing 29% of total commitments, with over half of this concentrated in transport and communications.
- ***Humanitarian assistance*** accounted for over a fifth of all allocable aid to the CEECs with 54% of this funded by ECHO. The countries of the former Yugoslavia taken together, took 88% of humanitarian aid commitments.
- ***Social infrastructure and services*** (principally education) also emerges as a major sector. In 1998, the Phare Democracy programme accounted for 15 m euro.

NIS (Chapter 7)

The New Independent States of the former Soviet Union began with the establishment of the Tacis programme in 1991 which has contributed 67% of all commitments since. The NIS have also received significant flows of food aid since 1990 funded by the Aid flows through the European Agricultural Guidance and Guarnatee Fund (EAGGF), and from 1993 large flows of humanitarian aid managed by ECHO.

- Aid was heavily concentrated in a limited number of countries, especially in the ***NIS*** where over one-third went to the Russian Federation, and nearly 10% to the Ukraine, though this is not disproportionate to their population, and one-third was regional.
- ***Economic infrastructure*** represented 30% of commitments for 1986-98. Of this, over 60% was allocated to energy (including nuclear safety) projects and programmes.
- ***Social infrastructure and services*** as with Phare, was principally committed to education, although between 1995-98 this dropped to 5% of allocable aid. Similarly Tacis contains a '*democracy programme*' concentrating on the transfer of parliamentary mechanisms and know-how to politicians on the strengthening of NGOs, and the transfer of skills to professional groups on democratic practices.

EC Aid in a Global Context (Chapter 8)

The growth in Community aid must be seen in the context of a generally upward trend in total OECD assistance to developing countries. However, while US aid remained constant in real terms, the EU Member States grew from $14.9bn in 1984 to $23.4bn in 1997. In 1995 the total aid disbursements of the EU Member States peaked at $32.5bn. Since then however total aid has slowly declined. Throughout the 1984-97 period, contributions from the EU Member States to the EC has continued to increase and contributions have tripled from $2.2bn to $6.6bn. Japanese aid has followed a similar pattern to that of the EU Member States reaching a peak in 1995 of $15.3bn after which it has slowly declined. In 1984 Japan's total aid was only half that of the US however by 1997 both the US and Japan contributed equal amounts of aid ($9bn).

- In real terms, world aid increased from an annual average of $56.4bn for 1986-91 to $67.3bn for 1992-97. This was very largely due to the growth in European Community and Member State aid, which saw their annual average increase by $10.1bn over the two time periods. The annual real terms average increase for Japan was $2.8bn, while for the USA it fell by $1.2bn, and for other DAC donors by $810m. In 1997 EC and Member State aid accounted for 55% of world aid.

- EC aid has seen its share of OECD aid rise from 6.2% for the 1986–91 period to 10.0% for 1992-97 (making it the fifth largest DAC donor), and its share of total European Union aid has increased from 13.9% to 19.0% over the same period.

- European Community aid accounted for a third of all multilateral aid, making the Community the largest 'multilateral' donor, followed by the International Development Association of the World Bank.

- The Community was the largest donor to sub-Saharan Africa, providing 13% of all aid to the region, more than the USA (10%) or Japan (9%), over the 1993-6 period.

- The Member States and EC together provided nearly 63% of OECD aid to the CEEC and NIS for the 1993-96 period.

- In the 1990s an average of 53.8% of average DAC bilateral aid went to the poorest countries (LLDCs and LICs), compared to 52.3% of EC aid.

1

The Nature of the European Community External Cooperation Programmes

EC External Cooperation Today

The European Community (EC) became the world's fifth largest aid donor in the 1990s, providing in 1997 $6.6bn or 12.2% of all aid disbursed by OECD countries. This reflects the rapid growth of the Community's external cooperation programme[1] over the past three decades, when it increased steeply in real terms and almost quadrupled a proportion of total OECD aid. European Community and European Union Member States' aid together accounted for well over half (55.3%) of total OECD aid in 1997 (see Figure 1.1).

Since the 1970s EC aid has changed not only in volume but also in terms of its regional composition. For the years 1996–97 EC aid disbursements[2] to sub-Saharan Africa averaged $2.0 bn per year (1997 prices), considerably larger than any other region. The volume of total OECD aid disbursed to sub-

Figure 1.1: OECD Aid in 1997 (disbursements $m)

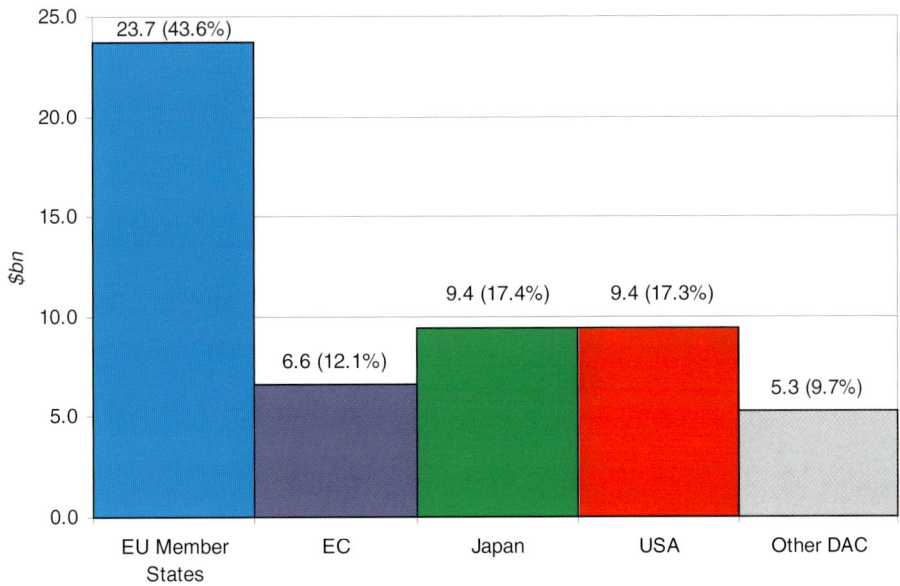

Source: European Commission/ODI database 1999; other data, OECD (1999), Development Co-operation. OECD: Paris

---

[1] 'European Community (EC) external cooperation' includes that portion of European Union external assistance that is managed by the European Commission and the European Investment Bank (EIB). It comprises all concessional flows to countries outside the EU, ie Official Development Assistance (ODA), and Official Aid (OA) to Part II of DAC aid recipients (mainly the CEECs and NIS).

[2] Disbursements is used throughout the book to refer to gross disbursements (the amount paid out each year) as opposed to net disbursements which also take account of capital repaid on concessional loans. The difference is of the order of 8% for 1996-98 when the sum of gross disbursements were 17.5 bn euro, and the capital repaid on concessional loans 1.4 bn euro.

Saharan Africa has fluctuated, but is significantly lower at the end of the 1990s than for the 1992–94 period, although EC aid to the region has in fact increased over the decade. The region has experienced a far sharper decline in its *share* of total allocable EC aid, averaging 30% of EC aid for 1996–97, down from over 70% at the beginning of the 1970s and 60% a decade later. In contrast, the share to a new group of beneficiaries, the Part II Central and Eastern European Countries (CEECs) and the New Independent States of the former Soviet Union (NIS), increased rapidly in the 1990s, with disbursements reaching an annual average of $1.3bn. for 1996–97, or 19% of all EC external cooperation, up from almost zero prior to 1990 (see Figure 1.2).

Countries in the Middle East and Southern Europe were the third largest beneficiaries of EC aid with average disbursements of $974 m for the 1996–97 period, and saw their share of total EC aid increase to 14%, up from under 6% in the 1970s and 1980s. Asia presently receives nearly $838m or 12% of EC aid, representing a significant decline from a peak of 21% in 1980–81. Latin America comes next with $680m per year for 1996–97 or 10%, up from under 6% in the 1970s and 1980s, followed by Africa north of the Sahara with $386m (6%) and finally Oceania which received some $70m per year, retaining a share of 1% of aid.

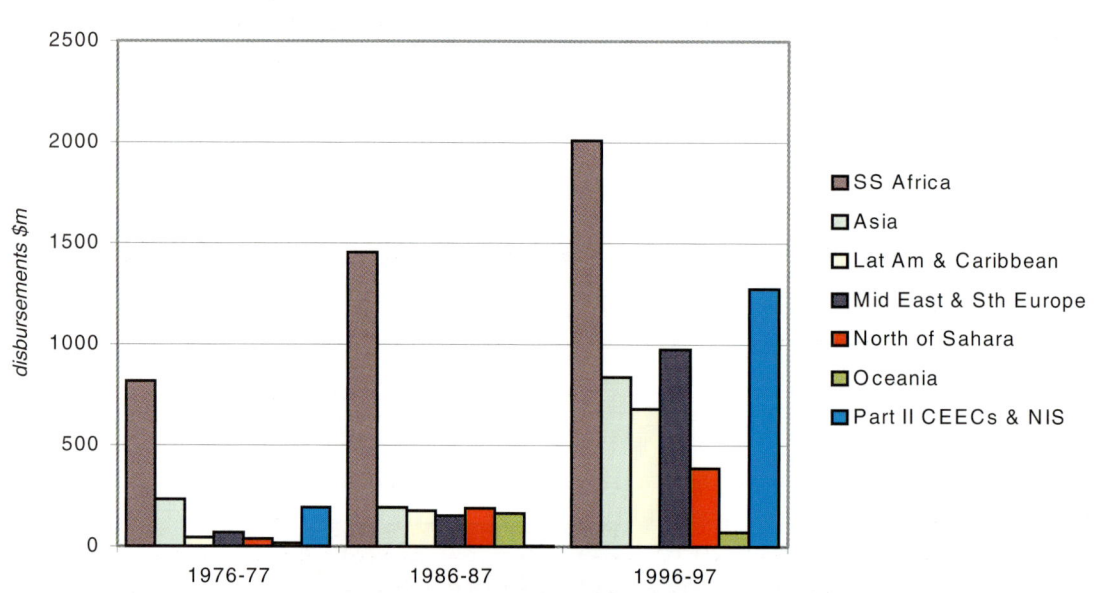

Figure 1.2: Distribution of EC External Cooperation by DAC Region (1976–97, average annual disbursements, $m, 1997 prices)

Source: 1986–97 data, European Commission/ODI database 1999; other data, OECD (1999), *Development Co-operation*. Development Assistance Committee, OECD: Paris. NB: for conciseness, OECD *Development Co-operation* reports are henceforth referred to as OECD (year of publication).

Main Trends in Size and Distribution

Since 1986 the pace of change has accelerated, and the main trends are analysed below. For the purposes of comparison, the introduction above and Chapter 8 examine aid disbursements in US dollars using the OECD DAC regional classification. The rest of the report, however, uses the Commission's own regional categories[3] and the euro[4], thus approaching an analysis which

---

[3] These are: Africa, Caribbean and the Pacific (ACP); Mediterranean and Middle East (MED); Asia and Latin America (ALA); and the Central and Eastern European Countries (CEECs) and New Independent States (NIS).

[4] For the sake of convenience the term euro is used to cover the ecu and the euro, since 1 ecu = 1 euro.

corresponds closely to the political and administrative realities which have influenced the development of the Community's external cooperation programme. *Commitments*, which represent a decision to commit a certain sum of aid, are used more often than *disbursements*, which indicate the amount actually spent in a country or region, since the commitments data provides fuller and more accurate information on the country allocation and the intended use of the aid.

Table 1.1: Major Recipients of EC External Cooperation (1970–98, share of total aid committed, %)

1970–74	%	1980–84	%	1990–94	%	1997–98	%
India	6.5	India	6.3	Poland	3.4	Egypt	5.5
Bangladesh	6.4	Ethiopia	4.3	Yugoslavia (ex)	3.4	Russian Fed	4.2
Senegal	5.5	Turkey	3.8	Egypt	3.0	Ethiopia	3.7
Mali	5.4	Bangladesh	3.4	Ethiopia	2.8	Morocco	3.1
Niger	5.1	Egypt	3.3	Russian Fed	2.2	Poland	2.6
Burkina Faso	4.5	Sudan	2.9	Côte d'Ivoire	2.0	Bosnia-Herzegovina	2.5
Madagascar	4.4	Tanzania	2.6	Romania	1.8	Yugoslavia (ex)	2.1
Zaire	4.1	Senegal	2.3	Soviet Union (ex)	1.8	Turkey	1.9
Ivory Coast	4.1	Somalia	2.2	Mozambique	1.7	Tunisia	1.8
Cameroon	3.7	Zaire	2.1	Hungary	1.7	South Africa	1.7
Chad	3.0	Morocco	2.0	Cameroon	1.6	West Bank/Gaza	1.7
Somalia	3.0	Ghana	1.8	Rwanda[a]	1.5	Romania	1.7
Mauritania	2.9	Madagascar	1.8	Nigeria	1.5	Bulgaria	1.5
Rwanda	2.2	Uganda	1.8	Bangladesh	1.5	Lebanon	1.3
Central African Rep.	2.0	Burkina Faso	1.8	West Bank/Gaza	1.5	Algeria	1.3
Top 15: % total EC	62.8	Top 15: % total EC	42.5	Top 15: % total EC	31.4	Top 15: % total EC	36.5

Note:
[a] includes 227 m euro for humanitarian action in Rwanda and Burundi for 1990–94

Source: 1970–84 data, OECD (1999); 1990-98 data, European Commission/ODI database 1999

The rapid rate of growth and change in regional composition of EC aid is reflected in the shift in its main recipients (see Table 1.1 and Appendix 1 for a comprehensive list). As the programme has grown overall the trend has been for the top 15 recipients to receive a smaller share of total aid, falling from nearly two-thirds for 1970–74 to around a third for 1990–94, though this rose again slightly to 37% for 1997–98. Although EC aid volumes to the Africa, Caribbean and Pacific (ACP) region have generally increased over the past decade (see particularly Figure 1.3 showing actual aid disbursements), the ACP programme has become less prominent in the overall EC aid programme. Thus in 1970–74, 13 out of 15 of the top recipients were ACP countries (all from sub-Saharan Africa and all but one francophone), by 1990–94 this had fallen to 6, and in 1996–97 to 2, with only one in the top five. Moreover, none of these highest-ranking ACP states were francophone. During the 1970–74 period 2 recipients from Asia, India and Bangladesh headed the list, but their position slipped every time period, and by 1997–98 there were no Asian recipients in the top 15. Instead the Russian Federation and five countries of Central and Eastern Europe (Poland, Bosnia-Herzegovina, ex-Yugoslavia, Romania and Bulgaria) have loomed large, along with five Mediterranean and Middle East countries and Africa two countries north of the Sahara.

Figure 1.3 illustrates the growth in the volume of EC external cooperation to every region over the decade. The most obvious development has been the sharp rise in cooperation with the Central and Eastern European Countries and to the New Independent States since 1990, following the introduction of the Phare and Tacis programmes. Though the trend in commitments and disbursements to each regional programme is generally upwards in all cases, trends in their share of the total programme vary (see Table 1.2).

Table 1.2: Regional Distribution of EC External Cooperation[a]
(1986-98, commitments and disbursements m euro)

	1986	1987	1988	1989	1990	1991	1992	1993	1994	1995	1996	1997	1998	Total
Commitments														
Total (euro)	2553	3857	4196	3314	3255	5567	6597	6800	7303	7344	7234	6515	8614	**73148**
ACP	1141	2632	2869	1994	1362	2123	2765	2774	3514	2599	1946	1127	2853	**29698**
South Africa	7	19	30	25	31	58	81	91	103	125	134	131	130	**963**
Asia	140	257	226	426	317	383	470	504	451	696	522	639	617	**5649**
Latin America	160	156	159	210	222	286	338	401	390	486	507	502	485	**4301**
Med & M East	401	149	309	511	386	1133	655	711	757	869	1189	1543	1368	**9981**
CEECs	–	2	1	52	683	845	1238	1541	1281	1446	1618	1541	1587	**11836**
NIS	0	0	20	0	5	615	679	592	593	821	702	583	1041	**5652**
Unallocable	704	643	582	96	249	124	370	185	213	301	615	450	534	**5068**
Share (%)														
TOTAL	100	100	100	100	100	100	100	100	100	100	100	100	100	**100.0**
ACP	44.7	68.2	68.4	60.2	41.9	38.1	41.9	40.8	48.1	35.4	26.9	17.3	33.1	**40.6**
South Africa	0.3	0.5	0.7	0.8	0.9	1.0	1.2	1.3	1.4	1.7	1.9	2.0	1.5	**1.3**
Asia	5.5	6.7	5.4	12.9	9.8	6.9	7.1	7.4	6.2	9.5	7.2	9.8	7.2	**7.7**
Latin America	6.3	4.0	3.8	6.3	6.8	5.1	5.1	5.9	5.3	6.6	7.0	7.7	5.6	**5.9**
Med & M East	15.7	3.9	7.4	15.4	11.9	20.3	9.9	10.5	10.4	11.8	16.4	23.7	15.9	**13.6**
CEECs	–	0.1	0.0	1.6	21.0	15.2	18.8	22.7	17.5	19.7	22.4	23.7	18.4	**16.2**
NIS	–	–	0.5	–	0.2	11.0	10.3	8.7	8.1	11.2	9.7	8.9	12.1	**7.7**
Unallocable	27.6	16.7	13.9	2.9	7.7	2.2	5.6	2.7	2.9	4.1	8.5	6.9	6.2	**6.9**
Disbursements														
Total (euro)	1669	1964	2644	2801	2886	4326	4720	4529	5507	5510	5334	5821	6710	**54420**
ACP	1057	1235	1542	1779	1703	2012	2592	1898	2445	2287	1899	1924	1952	**24326**
South Africa	3	13	23	19	34	48	66	62	58	46	29	60	72	**533**
Asia	138	125	132	271	250	261	300	264	246	369	503	528	456	**3843**
Latin America	53	72	94	146	176	196	231	273	247	275	323	319	370	**2775**
Med & M East	311	164	249	331	285	1012	468	594	581	578	601	794	943	**6911**
CEECs	3	0	0	12	360	348	501	789	1063	941	1118	1226	1951	**8312**
NIS	–	0	0	6	0	209	289	248	377	642	462	449	555	**3237**
Unallocable	103	356	604	238	77	240	273	403	488	373	399	520	410	**4484**
Share (%)														
TOTAL	100	100	100	100	100	100	100	100	100	100	100	100	100	**100.0**
ACP	63.4	62.8	58.3	63.5	59.0	46.5	54.9	41.9	44.4	41.5	35.6	33.1	29.1	**44.7**
South Africa	0.2	0.7	0.9	0.7	1.2	1.1	1.4	1.4	1.1	0.8	0.5	1.0	1.1	**1.0**
Asia	8.3	6.4	5.0	9.7	8.7	6.0	6.4	5.8	4.5	6.7	9.4	9.1	6.8	**7.1**
Latin America	3.2	3.7	3.5	5.2	6.1	4.5	4.9	6.0	4.5	5.0	6.0	5.5	5.5	**5.1**
Med & M East	18.6	8.3	9.4	11.8	9.9	23.4	9.9	13.1	10.6	10.5	11.3	13.6	14.1	**12.7**
CEECs	0.1	–	–	0.4	12.5	8.0	10.6	17.4	19.3	17.1	21.0	21.1	29.1	**15.3**
NIS	–	–	–	0.2	–	4.8	6.1	5.5	6.8	11.6	8.7	7.7	8.3	**5.9**
Unallocable	6.2	18.1	22.8	8.5	2.7	5.6	5.8	8.9	8.9	6.8	7.5	8.9	6.1	**8.2**

[a] The figures contained in this (ODI) survey differ from those reported by the European Commission to the OECD Development Assistance Committee (DAC). The two principal factors are: i) The ODI database excludes certain budgets lines which proved on further investigation not to qualify as Official Development Assistance (ODA) or Official Aid (OA); (ii) The ODI database includes several budget lines, of which by far the largest is EAGGF food aid, which are not included in the submission to the OECD DAC, but which do qualify as ODA or OA.

Note: in this and subsequent tables '–' indicates a zero figure, while '0' indicates a figure greater than zero but less than 0.5

Source: European Commission/ODI database 1999

Commitments to the ACP region declined from 67% of total allocable aid for 1986–90 to 29% for 1996–98. Other shifts in regional shares were, with the exception of the CEEC and NIS, very modest in comparison. Aid commitments to Latin America rose slightly from 6% to 7%, while the Mediterranean also benefited from an increased share, rising from 12% for 1986–90 to 20% for 1996–98. Cooperation with the CEECs and the NIS rose even more rapidly. These economies in transition received commitments of only 5% and 0.2% of the 1986–90 total, 90% of which was in 1990 when Phare had just begun and Tacis had not yet been created, a share which rose to 23% and 11% respectively during the 1996–98 period. Of the two regions, cooperation with the CEECs (75% of which is from Phare) grew most rapidly, rising from 845 m euro in 1991 to 1587 m euro in 1998, compared with a rise from 615 m euro to 1041 m euro for the NIS.

Figure 1.3 and Table 1.2 show that EC aid disbursements are usually lower than commitment levels, owing to the time lag between decisions to commit aid and the disbursement of those funds, the overall upward trend in committed aid levels and, of course, the suspension or cancellation of some commitments before they are disbursed. For the 1986–98 period total disbursements amounted to 74% of total commitments, though the ratio varied between different regional programmes, being lowest for the relatively new aid programmes, such as that to post-apartheid South Africa (56%). Similarly disbursements to the NIS for 1990–95 stood at 53% of commitments for the same period, rising to 57% for 1990–98 overall. These early difficulties in disbursements partly reflect the ambitious nature of these programmes. The programme to the CEECs saw a similarly low disbursement rate of 57% for 1990–95, which has since improved to 70% for 1990–98, paralleling the experience of the NIS.

However, there is also a lag in long-established programmes, notably those to Asia, Latin America and the Mediterranean and Middle East, for which total disbursements for 1986–98 totalled 68%, 65% and 69% of total 1986-98 commitments respectively. This may be partly explained by the fast growth of these programmes since the end of the 1980s. A further factor may be that Asia and Latin America (apart from several Caribbean countries, which are anyway grouped as ACP in these figures) are not eligible to receive support for Sysmin (which is confined to Lomé Convention countries) and receive only tiny amounts of Stabex and structural adjustment (the latter for some Latin American countries since 1997). Such funds, concentrated in sub-Saharan Africa, are by their nature quick-disbursing and undoubtedly contributed to the high ratio of disbursements to commitments (82%) through the long-established ACP programme. Many factors affect the rate at which aid is disbursed, including the different capacities of countries (or regions) to absorb and spend aid, as well differences in operational policies and procedures among Commission programmes. Not surprisingly disbursements follow a steadier trend than commitments, which can peak in a year when particularly large projects or programmes are agreed, whereas the following disbursements of funds are spread out more evenly (see Figure 1.3).

The Political Context

When looking at the shifts in volume of EC aid in Figure 1.2 and the main recipients shown in Table 1.1, it is clear that EC aid has been responsive to political and economic changes over the past three decades. Comparing four periods in time, 1970–74 (before the first enlargement of the European Economic Community (EEC) and essentially before the OPEC oil crisis); 1980–84 (as Africa's economic crisis was fully setting in, during Mexico's first debt crisis but before the accession of Spain and Portugal); 1990–94, (after the collapse of the Berlin Wall, the reunification of Germany and the end of the Cold War) and the most recent period 1997–8, after the conflict in the former Yugoslavia, the distribution of EC aid significantly reflects the political basis for European aid-giving over time. The origins and legal basis for the various EC aid programmes are discussed here in relation to political changes.

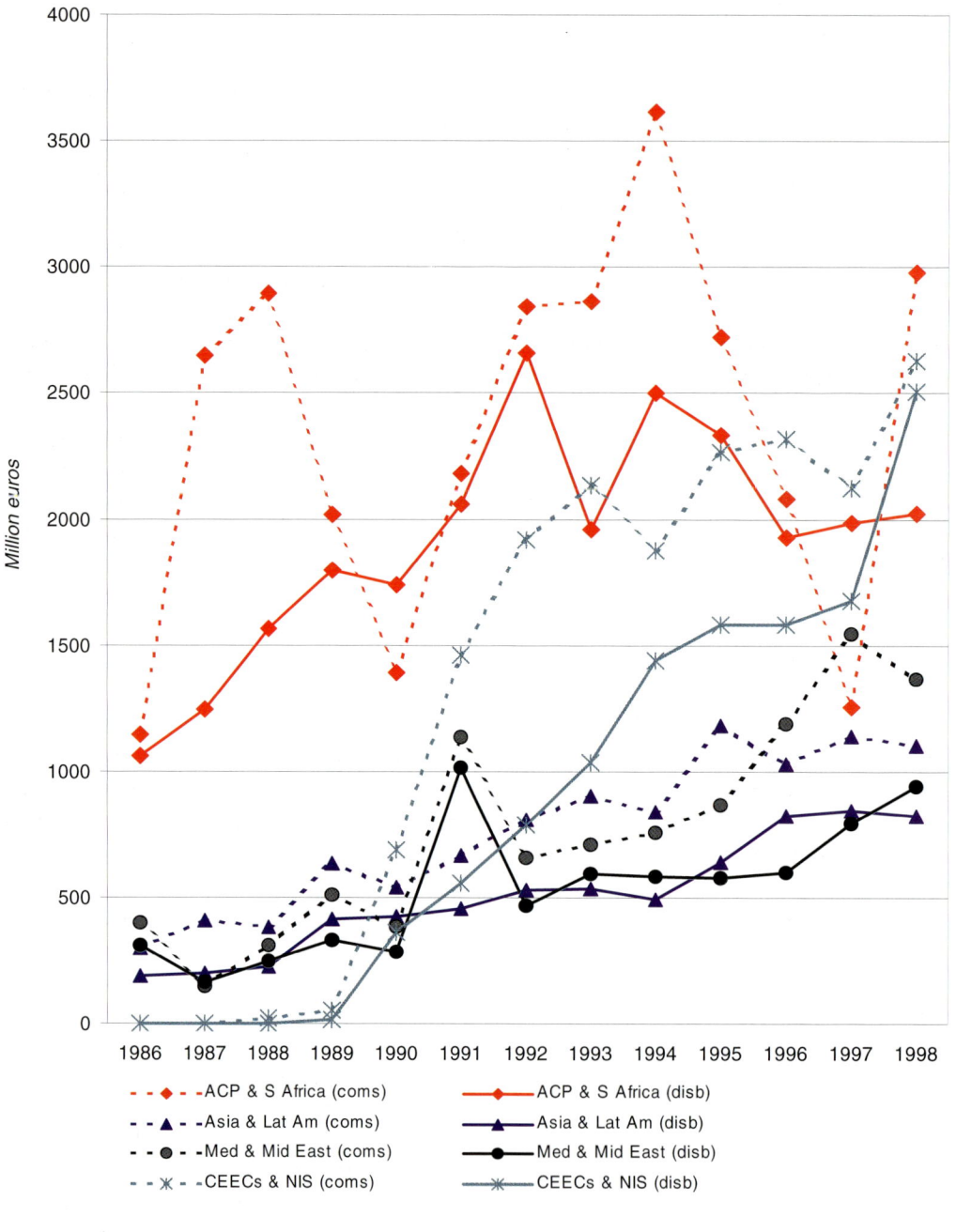

Figure 1.3: Regional Distribution of EC External Cooperation (1986-98, commitments and disbursements, m euro)

Source: European Commission/ODI database 1999

In the early seventies the only legal basis for EC aid was enshrined in the Treaty of Rome and the later obligations of the EEC under the Food Aid Convention. At the creation of the EEC in 1957 four of the then six member states (France, Belgium, the Netherlands and Italy) still had responsibility for dependent territories. Arrangements were therefore made under Part IV of the Treaty for their association with the Community, and the European Development Fund (EDF) was set up to supply them with financial aid. Algeria was also included in the original legal text, though shortly afterwards the EDF became restricted to sub-Saharan Africa. In 1963, eighteen former, mainly francophone, colonies (the Associated African and Malagasy States) reached an agreement under the Yaoundé Convention to continue the relationship set out in the Treaty of Rome. The Yaoundé agreement, conceived of in the context of Cold War decolonisation, reflected a recognition of the importance of offering the newly independent 'associated countries' benefits over and above those available from the Soviet bloc. It established as a guiding principle of the later European-ACP cooperation the contractual nature of the relationship, according to which the Community guarantees a certain level of technical and financial support while the partner 'associated' countries have a say in the choice of development strategy.

The other basis for aid was the supply of food aid, originally in kind from the surpluses generated by the Common Agricultural Policy, the biggest tonnage being in cereals, though the highest cost items were milk-powder and butter oil. The costs were charged to the EEC Budget and were not the subject of a fund. Regular EC programmes of food aid began in the late 1960s with the signature of the first Food Aid Convention in 1967. It is on the basis of such food aid that India and Bangladesh rank higher than the leading African recipients of EC aid in this period and why the region of Asia, with 9.1% of receipts, mitigates the otherwise strong dominance of sub-Saharan Africa overall (73.1%).

By the time of the second snapshot, 1980–84, the Community's legal powers to provide aid had been extended to 46 African Caribbean and Pacific (ACP) states following the accession of the United Kingdom to the EEC.[5] No longer 'associates', the enlarged group of countries selected for special aid and trade preferences included countries in the Commonwealth Caribbean and the Pacific, and in Africa included Ethiopia as well as the anglophone countries. The Yaoundé Convention with the francophone associates was replaced by the first Lomé Convention with ACP partners in 1975. This was renegotiated every five years thereafter until Lomé IV in 1990, which was renegotiated for ten years including a mid-term review (held in 1995), and has been extended to cover an increasing number of ACP partners. It expires on 29 February 2000 and will be replaced by transitional arrangements, which strengthen the elements of reciprocity within the ACP-EU relationship which were characteristic of the Yaoundé Conventions of the 1960s.

Also a new programme of financial aid starting in 1976, the ALA programme, had been approved on the initiative of the European Parliament, to cover the Asian and Latin American developing countries. Mediterranean protocols – with individual North African and Middle East states, sometimes called collectively the Maghreb[6] and Mashreq[7] agreements – had also been signed, which similarly drew on the EC Budget rather than being separately funded.

Thus, by the early 1980s EC aid had become global in its reach. Its share to Latin America and the Caribbean (at 5.9%) was below the DAC average, but otherwise the large, poor, South Asian countries, India and Bangladesh, were still high in the rankings (though largely because of food aid); Egypt (non-ACP) was there for the same reason, and the leading ACP country was no longer a francophone ex-colony but Ethiopia. Asia's share peaked at 20.6% of the total but Africa south of the Sahara, thanks to the Lomé Conventions and EDF funding, still maintained a dominant (60.4%) share.

Community external cooperation, as well as broadening its geographical reach, became more varied and deeper in nature, though this process happened at different rates in different regions. The number of aid instruments increased, as the traditional forms of assistance – financial and technical cooperation (e.g. for infrastructure and rural development) – were joined by new and sometimes innovative approaches, such as Stabex (system to stabilise export earnings) and Sysmin (the special facility for the mining sector) both under the Lomé Convention.

More recently, several new developments are apparent (see the third column of Table 1.1, for 1990–94). This is after the end of the Cold War, at the time of the signing of Europe Agreements with the successor states in Central and Eastern Europe and the Baltic of what were, until three years before,

---

[5] Commonwealth countries in Asia (Bangladesh, Ceylon, India, Malaysia, Nepal, Pakistan and Singapore) were excluded from this agreement.

[6] The Magreb countries are Algerica, Morocco and Tunisia.

[7] The Mashreq countries are Egypt, Jordan, Lebanon and Syria.

Communist regimes in COMECON. They reflect a time when aid is increasingly being given less for long-term social and economic development than for short-term political transformation, or as a response to conflict-induced emergencies. Emergency aid spending, in particular, more than tripled within three years. Phare (initially just for Poland and Hungary but rapidly encompassing all Central and Eastern Europe) and Tacis (for the ex-USSR) were rapidly initiated. The programme of aid to South Africa, hitherto channelled through NGOs in the region and itself transitional, was switched to support for government-led reconstruction efforts and then in support of the government's growth, employment and redistribution strategy (GEAR). Six out of the top 15 countries in 1990–1994 were East European 'countries in transition', to borrow the DAC's terminology.

Finally, the most recent (1997–98) period spans the time following the Maastricht Treaty on European Union, when the European Community resolved to form a political union, to forge a foreign policy, and define specific objectives for EC aid (see Box 1.1) and the Amsterdam Treaty which aimed to integrate respect for the environment and human rights into all external cooperation as well as rationalising decision making procedures (see Box 1.5). To the extent that this emerging foreign policy is global, the search for global reach is reflected in aid policies, with less priority than hitherto given to poorer countries (see also Chapter 8). It is also the time following the war in the former Yugoslavia and the initiation of the Obnova programme, as well as following the Barcelona Declaration and the new Euro-Mediterranean Partnership.

Of all 71 ACP states[8] only one – Ethiopia – ranks among the top five beneficiaries for 1997–98. The ACP's overwhelming dominance from the 1958–74 period is clearly over. Five of the fifteen leading places are taken by Eastern European countries; the Russian Federation also features. The prominence of emergency and rehabilitation assistance to the CEECs is reflected in the leading position of Bosnia-Herzegovina and ex-Yugoslavia. Bangladesh and India have dropped out and as a result the ALA countries no longer feature in the top 15 recipients of EC aid. Mediterranean countries however, as a consequence of the new MEDA budget line and concessional EIB loans, have become a lot more prominent with seven out of the top fifteen places. South Africa quickly moved up to tenth position following its abolition of apartheid and the holding of new elections.

Box 1.1 : The Maastricht Treaty and External Cooperation

The Maastricht Treaty put Community aid on a firm legal footing, and provided a general framework for overall Community aid policy. It sets out for the fist time common objectives for EC external assistance (art. 130u), namely, to foster:

- sustainable economic and social development of the developing countries, especially the poorest;
- smooth and gradual integration of developing countries into the world economy;
- the fight against poverty in developing countries; and
- the observance of human rights and fundamental freedoms and the development and consolidation of democracy and the rule of law.

The new emphasis is to increase the coordination and complementarity of the aid programmes of the Community and the Member States. A specific mandate was given to the European Commission to improve the coherence of policies and to take account of the above objectives when implementing other policies likely to affect developing countries (Art. 130v)

These policy prescriptions remained unchanged by the Amsterdam Treaty (signed on 2 October 1997; see Box 1.5).

There will be a further inter-governmental conference in 2000.

---

[8] South Africa joined the ACP in April 1997, but it can benefit only from certain parts of the Lomé Convention.

Evolution of the Main EC Aid Programmes

Cooperation with the ACP countries

The legal basis for the European Development Fund (EDF), which is the main component of aid to the ACP states, can be found in Part IV of the Treaty of Rome (art. 131–136). The Treaty provided for an aid allocation – the European Development Fund – financing from the European Investment Bank, and a free trade area between the EEC and the associated countries. This was continued into two Yaoundé Conventions signed in 1963 and 1968. After the extension of the associated group to include some of the Commonwealth countries following Britain's accession to the Community, the Convention was replaced in 1975 by the Lomé Convention. The free access the Yaoundé countries had enjoyed to the EEC up to then was replaced by non-reciprocal preferences for most exports to the EEC. In addition, the Sugar Protocol, a Commonwealth inheritance, was annexed to the Convention to benefit a selected number of sugar exporters. As far as aid is concerned, the dominant paradigm was 'partnership' both as a principle and in the definitions of (shared) powers and roles.

The Lomé Convention and its financial protocol have been extended three times since. Lomé II (1980–85) and Lomé III (1985–90) were also negotiated for five years, while Lomé IV was agreed for a period of 10 years (1990–2000) with two five-yearly financial protocols, for EDF 7 and 8. Over this period the beneficiaries of the Lomé Convention have increased from 46 to 71 ACP countries.[9] The current Lomé Convention and EDF run out in 2000. Negotiations on a successor agreement with the ACP were opened in September 1998 and are due to conclude in February 2000. There is increasing debate as to whether EDF aid to the ACP countries should be integrated into the external aid section of the general Budget of the European Communities. In addition, in 2000 the waiver from the World Trade Organisation for the EU's trade concessions will expire.

In addition to aid from the EDF, ACP countries have benefited from financial flows from the general budget of the European Communities. Budget lines have been introduced in order to respond quickly to a changing situation (eg humanitarian assistance, or support for banana-producing countries), or to create pilot funds for areas of cooperation which can later be integrated in the traditional cooperation agreements. The first budget line for external aid was introduced in 1967 for food aid under the Food Aid convention. The next two decades saw about 130 budget lines introduced for other areas of cooperation such as humanitarian assistance, women in development, the environment and population activities. At the end of the nineties, though, in the face of both budgetary restrictions and growing difficulties in managing this many budget lines, attempts have been made to rationalise the system and make it more transparent. A number of budget lines have been cut and the pace at which new lines are created has slowed.

Cooperation with the Mediterranean Countries

The agreements with Mediterranean countries were also stimulated by the Treaty of Rome (art 238). There were different agreements for various parts of the region, all established on a country-by-country basis between 1961 and 1980. Generally, the European Commission makes a geographical distinction between the North Mediterranean countries (Malta, Cyprus and Turkey) and East and Southern Mediterranean countries (Morocco, Algeria, Tunisia, Egypt, Israel, Jordan, Syria, Lebanon) and the West Bank/Gaza. The other Middle East countries receive little aid.

The cooperation agreements are of unlimited duration, but their financial Protocols had to be renegotiated every five years. No separate fund was established for the implementation of the Protocols but a special budget line (B7–4050 for Protocol 1 and 2, B7–4051 for Protocol 3 and 4) was created.

---

[9] In addition, a part of the EDF funds is reserved for twenty Overseas Countries and Territories (OCTs) which are constitutionally linked to France, The Netherlands and the United Kingdom.

Southern and Eastern Mediterranean countries have a history of political, social and economic relations with Europe, with formal institutional links with the Community dating back over thirty years. In 1990 the European Community introduced the New Mediterranean Policy, which sought to move towards a more comprehensive region-wide strategy, extending beyond trade concerns and traditional financial and technical cooperation. This approach led to increased attention being paid to the reform process in the Mediterranean countries and to the role of the private sector as an essential actor for the overall development in the region. This had the result of substantially increasing the budget for the region between 1991 and 1995, and placed particular emphasis on regional and horizontal cooperation (between non-state actors in the Mediterranean and the EU).

In 1995 a new stage in relations between the EU and the countries of the Mediterranean began at a ministerial conference in Barcelona. This set out priorities for a work programme in the Barcelona Declaration. In 1995, the European Council allocated increased funds to this Euro-Mediterranean Partnership for the years up to 2000, amounting to 4.7 bn euro, including in particular 3.4 bn euro for the single MEDA budget line. This Partnership includes a political dimension, as it seeks to reduce civil unrest and ease the migratory pressures from the region. It also aims at gradually moving towards a free trade area between Europe and South and East Mediterranean countries by 2010 (see Chapter 4).

In the case of the northern Mediterranean, Turkey, Cyprus and Malta have had an association agreement with the EC since 1963, 1970 and 1972 respectively with a view to creating a custom union. With Turkey, this stage has been reached since 1996. Cyprus, Malta and Turkey are candidates for accession to the European Union.

Cooperation with Asia and Latin America

The six original Member States of the EEC made no provision for Community aid to Asia and Latin America when drawing up the Treaty of Rome in 1957. Neither region enjoyed tariff preferences for their exports to the Community, nor financial support. It was not until the 1970s that the Commission and the Council of Ministers felt it necessary to extend aid to the so-called 'non-associated' countries (to distinguish them from the Yaoundé associated states). In 1970 the EEC introduced its Generalised System of Preferences and in 1976 a programme of financial and technical cooperation was set up, funded from the Budget, benefiting some 40 Asian and Latin American countries. Limited eligibility reflected the Community's desire to concentrate a quite modest budget on the poorest countries, though relatively affluent countries and territories such as Uruguay and Argentina were also included.

The programme's legal basis and objectives were not set out until 1981, in Council Regulation EEC No. 442/81. It was during the 1980s that the EC began to negotiate framework agreements with individual Asian nations, seeking to meet their specific development needs and with greater continuity, as well as to promote more predictable trading relations. By 1997 all developing Asian countries, bar the smallest,[10] have signed cooperation agreements with the EC, providing a legal framework for actions in fields as diverse as energy, rural development and the prevention of drug abuse. The EC's relationship with Asia was further reinforced at the Asia–Europe meeting (ASEM) first held in Bangkok in 1996 and repeated subsequently.

The 1990s also saw a deepening of cooperation agreements with Latin America. Since 1991 more ambitious 'third generation' agreements have been signed with all Latin American countries apart from Cuba[11]. These include a clause designed to safeguard 'democratic principles', while clauses on 'future developments' provide scope to expand. The overarching legal framework for the

---

[10] Bhutan and the Maldives.

[11] Although Cuba now has observer status within the ACP and might soon become an ACP state.

Community's programme to Asia and Latin America was redefined in a 1992 Council Regulation (EEC No. 443/92). This presented a new approach and a diversification of cooperation beyond the long-standing areas of financial, technical and economic cooperation, and especially food security and rural development, since it gave weight to areas such as human rights, democratisation and good governance, environment, and cultural exchange. The 1992 Regulation agreed a budget of 2750 m euro for the 1991–95 period, 10% of which was set aside for environmental initiatives. The Commission has greater autonomy and flexibility vis à vis the ALA developing countries than in the case of the ACP countries regarding countries it wishes to extend cooperation to, and the size of each country's annual budget (see also Chapter 5).

Cooperation with Central and Eastern European Countries

Phare: The Phare programme provides the great bulk of all EC external cooperation to the Central and East European Countries (75% of commitments, 1990–98) (see Table 6.2 in Chapter 6).[12] Phare became operational in January 1990 on the basis of a Council Regulation to support the process of transition to a market-oriented economy.[13] It started with Poland and Hungary and it was extended in September 1990 to include Bulgaria, the former Czechoslovakia (later the Czech Republic and Slovakia), the former GDR (until December 1991), Romania, and the former Yugoslavia. Subsequently in 1991 it was extended further to include Albania, Estonia, Latvia and Lithuania. Conflict in the former Yugoslavia and heavy German lobbying required that Slovenia be brought in separately in 1992, Croatia in July 1995, Macedonia in March 1996, and Bosnia from April 1996, though in the case of Croatia this was suspended shortly afterwards and Greece vetoed Community disbursements to Macedonia.

EU–CEEC relations began to take shape with the signing of the first in a series of Trade and Economic Cooperation Agreements in 1988, the priorities of which were to establish trading links and develop market access. The emphasis was on providing technical and financial support for the process of economic restructuring, and encouraging the changes necessary to build a market-oriented economy, provide private enterprise and help establish democracy. In June 1993 the focus of the Phare programme began to shift, with the decision of the European Council at Copenhagen that the associated CEECs so desiring should become members of the European Union when they were able to meet the necessary economic and political obligations. This second phase was cemented by the signing of association agreements, the so-called 'Europe Agreements', with 10 countries: Poland and Hungary (February 1994), Romania, Bulgaria, the Czech Republic and Slovakia (February 1995), Estonia, Latvia, Lithuania (all signed in 1995), and most recently Slovenia (signed in June 1997).

The Europe Agreements provide a basis of 'shared understandings and values' and are designed to speed progress towards greater convergence between the EU and the CEEC regions. Phare, originally a technical assistance programme, has become the financial instrument by which the objectives of the Europe Agreements may be achieved, underscoring the EU's support for the reforms undertaken by the CEECs to 'return to Europe'. This change of focus in the Phare programme was confirmed at the Essen Summit of December 1994, which built on the decisions of the Copenhagen Summit, and adopted a Pre-accession Strategy (see Box 1.2).

---

[12] Of the remainder, 12% was humanitarian assistance provided by ECHO and 4% was food aid through the European Agricultural Guidance and Guarantee Fund (EAGGF).
[13] Council Regulation No. 3906/89, 18.12.89. This was based on Article 235 of the Treaty of European Union, and was revised following the broadening of the programme beyond Poland and Hungary. Originally Phare stood for *Poland and Hungary Assistance for Economic Restructuring*.

At Luxembourg in December 1997, the European Council took historic decisions on the enlargement of the Union and defined the 'overall' enlargement process in a way which encompasses all candidate countries that wish to join the Union.

In 1998 new policy guidelines for the Phare programme were developed, taking into account its role in the creation of a larger 'family' of nations within an enlarged European Union. Instead of being driven by partner country demands, the new Accession Partnership will be focused on meeting the criteria for accession to the Union. The first priority will be 'institution building', designed to help the administrations of the partner countries acquire the capacity to implement the 'acquis communautaire', including the harmonisation of legislation, through the development of twinning programmes. The second priority is to help partner countries bring their industries and major infrastructure up to Community standards by promoting the necessary investment.

> **Box 1.2: The Essen Strategy**
>
> The key element of the strategy is the preparation of the associated states for integration into the internal market of the EU. To this end, a White Paper has been produced by the Commission setting up a plan to prepare for the adoption of the acquis communautaire (legislation and implementation and enforcement structures). The Essen Council reconfirmed support for other elements of an overall integration strategy, including:
> - the establishment of institutions guaranteeing democracy, the rule of law, human rights and protection of minorities;
> - integration through the development of infrastructure, including trans-European transport networks;
> - intra-regional cooperation between the CEECs;
> - environmental cooperation
> - cooperation in the fields of foreign and security policy, justice, culture, education and training.
>
> Under the Essen Strategy, Phare has become the major tool for meeting the aspirations of the CEECs for integration into the EU.

1998 also saw the adoption of the Accession Partnerships and the formal launch of the accession process with the ten candidate countries. The Accession Partnerships set out the priorities to be tackled in preparation for membership and the framework for all pre-accession assistance.

Cooperation through the Phare programme is funded exclusively from the EC Budget. The principal budget line (B7–5000, formerly B7–600) is directed at the economic restructuring of the CEECs, and committed 8.8 bn euro between 1990 and 1998 compared to total commitments to the region of 11.8 bn euro. The Cannes European Council of 1995 allocated some 6.7 bn euro to the main Phare budget line for the 1995–99 period. Humanitarian aid, funded via the European Community Humanitarian Office (ECHO), has also been very significant, with total commitments amounting to 1396 m euro. In addition, surplus food stocks have been transferred to the CEECs through the European Agricultural Guidance and Guarantee Fund (EAGGF), with an accounting value of some 412 m euro.[14] Other activities such as cross-border activities, nuclear safety, and support for NGOs are funded from separate budget lines which generally cover the CEEC and NIS jointly (see also Chapters 6 and 7).

In 1996 the Obnova programme was established to focus on reconstruction activities in the former Yugoslavia. It has committed of 587 m euro for the period 1996–98.

Cooperation with the New Independent States

Tacis: The Technical Assistance Programme for the former republics of the Soviet Union (the so called Commonwealth of Independent States) began operations in 1991. Tacis represents the central pillar of the European Commission's aid programme to the twelve New Independent States (NIS) and Mongolia.[15] The recognition by the USSR in 1986 of the European Community as a legal and economic entity opened the door to a closer relationship between East and West, and reflected a major shift in Soviet policy towards Europe. In December 1989 a Trade and Economic Cooperation

---

[14] The real value of this food aid, if measured at world market prices, would be considerably higher; estimates range from an additional 50 to 75%.

[15] These are: Armenia, Azerbaijan, Belarus, Georgia, Kazakhstan, Kyrgystan, Moldova, Russia, Tajikistan, Turkmenistan, Uzbekistan and Ukraine. See Chapter 7 for the levels of EC aid to each of NIS.

Agreement signed between the USSR and the European Community, aimed at strengthening and diversifying economic relations between them. This was given greater substance at the European Council in Rome in 1990, with the Member States' decision to support the Soviet authorities in their efforts to achieve fundamental economic and social reform in the Soviet Union. As a result Tacis was formally established by Council regulation No. 2157/91 of 15 July 1991, and Mongolia was included within the Tacis programme. In 1995, the NIS/Tacis Directorate within the Enlargement Service (then DG IA) of the Commission was reorganised in an attempt to integrate the management of the Tacis programme with all other areas of EC-NIS relations, including political, economic and trade issues. Since then, four-year indicative country programmes have replaced the three-year instruments. These are designed to provide a more comprehensive analysis of a more limited number of priority sectors, and will bind partner countries to longer-term political and economic reforms as a condition of Tacis support.

The legal basis of Tacis is the Tacis Regulation (EEC 1279/96). As with Phare, all assistance is drawn from the EC budget, the budget lines being B7–520, B7–528 and B7–536.[16] Commitments through Tacis amounted to 3.8 bn euro for the 1991–98 period, representing 67% of all EC commitments to the NIS. A second major source of aid to the region has been food aid through EAGGF, which amounted to over 1100 m euro, or nearly 20% of total commitments between 1991 and 1998, with 400 m euro going to Russia in 1998. ECHO provided over 400 m euro of humanitarian aid, and specific aid activities in the NIS or in the NIS and CEEC jointly were funded by several other budget lines. These include a budget line promoting democracy in the former USSR (B7–7010, earlier B7–521), humanitarian aid (B7–215) and several lines shared with Phare covering nuclear safety and support for NGOs, though the latter is very small (see Chapters 6 and 7).

EC Support for Regional Economic Integration

Support for regional cooperation has long formed an important part of Community cooperation with developing countries, and more recently with the economies in transition. As noted in Box 1.1, Article 130u of the Maastricht Treaty specifies that the EU's external aid policy shall foster 'the smooth and gradual integration of developing countries into the world economy'. This serves to reinforce the Community's belief that by assisting countries to compete in the regional market they can gradually improve their competitiveness in the global economy. Regional cooperation and particularly regional integration was given renewed priority in the Council Resolution of 1 June 1995.

The Commission views regional integration as part of a wider strategy to promote equitable growth by increasing competition, reducing private transaction costs, assisting firms to exploit economies of scale, encouraging inward foreign investment and facilitating macroeconomic policy coordination. The EU supports realistic regional economic integration initiatives among developing countries that are consistent with national economic reform programmes. This support usually comprises three interrelated areas:

- capacity building (including technical assistance, training and research) on the subject of regional economic integration at the level of regional institutions and national governments;
- assistance to the private sector to facilitate restructuring in the larger regional and world market including improvements in the financial sector;
- support to governments committed to implement regional integration to help them cope with net transitional effects on budgetary resources (see Chapters 3, to 7).

---

[16] The Council Regulation establishes the principles under which Tacis assistance is provided to the NIS and includes rules on the award of contracts.

Sources of European Community Aid

Figure 1.4 shows that three-quarters of all European Community external assistance was funded through the Community Budget for the 1996–98 period. Almost a fifth (18%) of aid was funded from the European Development Fund, and the remaining 7% from the European Investment Bank's (EIB) own resources. These proportions have changed considerably since the late 1980s. In the period 1986–88 the EDF was the major source of aid at 57%, with the budget providing only 36%. This shift in the relative weight of the EDF and Budget is largely as a result of aid flows to the CEECs and NIS through Phare and Tacis in the 1990s. EIB flows from its own resources, have fluctuated somewhat but averaged 7% over both time periods. In addition to own resource flows, the EIB also managed risk capital loans to ACP and Mediterranean and Middle East countries subsidised by the EDF and the budget respectively and totalling 1.9 bn euro for 1986–98.

**Figure 1.4: Sources of EC External Cooperation
(commitments, m euro; volume reflected in pie chart size)**

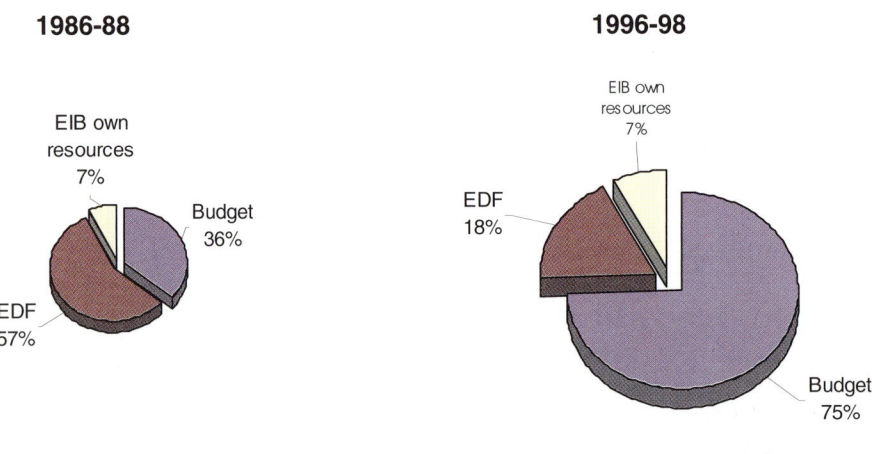

Source: European Commission/ODI database 1999

The EU Member States negotiate among themselves and with the ACP governments their contribution to the EDF, and the outcome is specified in the Internal Financial Agreement which is signed for every Lomé Convention (see Table 1.3). In contrast, their contributions to the Budget are obligatory, and are determined by applying an agreed formula[17].

While the contributions to the Budget are determined by formula, annual changes in the distribution of aid flows from the Budget are influenced by the decisions of the Council of Ministers setting out long-term expenditure plans. An important budgetary decision of this kind was taken during the Edinburgh Summit in 1992 (see Box 1.3) when the then twelve Member States voted an increase of the budget ceiling for external actions, which includes aid flows, to 6.2 bn euro by 1999. Other important budgetary decisions taken in more recent years, for instance the Cannes Summit in June 1995, have influenced the allocation of this budget to Eastern Europe and the Former Soviet Republics, the Mediterranean, Asia and Latin America and South Africa.

---

[17] This formula takes account of four main factors: (i) a levy on imports into the Community by the member state; (ii) a levy on production of certain agricultural products; (iii) a proportion of VAT collected in the member state; and (iv) member state's GNP, adjusted for any abatement agreed. Extra decisions taken throughout the year on unforeseen expenditure are determined by Member States' GNP only.

In 1999 a New Financial Framework for the years 2000–06 was agreed with the aim of improving the functioning of the annual budgetary procedure and cooperation between institutions on budgetary matters. This agreement forms the core of the Agenda 2000 financial package and contains a new financial perspective which establishes, for each of the years covered and for each heading and subheading, the amounts of expenditure in terms of appropriations for commitments, in 1999 prices. There are seven main headings including external action, reserves and pre-accession aid. External action will have its financial allocation increased slightly, throughout the period covered by the financial perspective, from 4.55 bn euro in 2000 to 6.0 bn euro in 2006. The emergency aid reserve and the loan guarantee reserve will remain at a steady level of 200 bn in each case. Pre-accession aid will be allocated 3.12 bn per year. The funds allocated will be divided between the agricultural instrument (0.52 bn per year), the pre-accession structural instrument (1.04 bn per year) and Phare (1.56 bn per year).

> **Box 1.3: The Edinburgh Summit**
>
> During the Edinburgh Summit in December 1992 the Council decided to increase the level of commitments for the Community's external actions paid for from the Budget. The ceiling was projected to go up from 4.45 bn euro in 1993 (6.4% of all commitments) to 6.2 bn euro (7.4%) in 1999, an increase of almost 40%. The Council agreed to allocate each year between 200 and 300 m euro of these funds to respond to emergencies and 300 m euro to a loan guarantee fund for lending to third countries. The Council made no decision on the geographical distribution of these funds, apart from indicating that 'an appropriate balance should be maintained, bearing in mind the Community's changing priorities'. At later Summits, such as the Essen and Cannes Summit, further commitments were made in favour of particular regions.

Table 1.3: EU Member States' Shares of EC Budget Aid and EDF

	EC Budget (% 1994)	EDF 7 (% 1990–95)	EDF 8 (% 1995–2000)	Total[b] (m euro)
Austria[a]	2.7	–	2.6	–
Belgium	3.8	4.0	3.9	243
Denmark	1.9	2.1	2.1	119
Finland[a]	1.4	–	1.5	–
France	18.3	24.4	24.3	1224
Germany	29.5	26.0	23.4	1716
Greece	1.4	1.2	1.2	81
Ireland	0.8	0.6	0.6	45
Italy	13.3	13.0	12.5	789
Luxembourg	0.2	0.2	0.3	12
Netherlands	6.1	5.6	5.2	359
Portugal	1.6	0.9	1.0	83
Spain	7.7	5.9	5.8	431
Sweden[a]	2.5	–	2.7	–
UK	15.5	16.4	12.7	954
Total	100	100	100	6046

[a] Contribution to the EC Budget of new Member States is for 1995.

[b] The volume of aid contributed to the aid Budget by each Member State was calculated by multiplying the share that the Member State is required to pay by total Budget expenditure in 1994 (4122 m euro). For the EDF, the Member State's negotiated share was multiplied by the annual average of the total value of the EDF for 1991–95 (1923 m euro).

Source: Report of the Foreign Affairs Committee of the House of Commons, 15 December 1994. Official Journal of the European Communities: 17 August 1991, The ACP-EC Courier Jan-Feb 1996.

Forms of EC External Cooperation

Official Development Assistance (ODA) and Official Aid (OA)

For aid flows to qualify as Official Development Assistance (ODA) they must meet specific criteria defined by the Development Assistance Committee of the OECD. These state that grants and loans must be undertaken by the official sector, with the promotion of economic development and welfare as its main objective. For loans to qualify they must be provided on concessional terms, with a grant element of at least 25%. Aid flows to countries in transition and more advanced (Part II of the OECD DAC List of Aid Recipients) are ineligible to qualify as ODA and are classed instead as official aid (OA).

The term 'aid' used in this inventory includes both ODA and OA, and therefore covers all external financial flows which have a degree of concessionality of at least 25%. The vast bulk (some 91%) of EC aid (as defined here) is grant aid, with only 9% provided as concessional loans (see below). Less concessional or 'hard' loans, such as macro-financial assistance and some EIB lending (see below) were also provided, but these are excluded from the EC aid total.

Out of total commitments of 73.1 bn euro for the 1986–98 period, 62 bn euro (or 84% of all EC aid described here) qualifies as Official Development Assistance. The 11 bn euro qualifying as Official Aid was split between the CEECs, which received 64% of it, and the NIS (see Table 1.4). It should be noted, however, that 38% of all EC aid provided to the CEEC region (4.5 bn euro) qualifies as Official Development Assistance, since Albania, and the states of former Yugoslavia are classed as developing countries (DAC Part I countries).[18] Not surprisingly the former Yugoslav states received the majority of this assistance. The share of EC aid to the NIS which counts as ODA is lower, at about 26%, since the major NIS recipients (the Russian Federation and Ukraine) are classed as countries in transition (Part II countries). Nonetheless commitments to developing countries within the NIS region amounted to 1.2 bn euro between 1991 and 1998, with Georgia and Azerbaijan (both over 190 m euro) being the largest recipients followed by Armenia (157 m euro) and then Kazakhstan and Tajikistan (both over 100 m euro).

Table 1.4: Regional Distribution of Official Development Assistance (ODA) and Official Aid (OA) (1986–98, commitments, m euro)

	1986	1987	1988	1989	1990	1991	1992	1993	1994	1995	1996	1997	1998	Total
Official Development Assistance (ODA)														
Total (m euro)	2553	3855	4176	3305	2678	4167	5232	5463	6102	5949	6004	5335	6843	61660
ACP	1141	2632	2869	1994	1362	2123	2765	2774	3514	2599	1946	1127	2853	29698
South Africa	7	19	30	25	31	58	81	91	103	125	134	131	130	963
Asia	140	257	226	426	317	383	470	504	451	696	522	639	617	5649
Latin America	160	156	159	210	222	286	338	401	390	486	507	502	485	4301
Med & M East	401	149	309	511	386	1133	655	711	757	869	1189	1543	1368	9981
CEECs	–	–	1	42	110	38	436	735	474	564	758	688	614	4461
NIS	–	–	–	–	–	23	116	62	199	308	333	255	243	1539
Unallocable	704	643	582	96	249	124	370	185	213	301	615	450	534	5068
Official Assistance (OA)														
Total (m euro)	–	2	20	10	578	1400	1366	1337	1201	1395	1230	1181	1771	11488
CEECs	–	2	–	9	572	808	803	806	807	882	860	853	973	7375
NIS	–	–	20	–	5	592	563	531	394	513	370	327	797	4113

Source: European Commission/ODI database 1999

---

[18] It should be noted that there is some dissatisfaction with anomalies in the OECD DAC categorisation of countries into Part I developing countries and Part II countries in transition. According to this system aid to Slovenia (a Part I country) counts as ODA while that to Bulgaria is OA (Part II).

EC External Cooperation in Loan Form

The small share of loans in total EC aid (9.2% and much less for the poorer developing countries) means that the EC is not among the aid donors which are building up debt problems for developing countries. In addition the Council Decision of 6 July 1998 commits the EC to participate in the heavily indebted poor countries (HIPC) initiative by making available grant resources to be utilised by eligible countries, which are all ACP states, to meet outstanding debt and debt service obligations towards the Community. This is to be financed from interest accrued on deposited funds. An initial amount of 40 m euro has been made available.[19] The Commission is currently recommending that this be increased and the scope be widened to include non-ACP countries also.

EIB loans: EC loans are managed by the European Investment Bank and come from two sources (see Table 1.5). By far the majority are loans from the EIB's 'own resources' – the proceeds of the Bank's borrowing on the capital markets – which are largely lent on terms similar to those to EU Member States. The vast bulk of these loans do not qualify as Official Development Assistance or Official Aid since they do not carry a subsidy of at least 25%. Such 'hard' loans are classed as 'Other Official Flows' and not included here. However, own resource loans to the ACP countries and some loans to Mediterranean and CEEC countries benefit from interest rate subsidies of 25% or more and therefore their total value is counted as EC aid.

Secondly, the Bank manages risk capital finance to ACP and Mediterranean countries, drawn from the EDF and the EC Budget respectively. This may be provided as equity or venture capital, or more usually as 'soft' loans, both of which are included as EC aid, and tend to be provided on a more flexible basis than own resource loans. Risk capital is provided mainly to poorer countries unable to take on further foreign debt, and its terms are similar to those of the World Bank's IDA.

In 1997–98 subsidised loans to the ACP and Mediterranean accounted for 13% of all EIB lending outside of the European Union, up from 8.8% of all EIB lending for 1990–95.

Table 1.5: Concessional Loans managed by the European Investment Bank, 1986-1998 (commitments, m euro)

	1986	1987	1988	1989	1990	1991	1992	1993	1994	1995	1996	1997	1998	Total
Overall total	408	375	417	439	231	624	406	437	679	573	874	541	719	6723
Of which:														
Own resources														
Total	349	185	236	313	188	491	284	357	412	349	771	487	361	4782
ACP	151	158	121	166	118	266	129	147	223	124	296	38	81	2017
Med & M East	198	28	115	147	70	225	156	163	189	193	445	414	210	2551
CEECs	–	–	–	–	–	–	–	47	–	32	30	35	70	214
Risk Capital														
Total	59	189	181	126	44	133	122	80	267	225	103	54	358	1941
ACP	59	185	172	114	36	119	119	75	239	225	99	19	272	1733
Med & M East	–	–	7	12	8	15	–	2	28	–	5	36	86	197
Latin America	–	4	2	–	–	–	3	3	–	–	–	–	–	11

Source: European Commission/ODI database 1999

The EIB managed a total of 6.7 bn euro of concessional loans for developing countries over the 1986–98 period. Over 70% of these were provided from the EIB's own resources, while the rest, which was provided as risk capital, came from the EDF (1.7 bn euro) and the Budget (208 m euro). Almost half (46%) of the loans provided to ACP countries were financed from the EDF as risk capital.

---

[19] Council Decision of 6 July 1998 concerning exceptional assistance for the heavily indebted ACP countries (98/453/EC).

Concessional loans to the Mediterranean and Middle East amounting to 1.6 bn euro were mostly (93%) financed from the EIB's own resources. The Asia and Latin America regions do, however, benefit from non-concessional loans with the EIB's mandate for 1997–99 having a ceiling of 900 m euro. The CEECs have benefited from concessional funding since 1993 receiving a total of 214 m euro.

Macro-financial assistance to third countries: Since 1990, countries in Central and Eastern Europe (Hungary, Czech Republic, Slovakia, Bulgaria, Romania. Estonia, Latvia, Lithuania and the former Yugoslav Republic of Macedonia), the NIS (Ukraine, Belarus, Moldova, Armenia and Georgia) and the Mediterranean (Algeria and Israel) have received macro-financial assistance from the Community (see Table 1.6). As a rule, this assistance is provided to support the balance of payments situation of partner countries and support macro-economic adjustment and structural reform efforts. It takes the form of loans granted on market terms managed by the Economic and Financial Affairs DG of the European Commission. Although the loans are provided at market rates, the rates are those obtained by the EU and are thus more favourable than the country would have obtained independently. The degree of concessionality is not sufficient, however, for the loans to qualify as ODA or OA, and they are not therefore counted under the EC aid total. Since 1998, some macro-financial assistance operations have included a grant element along with the loan, and in such cases the grant element is included in the EC aid total and classified as support for structural adjustment (see Chapter 2). In total 4.6 bn euro has been committed and 3.8 bn euro has been disbursed as macro-financial assistance, most of it (68% of disbursements) to the CEECs.[20]

Table 1.6: Macro-financial Assistance[a] to Third Countries
(1986–98, commitments and disbursements, m euro)

		1990	1991	1992	1993	1994	1995	1996	1997	1998	Total
CEEC	(commitments)	870	1220	410	–	255	–	–	290	–	3045
	(disbursements)	*350*	*695*	*705*	*270*	*70*	*80*	*40*	*95*	*265*	*2570*
NIS	(commitments)	–	–	–	–	130	255	15	265	150	815
	(disbursements)	–	–	–	–	*25*	*135*	*115*	*100*	*156*	*531*
Mediterranean	(coms)	–	588	–	–	200	–	–	–	–	788
(Algeria & Israel)	*(disbs)*	–	–	*438*	–	*150*	*100*	–	–	–	*688*
Total	**(commitments)**	870	1808	410	–	585	255	15	555	150	4648
	(disbursements)	*350*	*695*	*1143*	*270*	*245*	*315*	*155*	*195*	*421*	*3789*

[a] As a rule, this assistance is categorised as balance of payments support by the Economic and Financial Affairs DG. The exceptions are a loan to Hungary (870 m euro) and a loan to Israel (187.5 m euro), which were both labelled as structural adjustment loans. 265 m euro committed to Armenia and Georgia in 1997, of which 156 m euro was disbursed in 1998, was categorised as exceptional financial assistance.

As a rule, this assistance takes the form of long-term loans which do not qualify as ODA or OA, and are therefore excluded from the EC aid total. The exception is 18 m euro disbursed to Armenia and Georgia in the form of grants, which is also included in the overall EC aid figures.

70 m euro was committed to Albania in 1992 and a further 35 m euro in 1994 for balance of payments support. This was exclusively in grant form and is included in overall EC aid to the CEECs under the Phare programme heading, and thus not shown in this table.

Source: European Commission/ODI database 1999

---

[20] A full description of macro-financial assistance appears in the European Commission document COM(1999)580 of 15 November 1999.

The Management of EC External Cooperation

Management Structure

European Commission: The European Commission manages and executes the EC aid programme, and initiates proposals for legislation. Until 1985 all EC aid was managed by a single Directorate-General for Development. Responsibility for managing aid to Asia, Latin America and the Mediterranean was transferred in 1985 to a separate Directorate-General which, in the early 1990s, merged with DG I (foreign policy). The original Directorate General for Development, which became DG VIII (now Development DG), remained responsible for relations with the ACP countries and managed food aid, the largest aid component from the EC Budget. DG I not only covered North–South relations but also dealt with relations with Eastern Europe and the Former Soviet Union. DG I therefore managed the Phare and TACIS programmes, when they were established in the beginning of the 1990s.

In 1993 a new DG, DG IA was created to deal with political aspects of the Community's external relations (and its delegations), while DG I kept control over trade relations and 'North–South' issues. This situation changed again in 1995 when DG IB was set up to deal with relations with Asia, Latin America and the South and East Mediterranean; and in 1999 (see below). It is recognised that further enlargement of the European Union will bring further institutional changes in the European Commission.

Community relations with developing countries and with the CEEC and NIS (including their aid programmes) are managed by five different parts of the European Commission for which, three different Commissioners are essentially responsible. Loans and interest rate subsidies are managed by the European Investment Bank, based in Luxembourg, while the European Commission Directorate-Generals are all based at headquarters in Brussels. To assist in the implementation of the aid programmes overseas the European Commission has a relatively large number of delegations (see section on staffing below).

Since October 1999 the following picture has obtained:[21]

(i) *Development Directorate General – Commissioner Nielson*
This Directorate-General deals with external relations with the ACP and South Africa (in April 1997 South Africa became the 71st ACP country). It is responsible for the Lomé Convention, the post Lomé negotiations and also for some budget lines benefiting all developing countries such as non-emergency food aid and NGO co-financing. Commissioner Nielsen also heads ECHO. This Directorate covers the areas hitherto the responsibility of DG VIII.

(ii) *European Community Humanitarian Aid Office (ECHO) – Commissioner Nielson*
ECHO manages the humanitarian aid of the Community.

(iii) *External Relations Directorate General – Commissioner Patten*
This Directorate-General is responsible for Community relations with countries in the NIS, Mediterranean, Middle East, Latin America and most Asian developing countries. It has responsibility for programming and project preparation within the Tacis, MEDA and ALA programmes and is also responsible for budget lines on human rights and democratisation.

---

[21] It should be noted that at the time of going to press a major reorganisation was being prepared for decision in February 2000.

(iv) *Common Service for External Relations (SCR) – Commissioner Patten*
The SCR was set up in October 1997 as a new directorate general within the family of services responsible for external relations. It become operational in stages from July 1998 and is responsible for the technical, financial and legal aspects of implementing the Community's aid and cooperation programmes. It is also responsible for audits and evaluation. Its creation has led to considerable simplification and harmonisation of the main procedures for aid delivery, including procurement and contracting. The main effects will take place as soon as the necessary changes to existing legal provisions (Financial Regulations in particular) can be made.

(v) *Enlargement Service – Commissioner Verheugen*
The Directorate-General is responsible for relations with all pre-accession countries. It is responsible for policy on enlargement and the planning and negotiations of the programmes of pre-accession assistance including the Phare programme with the CEECs.

(vi) *Economic and Financial Affairs Directorate General – Directorate for International Matters – Commissioner Solbes Mira*
This Directorate is responsible for economic monitoring and dialogue with third countries. It also manages Community macro-financial assistance made available to these countries.

(vii) *Other DGs*
Other DGs in the Commission are involved in the delivery of the EC aid programme by providing technical support. For example, Eurostat has two Units specifically devoted to providing professional technical support to the design, implementation, monitoring and evaluation for either statistical cooperation projects or for statistical components of more general programmes.

All Commission spending is overseen by the European Court of Auditors, which checks that accounting rules have been complied with, as well as increasingly concerning itself with broader issues of effectiveness, relevance and impact.

European Investment Bank (EIB): Although the Bank's principal aim is to finance capital investment projects within the European Union, it also has operations in developing countries as discussed earlier. The European Investment Bank is an autonomous financing institution established by the European Community in 1958. The Bank, which has a 'triple-A' credit rating, on-lends the proceeds of its borrowing. It is owned by the EU Member States, which all subscribe to its capital, and is financially independent of the EC Budget. It has its own Board of Governors comprising the Finance Ministers of the Member States, and a Board of Directors, a Management Committee and an Audit Committee.

Staffing

The number of Commission staff managing the policy formulation and implementation of the European Community external cooperation programmes is shown in Table 1.7. This provides a guide to the number of headquarters staff working within the major Directorates General with direct responsibility for managing Official Development Assistance to developing countries and Official Aid to Part II countries in transition, though it should be noted that a major reorganisation is planned for decision in February 2000. The total number of staff at headquarters at October 1999 stood at 2171, with the largest number working within DG External Relations (35% of total staff), followed by the Common Service (SCR), with some 30% of total staff. However, it should be borne in mind that DG External Relations staff also have responsibility for activities which are not classified as ODA or OA, such as the EU's Common Foreign and Security Policy, and the management of external delegations (including in developed countries), for instance.[22] The SCR, therefore, contains the largest number of

---

[22] Since DG External Relations and DG Enlargement both contain staff with responsibilities which go beyond ODA and OA

staff with direct responsibility for managing (implementing) the Community's ODA and OA external cooperation programmes. DG Development, responsible for the planning and policies of the European Development Fund operations in ACP countries, contains 18% of total staff, while DG Enlargement, responsible for planning and policy towards the CEECS and NIS, contains some 10.5%. ECHO contains some 6% of total staff with responsibility for external humanitarian (relief) programmes.

The European Union currently has 106 delegations outside the EU, 91 of which (plus 14 offices) are situated in Africa, Asia, Latin America, the Mediterranean and the CEEC and NIS, covering 156 recipient countries. Between 1992 and 1999, 19 new delegations were opened, 11 of which were in the CEECs and NIS. Commission staff within the delegations totalled 1051, of which 654 were European Union officials and 380 were external staff (see Table 1.7).

Delegation staff have increased in the 1990s, though the precise changes in numbers are not readily available. Representation has always been better in the 71 ACP countries but has been reduced in recent years, which in 1999 have 48 delegations, 14 offices with a resident adviser and 3 offices with support staff only. Most of the countries in the Mediterranean region have delegations, while in the other regions only about half the countries have an EC delegation.

In practice, the level of responsibilities of the delegations varies from region to region, partly depending on the framework of the aid programmes, but in general the authority delegated to the field offices is limited. In the implementation of the Lomé Convention, delegates (Heads of Delegation) have authority, shared with the recipient government, to award study/technical assistance contracts up to 60 000 euro (80 0000 in the 8th EDF from 1997) and to approve contract awards after tender, under certain specified conditions, of up to 5 m euro. Delegates in the CEECs have been given similar authority in recent months.

Table 1.7: Staffing of the European Community External Cooperation Programmes (Following October 1999 Reorganisation)

DG	Officials	External Staff[d]	Total Staff
Headquarters:	1796	375	2171
DG External Relations[a]	662	107	769
DG Development	346	48	394
DG Enlargement[b]	185	43	228
ECHO	111	19	130
SCR	492	158	650
Delegation Staff[c]	654	380[e]	1051
Overall Total	2450	755	3222

[a] In addition to responsibilities with respect to ODA and OA, DG External Relations staff are also responsible for the Common Foreign and Security Policy (CFSP), management of external delegations, information for delegations, policy planning and coordination of policy on human rights and democratisation.
[b] In addition to responsibilities with respect to OA, DG Enlargement staff provide further assistance in support of the accession of CEECs to the European Union.
[c] It is currently not possible to break down Delegation Staff by indivdual DG
[d] Grade I: A grade equivalent. In addition there are 1475 staff at a lower level (grades II-V).
[e] Detached National Experts; auxiliaries; interimaires.

Source: European Commission, DG Development, Personnel Department, 1999.

activities, the total figures shown here exaggerate their weight in terms of absolute number and as a percentage of total staff. The precise number of such staff was not available. Therefore, the figures given for DG Development, ECHO and the SCR staff *as a percentage of total staff* with responsibility for ODA and OA programmes are an underestimate.

Administrative Costs

The DAC includes the following under the heading administrative costs: i) the administrative budget of the central aid agencies and executing agencies wholly concerned with ODA delivery; ii) a share of the total administrative costs of the executing agencies, proportional to the share of ODA disbursements in the agencies' total disbursements; and iii) administrative costs related to the aid programme borne by overseas representatives and diplomatic missions. All costs not appearing as part of the aid programmes, such as salary and overheads costs, must be included.

The European Commission calculates its administrative costs for submission to the Development Assistance Committee of the OECD. Costs for external cooperation are calculated by taking the percentage of the administration budget to the whole budget, and then applying this percentage to the Budget (B7) title. This method can only give an approximate cost, and is likely to underestimate the full cost as it does not take account of funding by the EDF, or EIB, though it does include all budget lines within B7[23]. It should be noted, however, that unlike some other donor organisations, EC administrative costs are not paid for out of the aid and cooperation budget and they therefore do not reduce the funds available for external cooperation.

Using this method the overall administration of the EC as a percentage of the total budget has varied between 3.2 and 3.3% of commitments for the years 1996–98 (3.4–3.5% of disbursements), and the costs of administering the external cooperation programme have been calculated as an annual average of 135 m euro (based on disbursement levels).

It is difficult to arrive at more accurate information on the costs of administration or compare between Directorate Generals, as these are not separated out in the budget, and Directorate Generals such as the Enlargement Service and the External Relations DG deal with many matters in addition to external cooperation.

An indication of the number of staff involved per 10 m euro committed can however be given. Table 1.8 provides a comparative analysis of the staffing levels of the various Directorates General responsible for EC external cooperation programmes in relation to their financial responsibilities. It indicates that DG External Relations is likely to be able to draw upon 2.8 staff for every 10 m euro of external assistance that it manages. At the other end of the spectrum lie the Common Service, with 1.2 staff per 10 m euro of commitments, and DG Development with 1.1 staff. In between are DG enlargement with 1.7 staff per 10 m euro and ECHO with 2.3 staff for every 10 m euro. However, it must be emphasised that these figures suffer from the same limitations as those indicated for Table 1.7, and must be treated as broad estimates. Thus, for instance, DG External Relations has responsibilities beyond managing ODA and OA programmes of external cooperation, and thus the number of staff available to manage each 10 m euro of commitments is in fact smaller than that shown in Table 1.8. The same qualification applies to DG Enlargement, which also in reality can draw on fewer staff than the 1.7 per 10 m euro indicated. Finally, when considering the relative high figure of 2.3 staff per 10 m euro shown for ECHO, it should be borne in mind that ECHO is responsible for managing the entire project cycle of humanitarian (relief) assistance, unlike other Directorates General which deal either with political selections and policy, or with implementation.

Decision-Making

Decisions on EC aid and cooperation policies are formally taken by the Council of Ministers (the Development Council) which adopts regulations and directives on the basis of the Commission's proposals (see Box 1.4 for an explanation of terms). The Development Council consists of the Ministers for Development Cooperation (or their equivalents) of the 15 Member States, but their resolutions are not binding on the Member States. Since the Maastricht Treaty, decisions on external

---

[23] Whereas all of Budget Chapter B7 is included in the DAC returns, this study, having had the opportunity to investigate further, has concluded that some lines do not qualify as ODA or OA and has therefore excluded them.

Table 1.8 Comparative Analysis of External Relations Group: Financial Responsibilities and Staffing Levels

DG	Financial Responsibilties	Forecast Commitments (m euro) 1999	HQ Staffing	HQ Staffing (per 10 m euro)
External Relations DG[a]	TACIS, MEDA, ALA, Balkans, Human Rights	2170	769	2.8
Development DG	EDF, Food Aid, NGO's, Thematic budget lines	3540[c]	394	1.1
Enlargement Service[b]	Preaccession instruments	1318 (2000: 3166[d])	228	1.7
ECHO	Humanitarian assistance	558[e]	130	2.3[f]
Common Service for External Relations (SCR)	All, except humanitarian assistance	5570[g]	650	1.2

[a] In addition to responsibilities with respect to ODA and OA, External Relations DG staff are also responsible for the Common Foreign and Security Policy (CFSP), management of external delegations, information for delegations, policy planning and coordination of policy on human rights and democratisation.
[b] In addition to responsibilities with respect to OA, Enlargement Service staff provide further assistance in support of the accession of CEECs to the European Union.
[c] EDF: 2600 + Budget lines 940
[d] Will be partly managed in collaboration with DG Economic and Financial Affairs
[e] 1998
[f] ECHO is responsible for the entire project cycle of humanitarian assistance
[g] Disbursements.

Source: European Commission, Development DG, Personnel Department, 1999.

---

aid financed through the EC Budget are now taken on the basis of qualified majority voting. This was extended under the Amsterdam Treaty of 1997 (see Box 1.5). The actors in the process of decision making and the instruments available to them are summarised below.

Actors	Instruments
European Parliament	Control of Commission's budget; Introduction of special budget lines to support policies.
EU Member States	Council of Ministers; EDF and other management committees; Contributions to the EDF
Council of Ministers	Formal power to issue resolutions and regulation
European Commission	Formal monopoly of policy initiation; Agenda setting

Budgetary decisions have to be taken jointly by Parliament and the Council, although Parliament plays the dominant role: it has the last word on non-compulsory expenditure, which includes Title 9 (part of Development Aid expenditure) and is responsible for the final adoption of the budget, which it can also reject as a whole. It only has a limited input on compulsory expenditure, which includes most Food Aid.

The European Commission produces a preliminary draft on the basis of estimates of the requirements of the Union and its institutions. This preliminary draft is sent to the Council, which acting by a qualified majority, makes amendments and then establishes the draft budget. The European Parliament can within limits propose modifications to 'non-compulsory' expenditure items: these must be adopted by a majority of the component Members of Parliament. Parliament may also, acting by a majority of its Members and three-fifths of the votes cast, reject the budget as a whole. Should it do so, the procedure must begin again from the start, on the basis of a new draft.

EC aid to the ACP countries supplied under the Lomé Convention is decided on an intergovernmental basis, also subject to majority voting. One of the consequences of this intergovernmental nature of Lomé spending is that the European Parliament has no formal role in controlling the expenditure of the EDF, although its Development Committee has 'monitored' decisions taken, eg. in the mid-term review of Lomé IV. The Parliament has also sought to exert influence by 'discharging' EDF spending each year, and in 1996 it refused to give such a discharge and asked that the EDF be budgetised (made part of the overall EC Budget). National parliaments of the Member States do have control over the EDF, which some exercise more than others. All other aid flows, apart from the EDF, are subject to the control of the European Parliament, which approves each individual budget line. In the past the Parliament has used its power to block financial protocols, such as in the case of Syria and Turkey.[24]

> **Box 1.4: European legislation**
>
> **Regulations** are general legislative measures which are binding and take effect directly in the national legal order, without need for national implementing measures.
>
> **Directives** are binding upon a Member State as to the result to be achieved but require implementing into national law before they are effective.
>
> **Decisions** are measures of an individual nature which may be addressed to individuals, to undertakings or to Member States and are binding on the addressee.
>
> **Conclusions, Communications, Declarations, Recommendations, Resolutions and Opinions** are rules of conduct which have no legally binding force. They are used as persuasive guides to the interpretation of other measures adopted by the EU or the Member States.

Policies relating to the Lomé Convention are decided according to the procedures set out in the Convention. Most areas for decision-making are shared by the Community and the ACP countries. Joint ACP–EC institutions exist at three levels: the Council of Ministers, the Committee of Ambassadors and the Joint Assembly (bringing ACP and EC Members of Parliament together) (see Chapter 3).

For the Community, rules on EDF decision making for the *ACP countries* are included in the Internal Financing Agreement. The Commission submits country programmes and projects to be financed from the EDF for approval by the Member States in the EDF Committee, which meets every month. The voting power of each Member State in the Committee is related to its contribution to the EDF, but it is rare that financing proposals are put to a vote. The Committee expresses an opinion and it is the Commission which has the formal power to approve or reject proposals. The Committee rarely expresses a negative opinion, but when it does the proposal is usually reconsidered at the next meeting to allow officials time to amend it. The Committee has more authority over programmable aid (National and Regional Indicative Programmes) than over non-programmable resources, such as Stabex.

> **Box 1.5: The Amsterdam Treaty and External Cooperation**
>
> The Amsterdam Treaty was signed on 2 October 1997. It is not an entity in its own right but is a series of amendments to the previous treaties. The key changes are as follows:
>
> **Decision-making procedures:** The role of qualified majority voting by the Council has been extended, and the decision-making procedures have been rationalised so that the co-decision, consultation and assent procedures are now dominant:
> - *Consultation*: Parliament's opinion is required, but can be ignored.
> - *Assent*: Parliament's agreement is required; it can approve or reject the proposal but cannot amend it.
> - *Co-decision*: Parliament may negotiate on draft legislation as a full partner with the Council.
> - Some areas are subject to *qualified majority voting* and others to *unanimity* within the Council. Co-decision was extended to development cooperation under ex article 130w, new article 179.
>
> **Sustainable development:** New article 6 attempts to integrate environmental protection into every aspect of EU policy making, 'with a view to promoting sustainable development'. (Article 6, Title II).
>
> **Consistency in external activities**: Article 3 of the Common Provisions inserted the obligation of the Council and Commission to co-operate in order to achieve the aim of ensuring consistency in its external activities in the context of its external relations, security, economic and development policies.
>
> **Human rights and fundamental freedoms**: The Common Provisions were amended to include the statement that 'The Union s founded on the principles of liberty, democracy, respect for human rights and fundamental freedoms'. (Article 6.1, Common Provisions)

---

[24] Following the cooperation procedure (art. 189c of the Maastricht Treaty), amendments made by the EP can only be rejected by the Council if there is unanimity.

A separate committee of Member States representatives (the 'Article 28 Committee'), meets five or six times a year to approve the allocation of interest rate subsidies and risk capital from the EDF managed by the European Investment Bank.

The overall financial framework for Community aid to *Asia*, *Latin America*, and the *Mediterranean* follows a five-year plan, though the authority to commit and disburse funds is granted on an annual basis only. Decisions are taken by the Commission, taking into account the views of the management committees of the ALA and MEDA programmes in which the Member States are represented. In practice, the Commission has greater scope to respond to changing political or economic conditions in these countries, and can vary amounts to individual countries providing it stays within the overall annual budget appropriation. Country strategy papers are drawn up by the Commission and discussed with delegations, the recipient country and the member states. The strategy is then placed before the ALA or MED committee for their opinion. A NIP emerges from this process. In 2000 a Regional Indicative Programme will also be prepared for the Mediterranean region.

As with the ALA and Mediterranean programmes, *Phare* and *Tacis* are funded through the Communities general Budget, determined by the European Parliament and the Council of Ministers. Multi-annual Indicative Programmes are prepared in cooperation with partner countries, indicating the nature of interventions for each sector. These programmes run for three years in the case of Phare, while for Tacis they have been extended since 1995 to cover four years. The shift from annual to multi-annual programmes has been found to accelerate the implementation of the EC's programmes, as well as providing scope for a more strategic approach. Commitments and disbursements, however, remain subject to the annual budget cycle of the Commission.

Operational programmes and the associated funds within the *Phare* programme are subject to approval by the Phare Management Committee. However substantial moves have been made towards decentralisation (increased responsibility for the Commission's Delegations in the partner countries) and deconcentration (transfer of responsibility to the partner countries themselves) (see Box 1.6). As a result, and thanks to the efforts of the SCR, 1998 saw a record total of contracting (1260 m euro), and the level of uncontracted funds available under Phare fell for the first time since the Programme began in 1990.

Decision-making in *Tacis* also places increasing emphasis on decentralisation, though it is less advanced than for Phare. Community attempts to strengthen political and economic ties with the New Independent States resulted in the establishment of a number of delegations which have also helped to strengthen Tacis' presence on the ground. Delegations (coordinating units) were established in Moscow in 1991, in Kiev (Ukraine) in 1994, and more recently in Almaty (Kazakhstan) and Tbilisi (Georgia). The intention is to open technical offices in

> **Box 1.6: Deconcentration and Decentralisation in the Phare Programme**
>
> **Deconcentration** is the transfer of the Commission's responsibilities for Phare programme implementation and supervision from its headquarters in Brussels to its Delegations in the partner countries, enabling decisions to be taken on the ground. It is supported by the Court of Auditors and the European Parliament as a means of reducing the duplication of control and decision-making processes between headquarters and the Delegations. The Head of Delegation now has the authority to approve all tender documents, to approve tender evaluations, and endorse contracts up to 5 m euro (as for the ACP countries).
>
> Deconcentration is being implemented in all the partner countries' Delegations. In order to ensure that they are able to manage the increased workload, extra staff are deployed and internal procedures are being improved.
>
> **Decentralisation** is the transfer of greater management responsibility from the Commission to the partner countries themselves. This means that, to the extent permitted by the European Communities' Financial Regulation, the implementation of national programmes will become the responsibility of the candidate countries, under the supervision of the European Commission, which remains ultimately responsible for the use of the funds.
>
> One of the aims of decentralisation is to prepare progressively the candidate countries to administer Community funds after accession. The intention is to establish, within limits and in a gradual manner, a relationship between the Commission and the candidate countries in which responsibility is shared, similar to that which exists with Member States for implementing the Structural Funds.

some partner countries with close links to a coordinating unit and reporting directly to Brussels. In addition to the regional committees of Member State representatives, there is a separate financial committee for food aid.

Project Design, Appraisal and Evaluation

Various initiatives have taken place in recent years on programme and project design and appraisal including the introduction of integrated project cycle management (PCM) from about 1992 and introduction of a Quality Support Group (QSG) in 1997. A new manual of financial and economic analysis of projects and programmes was issued in September 1997.

The Evaluation Unit is located in the SCR and evaluates all the external cooperation programmes of the European Commission except the Humanitarian (relief) aid provided by ECHO. It covers all geographical regions and the corresponding EC external cooperation programmes. The work programme of the Evaluation Unit is built around a rolling 1–2 year programme covering several dozen multi-project and often multi-country evaluations of sectoral programmes (e.g. health, education) and themes (e.g. regional cooperation, post-emergency rehabilitation). Evaluations compare the design and implementation of projects/programmes to actual outcomes by analysing their:

- **relevance** – to objectives and to in-country needs;
- **efficiency** – in providing inputs promptly and at least cost;
- **effectiveness** – in achieving planned outputs and immediate results;
- **impact** – on high-level objectives to which the results should contribute;
- **sustainability** – over time, usually after the inputs have all been provided and external support stops.

Evaluation is funded both from its own budget line (B7–6510), for which disbursements averaged 4.3 m euro for the years 1996–98, and from the EDF and other budget lines. Together the sums disbursed on evaluation totalled some 8.5 m euro in 1997. It should be noted that these figures only cover formally programmed evaluations. In addition, individual services within the Commission also carry out their own evaluation and monitoring activities for the purposes of improving management effectiveness, and which are not captured here.

2

How is EC External Cooperation Spent?

Categorising EC External Cooperation

Attempts to analyse where European Community aid as a whole has been spent (as distinct from parts reported on separately to the Council and Parliament), and what it has been spent on, have always been hampered by the inadequate or inconsistent categorisation of EC aid within the Commission. Except in the case of the EDF, data have been collected to meet internal administrative requirements rather than to facilitate an understanding of the development purposes of the aid. The EDF is currently the only programme which conforms to the reporting procedures of the OECD Development Assistance Committee, of which the European Commission is a member, although there is a commitment to improving the management information systems for all EC aid programmes. As a result, although a considerable amount of information is available on EC aid flows for 1986–98 it is difficult to use because of its diffuse and non-standardised nature.

This was addressed in 1997 in an EC/ODI publication, *Understanding European Community Aid*.[1] This analysis builds on this, and again collected data at a highly disaggregated level to permit the presentation of an overall picture of the nature of EC aid. The raw data available for each aid programme have been reclassified according to a standard sectoral classification, thus providing a basis for comparing the main regional programmes. The recategorisation of EC aid according to these instruments, sectors and subsectors yields reasonably comprehensive information, with only 8.2% of all EC aid commitments remaining unclassifiable by country or region, while 10.0% is unallocable by development purpose or sector.[2]

Data were collected for commitments and disbursements (where available) and not for the intermediary stage, used within parts of the Commission, called 'contracts' or 'secondary commitments'. In this study commitments are understood to correspond to an internal Commission act which precedes the signing of the project financing agreements with beneficiary governments or regional or other (eg NGO) entities. Disbursements represent the actual payments made to the governments or other bodies, and they follow a timetable specific to each project agreement and contract. The categorisation adopted is based on that used by the OECD DAC, but has been adapted to take account of the particularities of EC aid. Furthermore, by being based on the DAC sector codes it is hoped that this review of EC aid will also help the European Commission to fulfil its reporting requirements to the Development Assistance Committee. Five main instruments have been identified, with the fifth – Project Aid – subdivided into six sectors. These eleven headings correspond closely to the principal types of EC aid, and allow a more detailed picture to be presented than would reliance on the eight main categories used by the DAC.[3] Some of the instruments and sectors have in turn been

---

[1] Aidan Cox and Antonique Koning (1997), *Understanding European Community Aid: aid policies, management and distribution explained*. European Commission/ODI: London.

[2] For disbursements the unallocable is higher, which is why the present analysis is undertaken mainly on the basis of commitments.

[3] The DAC uses 10 main headings but 'Action relating to debt' fell outside the Community's remit for the 1986–98 period, though this is likely to change given recent commitments to support HIPC II. The category 'Administrative costs' cannot currently be discretely identified.

subdivided into subsectors giving a total of 26 categories.[4] The instruments and categories are listed below:

1. **Programme Aid**
   - Support for structural adjustment
   - Stabex
   - Sysmin

2. **Food aid (developmental)**

3. **Humanitarian Assistance**

4. **Aid to NGOs**

5. **Project Aid**

    5.1 **Natural Resources Productive Sectors**
    - Agriculture
    - Forestry
    - Fisheries

    5.2 **Other Productive Sectors**
    - Industry, mining and construction
    - Trade
    - Tourism
    - Investment promotion

    5.3 **Economic Infrastructure and Services**
    - Transport and communications
    - Energy
    - Banking, finance and business services

    5.4 **Social Infrastructure and Services**
    - Education
    - Health and population
    - Water supply
    - Other social infrastructure and services

    5.5 **Governance and Civil Society**

    5.6 **Multi-sector/Crosscutting**
    - Environment
    - Women in development
    - Rural development
    - Other multisector

6. **Unallocable**

It is currently not possible to categorise data on EC aid flows by 'theme'. There is an intention to introduce a 'marker' system for themes such as gender, direct assistance to poor people, participatory development, good governance and the environment. However implementation is insufficiently advanced to permit a thematic analysis in this study. This means that statistical data for Gender and Development or the environment, for example, include only funds allocated specifically to these themes, and therefore are likely to underestimate the EC aid contribution in these areas.

It is also not yet possible to draw out figures for support to Sector Wide Approaches (SWAPs). The funding for SWAPs is drawn partly from counterpart funds generated by programme aid and partly from funds falling under the category 'project aid'. Current data do not allow these to be differentiated.

---

[4] This represents a simplification of the DAC system, which uses 35 categories relevant to EC aid. The ODI categories, however, remain compatible with DAC codes.

Overview of the Main Instruments and Sectors of EC Cooperation

General trends in allocations to instruments and sectors are covered here, and a more detailed analysis is provided later in the Chapter and in Chapters 3 to 7. Over the 1986–98 period, aid through the four main instruments (programme aid, food aid, humanitarian assistance, and aid to NGOs)[5] has declined as a share of total allocable EC aid, from an average of 46% for 1986–90 to 43% for 1991–95, and to 36% for 1996–98.[6] Project aid, the fifth instrument, in contrast, increased from 54% for 1986–90 to 64% for 1996–98.

Yet these aggregate figures conceal a number of opposing trends, which are clearly shown in Figure 2.1. Aid through one instrument – humanitarian assistance – increased enormously. It more than doubled from 1986–90 to 1991–5 as a proportion of total allocable aid, to 13%, and rose again to average 14% for 1996–8, though it dipped in 1997 and 1998. This increase reflects the increased priority given to humanitarian assistance since the establishment of ECHO in 1992 and the EC's response to the crises in former Yugoslavia and Rwanda/Burundi. Aid through the other three instruments, however, either stagnated or decreased as a proportion of total aid, though even here the picture is not a straightforward one. Thus programme aid declined relative to total EC aid from 16% (86–90) to 13% (91–95) to 10% (96–98), due very largely to the negligible total for Stabex in 1993

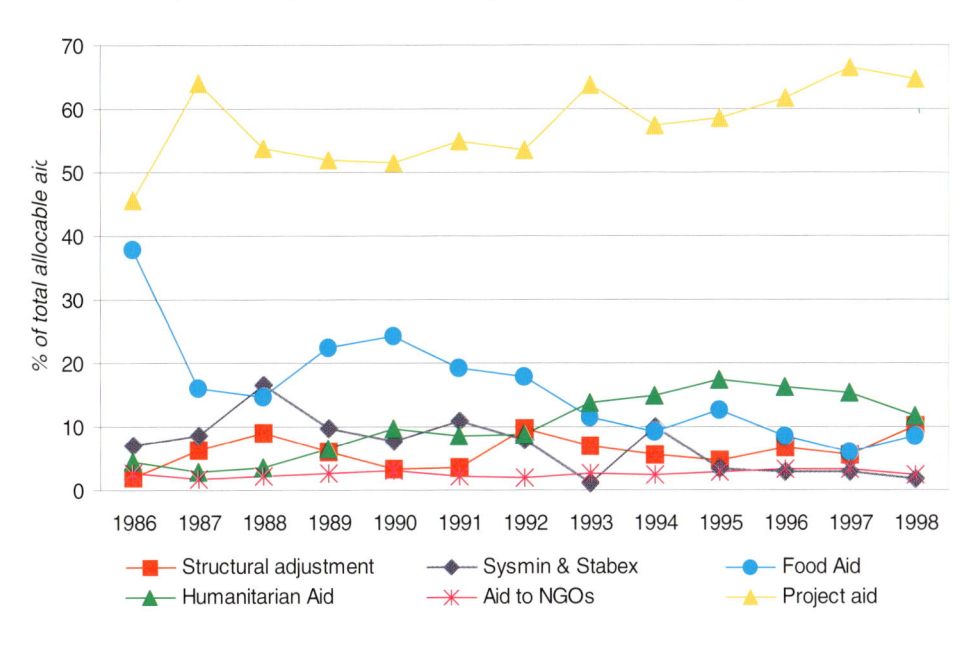

Figure 2.1: Main Instruments of EC External Cooperation (1986–98, commitments, % of allocable aid)

Source: European Commission/ODI database 1999

and 1997 and for Sysmin in 1998. Support to structural adjustment actually increased in absolute terms from an annual average of 180 m euro (86–90) to 382 m euro (91–95) to 526 m euro (96–98) and also

---

[5] For convenience the term 'instruments' will be used to refer to the first four instruments, while the fifth instrument will henceforth be referred to as 'project aid'.

[6] Trends in sectoral shares over time could be influenced by fluctuations in the proportion of EC aid that is unallocable by sector. To avoid this the shares cited in this chapter are expressed as a proportion of total allocable aid. For completeness, however, Table 2.1 includes the unallocable amount and expresses shares as a proportion of total aid, with the result that the sectoral shares shown in Table 2.1 are lower.

from 5.9% of total allocable aid (86–90) to 7.8% (96–98). Food aid, peaked in absolute terms in 1992, but has fallen since; declining as a proportion of allocable cooperation, from an average of over 21% for 1986–90, to 14% during 1991–95 and again to 8% for 1996–98 (Figure 2.2 and Table 2.1). Part of the most recent decline is due to the fact that some assistance provided through the food aid instrument is now classified under the agricultural and other sector headings. Aid committed to NGOs, largely through the co-financing instrument, maintained a constant share (2.5%) for the period 1986–95, rising to 3.1% for 1996–98.

A sketch of the trends in project aid reveals two main trends. One group increased in absolute terms during the three time periods (1989–90, 1991–95 and 1996–98): industry, mining and construction; tourism and investment promotion; transport and communications; banking, financial and business services; all social sectors; and governance and civil society. The second group peaked in absolute terms during 1991–95, and has fallen since; agriculture; forestry and fisheries; trade; environment; and energy. The exception is rural development which declined in absolute commitments from the first to the second time period, but then rose slightly.

In relative terms, aid to the natural resources sector declined considerably relative to the whole aid programme, falling from 13%, to 8%, to 4%. Aid to the 'other productive sectors' (industry, trade, tourism and investment promotion) fell in relative terms (from 8%, to 6%, to 6%), due to a decline in the share of aid to industry, mining and construction.

Aid to all other sectors and subsectors rose, or at least remained stable, relative to total EC aid over the two periods. The social infrastructure and services sector rose most, from nearly 6% during 1986–90, to nearly 13% for 1991–95, and nearly 19% for 1996–8. Within that the subsectors of education tripled as a share of total aid to 6%, health rose from 1% to 4% over the whole time period. Economic infrastructure also grew very significantly, over the first two time periods from 14% to over 21%. Aid to strengthen government and civil society also grew substantially,

Figure 2.2: Sectoral Allocation of EC External Cooperation to all Regions (1986–98, commitments, % of allocable aid)

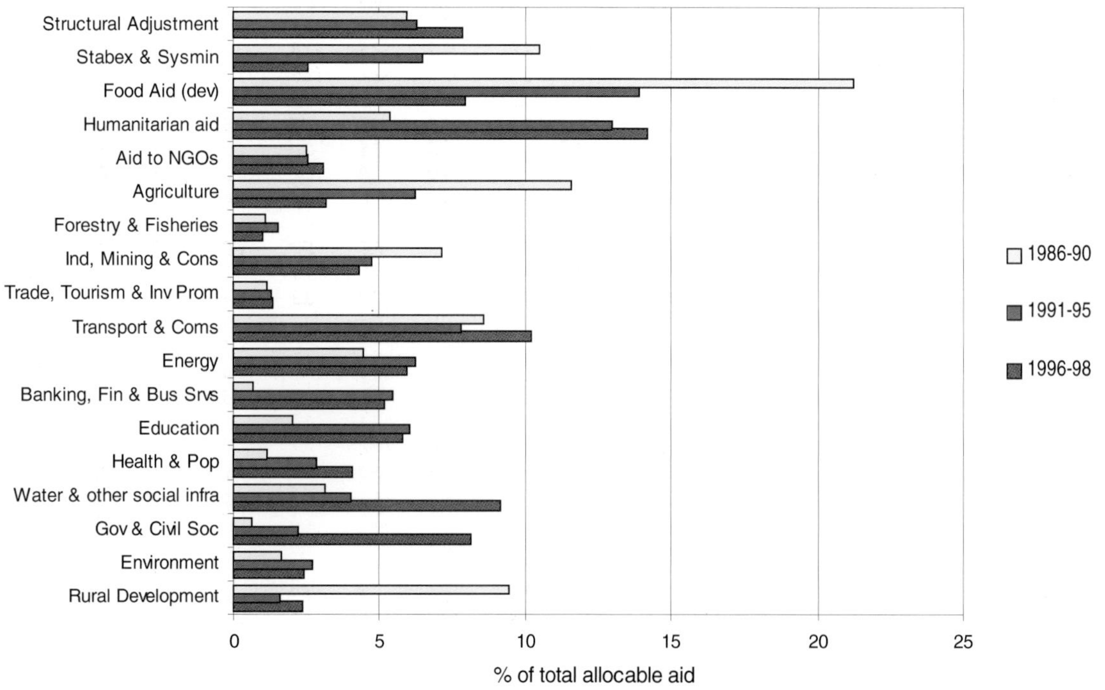

Source: European Commission/ODI database 1999

Table 2.1: Sectoral Allocation of all EC External Cooperation
(1986–98, commitments, m euro and % of total aid)

Commitmnts (m euro)	1986	1987	1988	1989	1990	1991	1992	1993	1994	1995	1996	1997	1998	Total
Programme Aid	159	529	983	487	339	716	1097	512	1048	512	624	489	974	8471
Structural Adjustment	37	222	351	189	104	183	608	444	376	297	435	321	822	4388
Stabex	122	308	566	283	220	515	397	4	615	131	155	–	152	3468
Sysmin	–	–	66	16	15	18	92	64	57	84	34	168	1	616
Food Aid (development)	665	568	563	681	741	950	1115	734	626	809	560	349	690	9051
Humanitarian Aid	80	100	135	198	299	423	543	870	1009	1117	1044	883	936	7639
Humanit excl rehabilitation	59	74	106	165	259	379	502	823	915	812	795	548	619	6057
Rehabilitation	21	27	29	32	41	44	41	47	94	305	249	335	317	1583
Aid to NGOs	49	65	83	86	95	115	125	168	175	193	214	201	204	1772
Natural Resources	163	560	464	322	414	443	432	568	483	452	178	224	437	5139
Agriculture	154	530	413	290	370	406	322	466	377	333	93	176	368	4297
Forestry	0	23	1	8	27	6	87	68	79	117	78	51	60	606
Fisheries	9	6	49	24	17	32	23	34	27	2	6	-3	9	236
Other Productive Services	214	245	306	274	215	380	314	402	387	363	242	310	592	4245
Industry, Mining & Construc	203	232	275	240	132	340	235	284	319	274	144	238	490	3405
Trade	7	13	16	21	48	28	45	61	24	27	9	5	43	346
Tourism	3	1	14	9	23	1	12	28	5	21	19	6	31	173
Investment Promotion	–	–	1	5	13	12	22	29	39	42	70	61	28	321
Econ Infrastructure & Servs	249	613	396	498	316	1009	993	1178	1395	1366	1425	1015	1850	12302
Transport & Comms	130	445	257	331	136	449	380	390	602	555	686	438	928	5728
Energy	112	166	132	162	102	276	320	367	491	446	474	287	434	3769
Banking, Finance & Bus Srvs	8	1	7	4	78	283	292	421	303	365	265	290	488	2806
Social Infrastructure & Servs	86	207	285	145	228	524	743	1042	745	882	1195	1342	1291	8713
Education	13	69	72	53	100	236	295	553	429	330	335	380	450	3314
Health & Population	24	47	56	26	22	146	168	209	115	227	270	235	313	1858
Water Supply	49	60	144	49	90	64	210	186	89	246	357	343	293	2179
Other Social Infra & Services	1	31	13	17	16	78	69	94	112	79	233	384	235	1362
Governance & Civil Society	3	12	17	12	53	58	120	165	207	117	504	612	525	2407
Multisector/Crosscutting	89	621	599	326	339	284	720	673	653	550	422	321	481	6079
Environment	4	4	16	50	172	106	160	164	140	250	226	113	146	1551
Women in Development	–	–	–	1	0	0	2	5	7	39	20	6	13	94
Rural Development	7	579	529	239	80	91	195	95	67	33	110	146	215	2385
Other Multisector	78	38	54	37	86	87	363	410	439	228	67	56	107	2050
Unallocable by Sector	796	335	365	286	216	666	394	487	573	981	827	769	632	7336
TOTAL	2553	3857	4196	3314	3255	5567	6597	6800	7303	7344	7234	6515	8614	73155

Commitments (%)	1986	1987	1988	1989	1990	1991	1992	1993	1994	1995	1996	1997	1998	Total
Programme Aid	6.2	13.7	23.4	14.7	10.4	12.9	16.6	7.5	14.4	7.0	8.6	7.5	11.3	11.6
Structural Adjustment	1.4	5.7	8.4	5.7	3.2	3.3	9.2	6.5	5.1	4.0	6.0	4.9	9.5	6.0
Stabex	4.8	8.0	13.5	8.5	6.8	9.2	6.0	0.1	8.4	1.8	2.1	–	1.8	4.7
Sysmin	–	–	1.6	0.5	0.5	0.3	1.4	0.9	0.8	1.2	0.5	2.6	–	0.8
Food Aid (development)	26.0	14.7	13.4	20.5	22.8	17.1	16.9	10.8	8.6	11.0	7.7	5.4	8.0	12.4
Humanitarian Aid	3.1	2.6	3.2	6.0	9.2	7.6	8.2	12.8	13.8	15.2	14.4	13.6	10.9	10.4
Humanit excl rehabilitation	2.3	1.9	2.5	5.0	7.9	6.8	7.6	12.1	12.5	11.1	11.0	8.4	7.2	8.3
Rehabilitation	0.8	0.7	0.7	1.0	1.3	0.8	0.6	0.7	1.3	4.2	3.4	5.1	3.7	2.2
Aid to NGOs	1.9	1.7	2.0	2.6	2.9	2.1	1.9	2.5	2.4	2.6	3.0	3.1	2.4	2.4
Natural Resources	6.4	14.5	11.1	9.7	12.7	8.0	6.5	8.4	6.6	6.2	2.5	3.4	5.1	7.0
Agriculture	6.0	13.8	9.8	8.7	11.4	7.3	4.9	6.9	5.2	4.5	1.3	2.7	4.3	5.9
Forestry	–	0.6	–	0.3	0.8	0.1	1.3	1.0	1.1	1.6	1.1	0.8	0.7	0.8
Fisheries	0.3	0.2	1.2	0.7	0.5	0.6	0.4	0.5	0.4	–	0.1	–	0.1	0.3
Other Productive Services	8.4	6.4	7.3	8.3	6.6	6.8	4.8	5.9	5.3	4.9	3.3	4.8	6.9	5.8
Industry, Mining & Construc	8.0	6.0	6.6	7.2	4.0	6.1	3.6	4.2	4.4	3.7	2.0	3.7	5.7	4.7
Trade	0.3	0.3	0.4	0.6	1.5	0.5	0.7	0.9	0.3	0.4	0.1	0.1	0.5	0.5
Tourism	0.1	0.0	0.3	0.3	0.7	0.0	0.2	0.4	0.1	0.3	0.3	0.1	0.4	0.2
Investment Promotion	–	–	–	0.1	0.4	0.2	0.3	0.4	0.5	0.6	1.0	0.9	0.3	0.4
Econ Infrastructure & Servs	9.8	15.9	9.4	15.0	9.7	18.1	15.0	17.3	19.1	18.6	19.7	15.6	21.5	16.8
Transport & Comms	5.1	11.5	6.1	10.0	4.2	8.1	5.8	5.7	8.2	7.6	9.5	6.7	10.8	7.8
Energy	4.4	4.3	3.2	4.9	3.1	5.0	4.8	5.4	6.7	6.1	6.5	4.4	5.0	5.2
Banking, Finance & Bus Srvs	0.3	0.0	0.2	0.1	2.4	5.1	4.4	6.2	4.2	5.0	3.7	4.4	5.7	3.8
Social Infrastructure & Servs	3.4	5.4	6.8	4.4	7.0	9.4	11.3	15.3	10.2	12.0	16.5	20.6	15.0	11.9
Education	0.5	1.8	1.7	1.6	3.1	4.2	4.5	8.1	5.9	4.5	4.6	5.8	5.2	4.5
Health & Population	0.9	1.2	1.3	0.8	0.7	2.6	2.5	3.1	1.6	3.1	3.7	3.6	3.6	2.5
Water Supply	1.9	1.6	3.4	1.5	2.8	1.1	3.2	2.7	1.2	3.3	4.9	5.3	3.4	3.0
Other Social Infra & Services	–	0.8	0.3	0.5	0.5	1.4	1.1	1.4	1.5	1.1	3.2	5.9	2.7	1.9
Governance & Civil Society	0.1	0.3	0.4	0.4	1.6	1.0	1.8	2.4	2.8	1.6	7.0	9.4	6.1	3.3
Multisector/Crosscutting	3.5	16.1	14.3	9.8	10.4	5.1	10.9	9.9	8.9	7.5	5.8	4.9	5.6	8.3
Environment	0.1	0.1	0.4	1.5	5.3	1.9	2.4	2.4	1.9	3.4	3.1	1.7	1.7	2.1
Women in Development	–	–	–	–	–	–	–	0.1	0.1	0.5	0.3	0.1	0.2	0.1
Rural Development	0.3	15.0	12.6	7.2	2.5	1.6	3.0	1.4	0.9	0.4	1.5	2.2	2.5	3.3
Other Multisector	3.1	1.0	1.3	1.1	2.6	1.6	5.5	6.0	6.0	3.1	0.9	0.9	1.2	2.8
Unallocable by Sector	31.2	8.7	8.7	8.6	6.6	12.0	6.0	7.2	7.8	13.4	11.4	11.8	7.3	10.0
TOTAL	100	100	100	100	100	100	100	100	100	100	100	100	100	100

Source: European Commission/ODI database 1999

particularly with the establishment of a budget line (B7–5053/B7–5220[7]) in 1992 to promote human rights and democracy, increasing from 0.6% to 2.2% and then to 8.2%. Aid targeted specifically at the environment became quite sizeable in the course of the 1990s, rising to nearly 3% of the entire aid programme. Finally, it should be noted that these figures have been calculated to avoid the possibility of double-counting (where aid flows are counted towards more than one sector).

EC External Cooperation Through Instruments

Programme Aid

The category 'programme aid' includes support for structural adjustment (which includes import support programmes initiated under Lomé III) and the EC's two distinct commodity support schemes – Stabex and Sysmin. The programme aid instrument is largely a feature of EC aid to the ACP, which received 89% of all commitments over the 1986–98 period, and where it accounted for over a quarter of all aid.

Support for structural adjustment is provided as import support, in kind or in foreign currency, to support the central budget of recipient countries. Most of these concessional funds benefit the ACP countries and have been financed from the EDF, though a small amount of structural adjustment support was allocated to Mediterranean, CEEC and NIS countries from the EC budget in recent years.

Import support for ACP countries has evolved substantially since 1986 when it was first introduced in the Commission. Initially ACP countries received support in the form of 'sectoral development and import programmes' (art. 188 of Lomé III). These programmes were designed to support economic growth and in particular to help redress the negative effects of reforms on the poor. Subsequently, in 1987, the 'Special Debt Programme' was introduced. This special facility provided import support to ACP countries which were heavily indebted and implementing a structural adjustment programme or which had undertaken macroeconomic adjustment policies acceptable to the EC. Under Lomé IV the Community's commitment to support structural adjustment programmes as negotiated with the IMF and World Bank was strengthened and a new facility for structural adjustment support was created (art. 243–250 of Lomé IV); 1150 m euro and 1400 m euro were allocated from EDF 7 (1990–95) and EDF 8 (1995–2000) respectively for this facility. (See Chapter 3 for further information on import support to ACP countries.)

From 1992 onwards, four south-eastern Mediterranean countries (Algeria, Morocco, Jordan and Tunisia) received structural adjustment assistance with a special facility of 300 m euro included in the off-protocol budget line which preceded MEDA. In 1992 and 1994 Albania received respectively 70 and 35 m euro for balance of payments support financed out of the Phare programme. In 1998, a new budget line (B7–531) financed some 18 m euro of exceptional financial assistance for Armenia and Georgia granted in conjunction with a long-term loan. Macro-financial assistance in the form of loans has also been provided to Mediterranean countries and the CEECs and NIS, although these are excluded from the present analysis since they do not qualify as ODA or OA (see also section on macro-financial assistance in Chapter 1.) The budget support mechanisms are likely to be strengthened in early 2000 under a new MEDA Regulation proposed by the Commission.

Stabex and *Sysmin* are financed by EDF contributions to ACP countries, with the exception of some Stabex-type assistance for some non-ACP countries in a number of years.[8] Stabex and Sysmin are therefore discussed further in Chapter 3.

---

[7] This has since become nine budget lines under the chapter B7–70

[8] Between 1987 and 1991 a special budget line analogous to Stabex existed in support of non-ACP least-developed countries Bangladesh, Nepal, Yemen, and Haiti (the last becoming a signatory of the Lomé Convention only in 1991). Information about this budget line is included in the section on Stabex in Chapter 5.

Between 1986 and 1998 almost 8.5 bn euro has been committed to programme aid. More than half of this (4.4 bn euro) was support for Structural Adjustment. The Stabex facility accounted for 44.1% (3.5 bn euro) of all programme aid commitments, while only 0.8% was committed through Sysmin. The quick-disbursing nature of programme aid is demonstrated by the high disbursement levels throughout the period with disbursements totalling 91% of total commitments.

Food Aid

Dating from 1967, food aid was the first instrument to be introduced outside the framework of existing cooperation agreements and financed from the EC budget. Food aid, which is provided on a grant basis, is provided to all regions without conditionality. Three forms of food aid can be distinguished: food security projects, emergency food aid and programme or structural food aid. The latter is sold on the local markets and generates counterpart funds which are managed in a similar way to those generated by general import support. These funds were initially intended for agricultural development, but this has changed since the DAC Principles of 1992 have indicated that counterpart funds should contribute to a country's general budget, rather than being tied to particular projects or sectors. Emergency food aid has become the responsibility of ECHO since its establishment in 1992, and a separate budget line was created for it in 1993.

Food aid originally responded to the need to dispose of European Community food surpluses, and was therefore managed according to the rules of the Common Agricultural Policy. It was managed in conjunction with the agricultural directorate (DG VI), but the main responsibility for its allocation and for negotiations with the recipients lay with DG VIII.

> **Box 2.1: Objectives of Food Aid and Operations in support of food security**
>
> - to promote food security;
> - to raise the standard of nutrition;
> - to promote the availability and accessibility of foodstuffs to the public;
> - to contribute to balanced social and economic development;
> - to support efforts to improve food production;
> - to reduce dependence on food aid;
> - to encourage independence in food by enhancing food production and/or purchasing power;
> - to contribute to initiatives to combat poverty.
>
> The allocation criteria for EC food aid are (i) food shortages, (ii) per capita income and the existence of particularly poor population groups, (iii) social indicators of the welfare of people, (iv) BoP situation of the country, (v) the economic and social impact and financial cost of the proposed action and (vi) the existence of a long-term policy on food security in the recipient country. The last criterion has been introduced recently.
>
> Source: Council Regulation 1292/96, 27.6.1996

In 1982 a first step was taken to transform food aid into an independent policy aimed at development objectives. A further step was taken in 1986 when food aid was dissociated from the Common Agricultural Policy, and further emphasis was put on purchasing the products in developing countries ('triangular operation') or in the specific country of destination ('local purchase'). New procedures for the mobilisation of products in the Community were introduced in 1987, following which DG Development also became responsible for the execution of the aid. However, DG Agriculture remained responsible for the initiation of the mobilisations. In 1996 the preferential procurement of products in the Community was abandoned. Procurements in third countries are either handled exclusively by the Common Service for External Relations (SCR) or entrusted to the beneficiary organisations.

The 1986 Council Regulation which defined policy and management guidelines for EC food aid was superseded by a Regulation in June 1996 which sought to take into account the objectives of the Treaty on European Union, and further stressed the need for coordination of policies and practice of the Member States and the Community. It focuses on the need for a long-term sustainable solution to the problem of food insecurity and emphasises the importance of development operations that are geared to stimulating local production and trade. The Regulation calls upon the Community to enhance the flexibility with which funds can be directed towards operations in support of food security. In addition to conventional food aid, the EC programme may now finance almost any type of support for the development of those sectors that affect food security. These actions are considered to be a significant element of the fight against poverty (see Box 2.1).

Food aid and food security projects may be implemented by the recipient countries, international bodies, NGOs, or directly by the Commission, the latter accounted for 55% in 1997. In 1998 nine regional multidisciplinary teams were established to analyse the food security situations of priority countries in order to develop a food security strategy. Food aid has traditionally represented a large proportion of EC aid, and over the 1986–98 period it formed the second largest sector after economic infrastructure and services (see Table 2.1). Commitments to the sector accounted for as much as 40–50% of EC Budget aid in the late 1980s, and fluctuated between 13% and 26% of total EC aid. In recent years, however, the importance of food aid has declined significantly as more of the budget line is devoted to food security projects. Between 1996 and 1998 it accounted for between 5% and 8% of all EC aid. In late 1999 the Commission launched an evaluation of the implementation of the 1996 Resolution on Food aid.

The main recipients of developmental food aid are listed in Table 2.2. From 1989 onwards the country allocation of a substantial share of food aid is available. For 1986–88 the geographical distribution cannot be provided by the Commission's own food aid authorities and so has to be classed as 'unallocable'. This is obviously unsatisfactory, especially for a period following the major African food crisis of 1984-85. From 1996 aid has been focused on a small number of priority countries: ones with a very high level of food insecurity and very low income[9]; countries in crisis[10]; and those with a high level of structural food insecurity with a high dependence on food imports[11].

Humanitarian Assistance

EC humanitarian assistance encompasses a broad range of actions, from providing emergency relief to victims of natural disasters and wars, to disaster prevention and preparedness, to coping with refugees, or to carrying out short-term rehabilitation and reconstruction work. The boundaries between these activities inevitably overlap, and the distinction between humanitarian and development assistance is itself far from explicit. However, relief, rehabilitation and development may be linked in a continuum whereby long-term 'development' can reduce the need for emergency relief, effective emergency 'relief' can contribute to development, and better 'rehabilitation' can ease the transition between the two.[12] Account is taken of this by differentiating between rehabilitation assistance and other humanitarian aid (mainly relief actions). For the EC, the explicit aim of relief operations is to save the lives of victims of emergency situations and reduce their suffering. Rehabilitation provides an intermediate strategy of reconstruction, improvement of infrastructure and services, and institutional reinforcement, all aiming at the resumption of sustainable development.

---

[9] Yemen, Ethiopia, Madagascar, Angola, Malawi, Mozambique, Haiti, Nicaragua, Peru, Bolivia, Bangladesh, Burkina Faso and Niger.

[10] Liberia, Sierra Leone, North Korea, Rwanda, Sudan, Somalia, Palestinian Administrative Areas, Guatemala and Afghanistan.

[11] Cape Verde, Honduras, the Programme for the Caucasus and Central Asia, Armenia, Azerbaijan, Georgia, Kyrgyz Republic and Tajikistan.

[12] This is elaborated in COM(96) 153 final, 30.4.1996, *Communication from the Commission to the Council and the European Parliament on Linking Relief, Rehabilitation and Development*.

Table 2.2: Main Recipients of Developmental Food Aid 1986–98
(1986–98, commitments, m euro)

	1986	1987	1988	1989	1990	1991	1992	1993	1994	1995	1996	1997	1998	Total
ACP	6	–	14	248	224	410	279	331	365	337	148	145	138	2643
Ethiopia	–	–	–	68	41	106	75	56	74	89	26	61	45	641
Sudan	–	–	–	28	38	109	27	27	22	6	0	2	34	293
Mozambique	–	–	3	38	44	41	24	46	12	20	23	11	0	262
Angola	–	–	3	11	5	21	10	17	39	47	26	13	16	207
Malawi	–	–	3	11	12	19	17	5	30	26	6	1	13	142
Rwanda	–	–	–	1	1	2	6	23	41	34	2	16	1	127
Liberia	–	–	–	0	4	11	4	26	14	2	6	15	8	91
Somalia	–	–	1	7	5	14	34	6	1	0	12	0	8	90
Kenya	–	–	–	6	5	7	12	15	15	12	–	1	7	81
Haiti	–	–	–	9	9	7	6	8	8	10	11	12	0	80
Eritrea	–	–	–	–	–	–	–	31	24	10	–	–	–	65
Uganda	–	–	–	8	11	8	9	10	10	4	–	–	–	60
Asia	–	–	19	173	81	69	100	56	63	98	39	80	81	859
Bangladesh	–	–	0	49	31	30	36	30	30	49	38	23	48	364
China	–	–	17	44	22	10	3	8	12	11	–	–	0	128
India	–	–	–	40	5	4	37	5	4	5	0	0	2	101
Korea DPR	–	–	–	–	–	–	–	–	–	–	–	47	31	79
Pakistan	–	–	1	19	8	22	15	1	0	2	–	–	–	68
Latin America	–	–	6	67	58	55	48	56	50	52	51	9	0	453
Peru	–	–	3	11	14	14	17	16	24	22	36	1	–	157
Nicaragua	–	–	1	11	11	8	11	13	6	6	9	0	0	76
Bolivia	–	–	3	11	6	9	7	7	0	8	0	4	–	55
	–	–	–	4	8	5	6	5	4	10	2	0	–	45
Med & Mid East	–	–	3	111	73	77	67	76	48	57	6	8	7	533
Egypt	–	–	–	47	31	16	31	27	17	18	–	–	–	188
Tunisia	–	–	–	21	12	7	8	6	3	17	5	–	–	80
West Bank/Gaza	–	–	–	5	4	19	8	11	16	8	0	–	5	76
CEECs (EAGGF: 420m euro)	–	–	–	43	183	63	64	94	8	–	–	1	–	456
Regional Phare	–	–	–	7	183	63	20	0	–	–	–	–	–	274
Albania	–	–	–	–	–	–	44	75	5	–	–	1	–	124
NIS (EAGGF: 1117 m euro)	–	–	–	–	–	207	254	64	29	167	112	35	400	1269
Soviet Union (former)	–	–	–	–	–	207	210	19	12	–	–	–	–	448
Russian Fed	–	–	–	–	–	–	–	–	–	–	–	–	400	400
Regional Tacis	–	–	–	–	–	–	–	–	17	163	–	–	–	180
Baltic States	–	–	–	–	–	–	44	44	0	–	–	–	–	89
Georgia	–	–	–	–	–	–	–	–	–	0	36	16	–	52
Unallocable	659	568	521	39	121	69	303	57	63	98	204	71	64	2837
Total	665	568	563	681	741	950	1115	734	626	809	560	349	690	9051
Food Aid as Share of Total Budget Aid (%)	51.2	44.4	44.8	46.6	35.0	25.7	27.6	17.3	15.2	15.7	10.3	6.5	11.6	19.9
Food Aid as Share of Total EC Aid (%)	26.0	14.7	13.4	20.5	22.8	17.1	16.9	10.8	8.6	11.0	7.9	5.5	8.2	12.5

Source: European Commission/ODI database 1999

Table 2.3 shows the growth in humanitarian assistance from 1993 to 1995, when it rapidly increased to over 1 bn euro, peaking at almost 15% of all EC aid in 1995, and then falling to 10.5% in 1998. With commitments totalling 7.7 bn euro over the 1986–98 period, humanitarian aid was the fifth largest sector, and in 1998 was the fourth largest (after economic infrastructure, social services and programme aid). The peak in 1995 reflects the increase in overall expenditures on humanitarian aid by EU donors as a whole in response to a sequence of major relief operations in Somalia, Bosnia and the Great Lakes Region in Africa, and the additional impetus given to humanitarian aid within the Commission by the establishment of the European Community Humanitarian Office in 1992 (see Box 2.2). This was created in order to respond more efficiently to humanitarian crises, and has at the heart of its approach an emphasis on the need for a better relationship with NGOs. In May 1993 it adopted

Framework Partnership Agreements as the basis for this, with the objective of regularising relations and simplifying decision-making. A new Framework Partnership Agreement came into force in 1998.

In 1994 the Commission's rehabilitation programmes received a boost, doubling in 1994 and tripling to 300 m euro in 1995, following the Council decisions in 1993 setting out guidelines for the Special Initiative for Africa. This approved additional funding for rehabilitation activities in Africa following the cessation of conflicts in the Horn and southern Africa. Not surprisingly, therefore, 80% of rehabilitation aid was concentrated in sub-Saharan Africa in 1995, despite the difficulties experienced by a number of countries in absorbing this assistance. The Obnova programme, established in 1996, focused on reconstruction activities in the former Yugoslavia and has maintained the level of rehabilitation commitments, with Central European countries taking over as the main recipients.

> **Box 2.2: European Community Humanitarian Office (ECHO)**
>
> The Commission formally created ECHO on 1 April 1992, though it did not become fully operational until the beginning of 1993 when it received adequate levels of staff. ECHO assumed responsibility for emergency food aid as well as non-food (eg medical) humanitarian aid. ECHO was put on a legal footing only in July 1996 (Council Regulation (EC) 1257/96). This set out the following objectives:
> - to save and preserve life during emergencies and their immediate aftermath;
> - to provide assistance and relief during longer-lasting crises;
> - to finance the transport of aid and make it accessible;
> - to carry out short-term rehabilitation and reconstruction;
> - to cope with refugees, displaced people and returnees.

In 1996, two Regulations relating to humanitarian aid and to rehabilitation and reconstruction were adopted by the Council of Development Ministers, both emphasising the need to strengthen the coordination of EC aid with that of the Member States.[13] The Regulation on humanitarian aid outlines criteria for selecting non-governmental partners for funding, and supports increased cooperation between NGOs in the Member States and their equivalents in recipient countries. The importance of ensuring greater coherence and continuity across the fields of humanitarian aid, rehabilitation and development is underlined in the Regulation on rehabilitation and reconstruction. The Community's priorities are defined as relaunching production on a lasting basis, the rehabilitation of basic

Table 2.3: Sources of Humanitarian Assistance
(1986–98, commitments, m euro and % of total aid)

	1986	1987	1988	1989	1990	1991	1992	1993	1994	1995	1996	1997	1998	Total
Total Humanitarian Aid	80	100	135	198	299	423	543	870	1009	1117	1044	883	936	7639
Total Humanitarian excl Rehab	59	74	106	165	259	379	502	823	915	812	795	548	619	6057
Total Rehabilitation	21	27	29	32	41	44	41	47	94	305	249	335	317	1583
Humanit. aid as % of total EC Aid	*3.1*	*2.6*	*3.2*	*6.0*	*9.2*	*7.6*	*8.2*	*12.8*	*13.8*	*15.2*	*14.4*	*13.6*	*10.9*	*10.4*
Sources:														
ECHO	–	–	–	–	–	–	–	516	499	642	647	438	480	3223
Humanitarian excl Rehab	–	–	–	–	–	–	–	516	499	642	647	438	480	3223
EDF	8	31	56	78	50	53	87	118	255	205	100	20	64	1124
Humanitarian excl Rehab	8	28	55	76	50	53	86	117	255	30	53	-2	38	848
Rehabilitation	–	3	–	1	–	–	–	1	–	175	47	22	26	276
Portion of EDF mangd by ECHO	–	–	–	–	–	–	–	90	263	46	7	7	37	450
Other Budget Lines	72	70	80	120	249	370	456	236	255	271	297	426	392	3293
Humanitarian excl Rehab	51	46	51	89	209	326	415	190	161	140	95	112	101	1986
Rehabilitation	21	24	29	31	40	44	41	46	94	131	202	313	291	1307

Note: There is an inexact correspondence between EDF and ECHO estimates of the portion of EDF funds managed by ECHO. This is revealed in the figure for 1994, for instance, which shows the portion of EDF funds managed by ECHO to be larger than the estimated EDF funds available for humanitarian aid in that year.

Source: European Commission/ODI database 1999 and ECHO

---

[13] Regulations (EC) No. 1257/96 of 20.6.1996 and (EC) No. 2258/96 of 22.11.1996, respectively.

infrastructure, the social reintegration of refugees, displaced persons and demobilised soldiers, and rebuilding local institutional capacities. [14]

In 1998 ECHO confirmed its readiness for greater involvement in disaster preparedness and prevention, notably through the DIPECHO programme which has been put into effect in South East Asia, Bangladesh, Central America and the Caribbean. In 1999 the Council adopted a Joint Action on the basis of Article K.3 of the Treaty on European Union, establishing projects and measures to provide practical support in relation to the reception and voluntary repatriation of refugees, displaced persons and asylum seekers, including emergency assistance to persons who have fled as a result of recent events in Kosovo.

ECHO provided humanitarian assistance to over 60 countries in 1998, as well as managing a disaster preparedness programme in high-risk areas of the world. From 1993 onwards most humanitarian aid (3.2 bn euro, or over 42%) has been financed through ECHO's budget lines, and a further 450 m euro has been financed from the EDF but managed by ECHO (see Table 2.3). In addition to these EDF funds managed by ECHO, the EDF has also provided and managed over 670 m euro of humanitarian aid since 1986. Other budget lines have also provided some 3.3 bn euro of humanitarian aid during the 1986–98 period. These have either been created to meet specific needs (eg B7–4210: aid to the UN refugee programme in the Palestinian Administrative Areas; B7–2120 – now B7–3020 and 3120: aid for refugees and displaced persons in Asia and Latin America), or are the major budget lines for regional programmes, part of which is spent on humanitarian aid (eg B7–30: Asia; and B7–50: Phare).

The greatest proportion of humanitarian assistance has been channelled to Central and Eastern Europe, largely to the states of former Yugoslavia which together received 2.2 bn euro over the eight years 1992–8 (see Table 2.4), making the EC the largest donor. Sub-Saharan African countries have traditionally been the largest recipients of EC humanitarian assistance, with Rwanda and Burundi ranking as by far the largest recipients within the region. Angola has also been a major recipient of both relief and rehabilitation aid as a result of its 35-year war, while Sudan, Mozambique, and Somalia and have been steady recipients of humanitarian assistance. The Mediterranean and Middle East region received some 12% of all humanitarian assistance, Asia 11%, the NIS 6% and Latin America 6%.

In the last few years the EC has also developed policies on peace building and conflict prevention reflected in the Common Position and Council Conclusions adopted by the General Affairs Council on 2 June 1997[15] and the Conclusions adopted by the Development Council on 30 November 1998[16].

Aid to NGOs

EC aid supports the work of NGOs both by 'contracting' them to provide particular services and through its co- financing scheme (see Box 2.3). EC aid *through* NGOs, where the NGO is contracted to implement Commission-designed projects and programmes, is accounted for under the total of aid to the particular sector (e.g. agriculture, or humanitarian aid). The amount of EC aid through NGOs is significant, but there is no reliable way at present to quantify it.

---

[14] The latest statement of commission policy on humanitarian aid is contained in communication COM(99)468 entitled "Assessment and Humanitarian Activities".

[15] *Conflict prevention and resolution in Africa*, Common Position and Council Conclusions adopted by the General Affairs Council on 2 June 1997.

[16] *The role of development cooperation in strengthening peace-building conflict prevention and resolution*, Conclusions adopted by the Development Council on 30 November 1998.

Table 2.4: Regional and Country Distribution of EC Humanitarian Aid (1986–98, commitments, m euro)

	1986	1987	1988	1989	1990	1991	1992	1993	1994	1995	1996	1997	1998	Total
ACP	18	36	61	83	72	79	117	144	348	417	435	167	179	2156
Rwanda/Bur Emergcy	–	–	–	–	–	–	–	–	177	82	–	–	–	259
Angola	–	3	1	6	9	10	19	14	32	83	27	46	6	255
Sudan	6	1	26	22	8	15	9	10	24	19	12	22	34	207
Somalia	–	1	0	1	1	11	41	32	8	7	51	8	5	166
Mozambique	–	5	4	17	6	8	19	11	13	15	16	8	2	124
Congo (Zaire)	–	–	1	1	1	3	–	8	11	89	6	–	1	120
Rwanda	–	–	1	–	1	1	3	12	9	5	63	6	3	104
Ethiopia	4	10	18	19	7	9	4	1	3	2	3	4	2	86
Liberia	–	–	–	–	7	9	5	10	7	6	1	3	31	79
Haiti	5	–	–	–	–	0	1	2	18	18	17	9	2	72
South Africa	–	–	–	2	1	–	1	0	0	–	–	–	–	3
Asia	2	17	10	37	20	65	84	88	90	95	95	93	123	819
Afghanistan	1	–	7	1	5	4	19	20	27	21	60	29	51	244
Bangladesh	–	11	1	22	–	33	5	19	5	3	2	1	9	112
Cambodia	–	–	–	–	3	2	14	11	15	21	5	9	12	91
Viet Nam	0	–	–	0	0	10	22	25	2	11	0	2	1	74
Pakistan	–	–	–	4	5	7	10	2	24	0	1	3	2	58
Latin America	3	1	9	29	12	16	22	32	59	59	56	61	73	432
Nicaragua	0	–	4	1	5	5	6	5	22	16	9	9	4	86
Guatemala	–	1	2	0	0	1	1	6	10	10	22	19	7	80
Cuba	–	–	–	–	–	–	–	8	14	15	9	10	9	65
El Salvador	1			3	3	3	13	6	3	4	7	3	4	50
Med & Mid East	57	33	25	39	34	172	34	70	85	94	108	64	91	904
West Bank/Gaza	57	27	24	24	26	59	29	40	50	52	56	42	49	535
Iraq	–	–	–	–	–	111	3	22	23	25	30	3	14	230
Lebanon	0	5	–	8	1	0	–	2	4	12	14	5	5	56
Algeria	–	0	–	0	–	–	–	1	3	5	7	8	17	42
CEECs	–	2	–	8	105	80	282	441	310	272	294	432	383	2608
Yugoslavia (ex)	–	–	–	–	30	14	210	420	300	269	291	337	349	2222
Albania	–	–	–	–	–	10	50	10	9	1	2	16	11	109
Romania	–	–	–	5	13	35	22	10	–	1	0	–	1	87
NIS	–	–	19	–	5	11	4	75	92	137	54	36	49	482
Tajikistan	–	–	–	–	–	–	–	–	10	16	14	15	20	75
Soviet Union (former)	–	–	10	–	5	6	4	51	–	–	–	–	–	75
Russian Fed	–	–	9	–	1	5	0	–	10	30	9	4	6	74
Azerbaijan	–	–	–	–	–	–	–	–	19	29	9	6	9	72
Georgia	–	–	–	–	–	–	–	–	18	27	10	6	8	69
Armenia	–	–	–	–	–	–	–	–	19	24	5	2	2	52
Unallocable	–	12	12	–	51	1	–	21	25	43	2	31	38	234
Total Humanitarian Aid	80	100	135	196	299	423	542	870	1009	1117	1044	883	936	7636

Source: European Commission/ODI database 1999

Commission aid *to* NGOs through the co-financing scheme is examined separately, since in this case the initiative remains with the NGO itself, and it is this figure which is listed in the sectoral tables. It should be emphasised, however, that the distinction between aid *to* and aid *through* NGOs is rather blurred, owing to the difficulty of judging the degree of autonomy and initiative enjoyed by NGOs. It is possible, therefore, that this analysis underestimates the amount of EC financing to NGOs.

In 1997, the Council of Ministers approved a common position on the regulation on co-financing of NGOs. This document states explicitly that NGO co-financing should aim at poverty reduction as well as on enhancing the target group's quality of life and development capacities. Support through NGOs is currently governed by Council Regulation (EC) No 1658/98 of 17 July 1998 on co-financing operations with European non-governmental development organisations (NGOs) in fields of interest to the developing countries.

The Commission has co-financed development projects undertaken by European development NGOS and their local partners in developing countries since 1974 and programmes in Europe to raise awareness on development issues since 1979. Only European based NGOs can apply on behalf of Southern partners.

The NGO co-financing scheme provides funds up to a maximum of 500,000 euro for any one project for a maximum of five years. The Commission contribution is normally up to 50%, though in some circumstances up to three-quarters of the cost may be borne by the EC while NGOs must provide from their own resources at least 15% of the total expenditure required to implement a project. The mechanism is intended to offer rapid co-financing, which is sufficiently flexible to take account of the diversity of situations in which NGOs work. It is seen as a response to the commitment and support shown for years by the European public towards non-governmental efforts to improve the living conditions of the poor.

EC aid to NGOs has increased significantly in recent years, doubling from an annual average of 76 m euro in 1986–90 to 155 m euro for 1991–5, and rising again to 206 m euro for 1996–8; in line with the growth in EC aid overall. The vast majority of aid to NGOs was funded through the co-financing budget line B7–6000 (formerly B7–5010), which dates back to 1976, and went mainly to the ACP and Latin American regions, each receiving a over a third of allocable funds for 1986–98. Ethiopia was the largest ACP recipient, receiving some 40 m euro over the period, while Kenya received 34 m euro and Uganda, Burkina Faso, the Democratic Republic of Congo and Tanzania each received slightly under 25 m euro. Brazil was the largest Latin American recipient (93 m euro). NGO actions in Chile received 73 m euro, while Peru, Bolivia and Nicaragua were all major recipients, each receiving about 50 m euro over the 1986–98 period. The Asian region received some 18% of allocable NGO aid, with India (75 m euro), the Philippines and Cambodia (around 30 m euro each), and Vietnam and Bangladesh (around 24 m euro) ranking largest; Cambodia and Vietnam until 1996 benefiting from individual budget lines (B7–6005[17] and B7–6004[18] respectively). The Phare programme provided some 100 m euro for NGO activities in the Central and Eastern European countries (7%), while the NGO activities in the NIS received much smaller amounts. Likewise the Mediterranean and Middle East benefited relatively little from this instrument, receiving 5% of funds, most of which went to the Lebanon and the West Bank/Gaza.

Box 2.3: NGO co-financing

The main pillar of the Commission's support to European NGOs is through the co-financing programme which began in 1976, and which has since provided over 1.7 bn euro of aid. The EC's support goes both to NGO development projects in countries in the South and to their activities to mobilise public opinion in favour of development and fairer international relations between North and South. NGOs are seen as vehicles by which official aid can reach the poorest and most marginalised people. The Commission supports the role of NGOs in encouraging participatory development and the creation of a democratic base at grass roots level. The basis of the EC's support to European NGOs is the support that they give to their partners in the South.

The NGO Liaison Committee is the central point of contact for dialogue between development NGOs and the Commission. It seeks to represent partner NGOs (some 900) in dealings with the European institutions, and also acts as a forum for discussion between European NGOs themselves.

Project Aid

This section complements the discussion of the main trends in the sectoral composition of project aid outlined earlier with a more detailed analysis of some of the sectors. The distinction between the four instruments and project aid is in many ways an imperfect one, since aid through instruments such as structural adjustment, Stabex, NGOs or humanitarian aid may be designed to assist the social and economic infrastructure sectors, natural resources or governance and civil society, among others. However, the double counting of sectors/instruments would be unhelpful in an inventory. Of particular

---

[17] Formerly B7–5015

[18] Formerly B7–5014

importance is the way in which counterpart funds generated by the structural adjustment facility may be used to support social sectors (health and education in particular), and the relative importance of these flows is discussed below with respect to the health sector. EC aid to NGOs provides a second example of how the line between aid through instruments and project aid may become blurred. While aid *to* NGOs is discussed as an instrument of EC aid in this analysis, since their funding through the co-financing facility is not focused on particular sectors, it is of course true that NGO activities will contribute to many project aid sectors (particularly the social infrastructure and services sector). These qualifications apart, examining project aid as a distinct category remains a useful mechanism by which EC aid can be better understood.

Natural Resources Productive Sector

Agriculture and Rural Development: Although the areas of agriculture and rural development are treated discretely in the OECD DAC sectoral categorisation and are presented separately in this book, the two are closely related in the Community's aid programme. For this reason they are considered together in this section.

Support for rural development and agriculture in developing countries has traditionally been a very important focus of EC aid. Taken together, they accounted for over one-fifth (3.2 bn euro) of all aid in the late 1980s. This has been particularly true of the ACP region, which received nearly 70% of all EC aid to rural development and agriculture for 1986–95. The preponderance of this sector in the late 1980s reflects the evolution in the priorities of the Lomé Convention. In the early 1980s (Lomé II) self-sufficiency and food security were high priorities, while in the late 1980s Integrated Rural Development Projects became the new priority area under Lomé III (1985–90). These projects often involved a mix of micro-projects for the improvement of the living conditions of the rural population. This ambitious attempt to provide a comprehensive approach to combating rural poverty generated rather disappointing results, and in the 1990s it gave way to a focus on sustainable development and the environment.[19] In the early 1990s, therefore, funds for integrated rural development amounted to less than 2% of all EC aid, rising slightly in the latter half of the decade, and aid to agriculture fell to 6% for 1991–95 and again to 3.7% for 1996–98.

Forestry and the Environment: Just as *tropical forests* became a major international concern in the first half of the 1990s, so the profile of EC aid to this sector rose for the years 1992–95. Aid to the sector amounted to an annual average of only 12 m euro for 1986–90, or 0.3% of total allocable aid. It increased six-fold to 71 m euro for 1991–95, accounting for 1.2% of total aid, falling slightly to an annual average of 63 m euro for 1996–98. This rise directly reflects various policy initiatives since 1989. In October 1989 the Commission prepared a policy document on the conservation of tropical forests, and at the European Council in Dublin in June 1990 it was agreed to set in motion an EC tropical forestry programme, with a particular focus on Brazil. To this end a specific budget line was created in 1991 (B7–6201, formerly B7–5041) at the behest of the European Parliament.[20] This complemented existing expenditure in forestry, largely through the European Development Fund and the main financial and technical cooperation line to Asia (B7–3000). The EDF provided some 107 m euro to the ACP countries between 1986 and 1998, with a further 77 m euro coming from the budget which also committed 177m euro to Asia and 125 m euro to Latin America between 1992 and 1998.

Forestry had been viewed largely as a component of rural development, but since 1992 EC forestry projects have enjoyed a higher profile. Forestry conservation measures were formalised in Council Regulation EC No. 3062/95 of December 1995, setting out the priority areas for the 1996–9 period

---

[19]The performance of the rural development sector was evaluated in an EC Evaluation Report in March 1994.

[20]Operations to promote tropical forests were formalised in Council Regulation EC No. 3062/95 in December 1995. Some forestry conservation measures were also funded under the environmental label.

and allocating some 200 m euro over the four years. This was followed by a Council Resolution on *Forests and Development* (12282/99), of 11 November 1999. In addition to the emphasis on protecting primary tropical forests and their biodiversity, it highlights the importance of developing a system to certify wood produced in sustainably managed forests, of information on forest dwellers, and of research. A similar approach was incorporated into the fourth Lomé Convention during the mid-term review in 1995.

In March 1997, revised guidelines to improve the quality of tropical forest assistance were issued by the Commission, stressing the links between economic, social and environmental factors. Recent projects place greater store on cooperation with EU Member States, NGOs, and international organisations, as well as initiatives in developing countries themselves. There are numerous examples of co-financed projects with Member States, particularly in Latin America, and the environment and tropical forestry have featured in recent agreements with Asian and Latin American countries including Brazil, Indonesia and Peru. The largest recipients of EC forestry aid since 1992 were Indonesia (79 m euro), Brazil (62 m euro), India (29 m euro), Philippines (28 m euro), and Morocco (24 m euro).

The Commission currently does not have a consistent definition of projects with the *environment* as their primary aim. The DAC have not yet agreed guidelines for the definition of 'environment' projects, and there is no consistent approach among other donors.[21] The fact that many activities which are classified under other sectoral headings, such as agriculture, forestry or industry, may also contribute to environmental objectives compounds the difficulty of forming a clear picture of EC aid for the environment. Our analysis takes as its starting point those activities funded by the budget line specifically created to promote environmental conservation in developing countries (B7–6200, formerly B7–5040), for which commitments totalled 150 m euro between 1986 and 1998. It also includes those projects funded from a variety of budget lines where the project title indicates a specific environmental focus. Budget line B7–8110, managed by the Environment DG, has a global brief on environmental issues, not restricted to recipients of ODA and OA. Those activities which do count as ODA or OA are included. An attempt has been made to avoid double counting.

Until a firm definition of environmental projects is adopted and projects are classed accordingly, attempts to assess the EC's contribution in this area will remain approximate. Table 2.1 indicates clearly the growth in commitments to the 'environmental sector' since the end of the 1980s. Annual average EC aid to the environment for 1986–90 stood at 49 m euro rising to 164 m euro for 1991–5, before falling slightly to 162 m euro for 1996–98. This represents changes in its share of total allocable aid from 1.6%, to 2.7%, to 2.4%. In the 1990s the Phare programme has committed large sums to environmental activities in Central and Eastern Europe, amounting to some 590 m euro or 40% of aid in this sector (1990–8). The Mediterranean and Middle East ranked second in the 1990s with 290 m euro (20%), followed by Asia with 240 m euro, the ACP with about 154 m euro, the Newly Independent states with 90 m euro and Latin America with around 55 m euro (nearly 4%). Environment as a crosscutting issue is dealt with later in this Chapter.

Fisheries: Aid to fisheries amounted to 236 m euro between 1986 and 1998. Over half of this went to the fisheries sector in ACP countries, though the largest single beneficiaries were India, Mozambique and Algeria. Assistance to the sector used to be concentrated on infrastructure improvements, but support to artisanal fisheries grew in the 1980s, and in recent years assistance has been focused on human and institutional development. The EU Development Council called in June 1997 for more attention to the local fishery sector and the sustainability of its resources, as well as full implementation of the FAO Code of Conduct for Responsible Fisheries (1995).

---

21 For further details and for a thorough attempt to provide a more complete inventory of environmental projects see the Inventory of Environment and Tropical Forests Programmes, May 1996, Environmental Resources Management, London.

The assistance to the sector is mainly in the form of support to: (i) efforts for greater coherence through rule-setting and enforcement, and improving information; (ii) the private sector to increase competitiveness; (iii) research; and (iv) resource conservation and protection. In addition to technical and financial assistance, a specific budget line was created in 1993 for the international fisheries agreements (B7–800). However, while developing countries (and Greenland) are the recipients of these funds (nearly 1.3 b euro for 1993–8), this has not been included as EC aid since the funds represent compensation for access for EC vessels in their waters. The main beneficiaries of these funds in 1998 were Morocco, Mauritania, Angola and Senegal.

Other Productive Sectors

This encompasses a wide range of activities including industry, mining, construction, trade policy and administration, tourism policy and management and investment promotion. The largest subsector by far is industry, mining and construction, for which commitments totalled 3.3 bn euro, or nearly 80% of all aid to the sector. The vast bulk of resources to this sector has gone to ACP countries, principally Mauritania and Nigeria which received 185 m euro and 170 m euro respectively and Zambia, Papua New Guinea and Mali each of which received over 100 m euro. The Mediterranean and Middle East region was also a major recipient with 950 m euro. Egypt received most of this with 580 m euro, over 300 m euro of which was own resources loans from the EIB.

ECIP: EC aid for investment promotion represented the fastest growing subsector, in relative terms, increasing from a total of only 19 m euro for the 1986–90 period to an annual average of 29 m euro in the 1990s for 1991–95 and again to 53 m euro for 1996–98. The primary factor behind this growth has been the development and success of the European Community Investment Partners scheme (ECIP), though a number of the regional programmes are now developing complementary schemes for example MED-Invest and AL-invest work upstream of the ECIP programme by putting firms in contact with each other.

> **Box 2.4: European Community Investment Partners scheme (ECIP)**
>
> ECIP's objective is to facilitate the creation, in 60 developing countries in Asia, Latin America, the Mediterranean and South Africa, of private joint venture investments that contribute to the economic development of those countries. It provides finance at all stages in the gestation and realisation of EU/local joint venture private investments. ECIP is managed from Brussels in a decentralised way through a network of 108 ECIP financial institutions and investment promotion agencies.

The Commission developed ECIP during a pilot phase (1988–91) as an instrument to help Member State private sector firms wishing to invest in Asian, Latin American and Mediterranean developing countries, and which would also respond to the increasing interest expressed by firms in developing countries in joint ventures with European firms (see Box 2.4). The scheme was originally limited to 28 countries, but now extends to 60 countries in the three regions and to South Africa. Support is provided by five financing facilities each targeting a different stage in the creation and early life of a joint venture (see Table 2.5).

Table 2.5: ECIP Facilities

	Facility 1	Facility 2	Facility 3	Facility 4	Facility 1B
Type of operation	Identification of potential joint venture projects & partners	Feasibility studies or pilot projects	Joint venture capital requirements	Training, technical or management assistance	Preparation of privatisation or 'build operate transfer' or 'build operate own' scheme
Max amount available (euro)	100 000	250 000	1 000 000	250 000	200 000
Type of finance	Grant	Interest-free advance	Equity holding or equity loan	Interest free loan or grant	Grant

Source: European Commission

The success of ECIP during its pilot phase led to the scheme being given a formal legal and budgetary basis with the adoption by the Council of Ministers on 3 February 1992 of Regulation EC No. 319/92. The budget made available was increased from 30 m euro for 1988–91 to 110 m euro for 1992–94. A new ECIP Regulation approved in January 1996 (EC No. 213/96) expanded the scheme to 60 countries and takes account of the investment needs of developing countries in infrastructure and utilities projects by providing a new grant facility (up to a ceiling of 200 000 euro) for the improvement or privatisation of utilities and environmental services. This Regulation indicated a financial commitment of 250 m euro for 1995–99.

Economic Infrastructure and Services

The category of economic infrastructure and services covers a broad array of activities, ranging from transport and communications, to energy, banking, and business services. Total aid to the sector amounted to 12.3 bn euro over the 1986–98 period, or 16.8% of all aid, making this the largest sector of all. EC aid for these activities is, however, heavily concentrated in three regions, which together receive nearly 87% of the total. The ACP region is allocated commitments of almost 45% of all aid for economic infrastructure and services for the 1986–98 period. Of the remainder, 23% of Commitments go to the Central and East European countries, and the NIS 15%. There were differences in the precise type of aid going to each region, with the ACP receiving a particularly large share of aid in the transport and communications subsector (66% of this subsector aid going to the ACP[22]), while the CEECs received 19% and the Mediterranean and Middle East 7%. In contrast, nearly half of all aid to the banking, financial and business services subsector was concentrated in the CEECs, reflecting the concentration of the Phare programme in these areas. Of the remainder, the largest part (370 m euro) went to the Mediterranean and the Middle East and 342 m euro to the ACP. Finally, almost half of all EC aid to the energy subsector went to ACP countries, with nearly a third going to the NIS, due in part to concentration there on nuclear safety. The CEECs received a total of 1945 m euro, for energy and transport and communications, most of which could not be differentiated between the subsectors in the available data. Information technology actions are acquiring increasing importance in the cooperation actions of the Commission.

> **Box 2.5: Micro-finance**
>
> On the Commission's initiative, a group of Member State experts took a closer look at micro-finance in 1997. Discussion identified potentials and constraints of micro-finance as an instrument for poverty reduction. It stressed the need for a multi-level approach that gave high priority to coordination of donor assistance and centred around:
>
> *A multi-level approach:* credit at the grassroots level alone is not sufficient. It advocated a balance between the provision of capital, institutional and technical support and stressed the particular need to address framework conditions for micro-finance in the policy dialogue.
>
> *Careful targeting.* In the view of the Commission there were '*already too many funds chasing too few viable institutions*'. It pleaded therefore for a careful approach that would take due account of the limited absorption capacities of existing organisations and gradually strengthen their institutional and financial viability.

Micro-finance: Micro-finance has played an increasing role in the Community's development assistance, though it is not currently possible to isolate all the funds spent on this sub-sector, as many can be, by the titles of the programmes and by the EDF Global Allocations for Microprojects. The 1996 Council Resolution on Human and Social Development mentions micro-credits as an instrument for improving the productive potential of the poor and more equal access to economic resources. The Council Resolution of 28 November 1997 calls for support to microfinancing institutions stressing the role micro-finance can play as an instrument for tackling income poverty and generating growth complementary to social sector and macro-economic support (see Box 2.5). The Resolution underlined that support for micro-financing institutions, should be geared to those '*sections of the population which do not have access to the services of the formal financial sector, particularly the poor and women*'. Methodological guidelines were produced in May 1998.

---

[22] However the percentage is distorted by 540 m euro of the sector to the CEECs not being differentiated between energy and transport and communications.

Social Infrastructure and Services

Health and Population: The health and population sector has witnessed very significant growth since 1986, with commitments rising from an annual average of 35 m euro for the 1986–90 period to an annual average of 170 m euro for 1991–5, rising again to 273 m euro for 1996–8. Its corresponding share of total aid rose from 1%, to nearly 3%, to over 4.5%. In the 1990s Community aid, in accordance with agreements with the Member States,[23] has emphasised health policy with the aim of strengthening coordination between Community and Member State aid, and developing strategies for action in areas such as drugs policy and HIV/AIDS (see Box 2.6).

The ACP region (mainly sub-Saharan Africa) received about a third of the 1.9 bn euro committed between 1986 and 1998. In addition, according to a 1996 study by DG VIII the health sector has also benefited substantially from an allocation of 369 m euro of counterpart funds generated by structural adjustment financing to the ACP between 1991 and 1995.[24] About 60% of recent commitments (EDF 7 and 8) have focused on supporting the decentralisation of health systems, and improving the quality of and access to prevention and care services.

Support for the health and population sector in Latin America grew significantly in 1995, reaching 68 m euro. This was drawn mainly from the technical and financial cooperation budget line (B7–3010), but it has not maintained this level, dropping to an average of 17 m euro for the following three years. In addition, the majority of rural development programmes include components related to health, such as water supply and sanitation and the construction of health centres. Asia also saw an increase in 1995, with a further significant rise in 1996, bringing its total for the period to nearly 400 m euro. Commitments to the CEECs and the NIS were significantly less than to the other regions.

In the specific field of HIV and AIDS, programmes have been adopted, notably in Mozambique and Tanzania, to support national strategies to reduce the spread of the virus. Research has also been financed into the management of sexually transmitted diseases and blood safety. From 1987 to 1996, 236 m euro were committed to the HIV/AIDS subsector through a specific budget line (B7–6211),[25] though additional funds have also been committed and included in the general health figures given above, not all of which are possible to separate out. Of HIV/AIDS funds that could be allocated by region since 1996, 51% went to the ACP, 28% to Asia, 10% to Latin America, and over 5% to the Mediterranean and the Middle East.

> **Box 2.6: HIV/AIDS**
>
> The EC has been running a HIV/AIDs programme since 1987. A new programme was launched in 1998 which aims to emphasise:
> - monitoring and surveillance of the epidemic and the risks related to it;
> - early interventions targeted at specific populations;
> - information and prevention measures aimed at those most vulnerable to acquiring and transmitting the virus;
> - providing affordable community-based care for the poorest and neediest people affected by ADIS;
> - scientific learning and training.
>
> New funds include:
> - 45 m euro from 1997-1999 on the special HIV/AIDS budget line for all developing countries;
> - 20 m euro for a 5 year regional programme under the 8th EDF.

Education and Training: Community aid policy was clarified in a Council Resolution on Education and Training in developing countries in 1994. The priority areas were increasing access to education, redressing the bias against the education of girls and disadvantaged groups, and improving the quality

---

[23] These were reflected in Resolutions adopted by the Development Council in May 1994.

[24] Under EDF 5, 139 m euro was provided for the health sector (including HIV/AIDS) through project aid, and 455 m through counterpart funds. The corresponding figures for EDF 6 were 183 m and 44 m euro respectively, and for EDF 7, 406 m and 563 m euro.

[25] Council Regulation (EC) No 550/97 of March 1997 on HIV/AIDs related operations in developing countries.

of education. Following the adoption of the 'Horizon 2000' declaration, enshrining education and training as part of the priority areas of European cooperation, support for basic education has been given pre-eminence, though unfortunately data on the precise share of aid to basic education are unavailable.

Increasingly the Commission provides sectoral support to education ministries. Under the terms of the Maastricht Treaty, increased EU donor coordination is required, and this has been piloted in a number of countries: Ethiopia, Burkina Faso, Côte d'Ivoire, Peru, Mozambique, India and Tanzania.

EC aid to the education sector totalled 3.3 bn euro over the 1986–98 period, the largest percentage going to the CEECs (30%). Poland was the second largest single recipient overall with 240 m euro (7.3%). The ACP region including South Africa came next with 817 m euro (25%), with South Africa the largest recipient overall with 260 m euro (7.9%). As with health, however, the ACP region also benefited from counterpart funds from structural adjustment assistance channelled towards education. These represented 280 m euro for 1991–5, doubling commitments for that period to the ACP (see Box 3.1 in Chapter 3). Commitments to the Mediterranean and Middle East amounted to 14.2% within which the Palestinian Administrated Area was the biggest recipient (150 m euro), followed by Egypt with 100 m euro. Asia received only slightly less at 13.3% with most going to India (160 m) followed by the NIS with 12.5% with most going to the Russian Federation (200 m euro). Commitments to Latin America accounted for almost 5% of total EC aid to education.

Cross-cutting issues

Governance and Civil Society: Since 1990 the Community has reinforced its policies in support of democratisation and human rights, underlined by a Council Resolution in November 1991 emphasising the linkages between human rights, democracy and development.

In 1994 the European Parliament launched the European Initiative for Democracy and Human Rights to bring a series of budget headings specifically dealing with the promotion of human rights together in a charter of their own (B7–70) entitled 'European Initiative for Democracy and the Protection of Human Rights'. The legal base is provided by Council Regulation (EC) No 975/1999 of 29 April 1999. The budget lines provide technical and financial aid for operations aimed at:

- promoting and defending the human rights and fundamental freedoms proclaimed in the Universal Declaration of Human Rights and other international instruments concerning the development and consolidation of democracy and the rule of law;
- supporting the processes of democratisation;
- support for measures to promote respect for human rights and democratisation by preventing conflict and dealing with its consequences, in close collaboration with the relevant competent bodies.

Aid under the banner of governance and civil society averaged over 130 m euro a year over the 1991–95 period, or a little less than 2% of the total, rising to an average of over 545 m euro a year for 1996–98 or over 7%. In addition to support for electoral processes such as election monitoring, actions to strengthen judicial institutions or parliaments, the creation of ombudsmen, the independence of the media, and civil society have been funded.

Support for good governance also includes technical co-operation provided to strengthen economic management and development planning by government. An example in this area is support for strengthening the capacity of national statistical systems in order to improve the quality and timeliness of data on which policy planning decisions are made.

One approach to this subsector is that of decentralised cooperation (DC) (see Box 2.7). This was formally introduced in articles 20 to 22 of the fourth Lomé Convention. Likewise DC is included in Council Regulation 443/92 relative to economic cooperation with Asia and Latin America. A specific DC budget line has been introduced. In 1998 Council Regulation (EC) No 1659/98 of 17 July 1998 set aside a sum of 18 m euro to finance decentralised cooperation for the period 1999–2001.

Poverty reduction: Two Council resolutions set out key strategic principles for the Community's current approach towards poverty reduction in partner countries: *The 1993 Council Resolution on the Fight Against Poverty* spells out a number of broad policy objectives and principles for incorporating the objective of poverty reduction in its external aid programmes. It stresses that the fight against poverty should be a central theme of policy dialogue and all cooperation agreements between the Community and developing countries. *The 1996 Resolution on Human and Social Development* (HSD) endorses the conclusions of the Copenhagen Summit: it defines priority areas for poverty-oriented intervention and puts the fight against poverty in the context of people-oriented development.

> **Box 2.7 Decentralised cooperation**
>
> Decentralised cooperation emerged in the 1980s with the aim of enabling the EC to contribute outside the conventional external aid framework. In DC activities, the central government facilitates but does not have a direct involvement. Funds are channelled directly to NGOs and organisations outside the formal governmental apparatus, and to local public authorities.
>
> Decentralised cooperation activities are designed to promote:
>
> - A more participatory approach to development, responsive to the needs and initiatives of the population in the developing countries;
> - A contribution to the diversification and reinforcement of civil society and grassroots democracy;
> - Mobilisation of decentralised cooperation agents in the Community and the developing countries in pursuit of these objectives.

In 1998 a Discussion Note of the Commission reviewed progress against the 1993 poverty reduction objectives. On the basis of this note, the Council reached conclusions, including that the policy remained valid, but that the operational strategy had been inadequate to realise the objectives. In essence, the EC had focused on stimulating economic growth and support to basic social services but had not really tackled the political or international dimensions of poverty reduction. It called for greater efforts in the fight against poverty, dealing with inequality and social exclusion and for a more balanced approach between growth on the one side and distribution and the fight against inequality on the other. The Council invited the Commission to set out an action plan and an operational framework against which progress in future could be measured.

In responding to this requirement, the Directorate General for Development has already undertaken several actions to strengthen the focus on poverty reduction and institutional capacity to fulfil this objective (see Chapter 3).

Gender: The first Council Resolution on integrating gender issues into development[26] emphasised the importance of 'mainstreaming' gender analysis into the conception and design of development policies and interventions, and of the importance of capacity building on gender issues and gender-sensitive approaches. It reflects the political commitments undertaken at the Fourth World Conference on Women (Beijing, 1995).

In 1997 the Commission published a progress report on the integration of the gender question into its external aid programmes.[27] This reveals efforts to raise awareness and strengthen the Commission's and its partners' capacities to take account of gender aspects systematically in development projects, programmes and to integrate gender aspects into the different regional and sector policies. Furthermore, a number of sector policy documents have been reviewed to mainstream gender issues

---

[26] Council of Ministers of the European Union 1995. *Integrating gender issues in development cooperation*. In: Report on the 1897th Council meeting –Development, Brussels, 20th December 1995, Press 12847/95: 10.

[27] Commission des Communautés Européennes 1997. *Intégration des questions de genre dans la coopération au développement. Rapport d'état d'avancement 1997*. Brussels, SEC (97) 2067.

more thoroughly, including a series of Council Regulations for special budget lines, including on AIDS, environment, family planning and humanitarian aid. On the institutional front, gender focal points have been established throughout the External Relations DG and the Development DG.

Most of the activities in the field of awareness building have been financed from a special budget line B7–611.[28] This budget line provides resources for technical advice, training, working materials and research promoting the integration of gender questions, but not for small projects. These can be financed from a number of other budget lines such as the one for NGO co-financing. On 30 March 1998 the Council adopted a Common Position with a view to adopting a Council Regulation on integrating gender issues into external cooperation. This accompanied a financial commitment of 25 m euro for the period 1999–2003.

Environment: Integration of environmental issues into external cooperation programmes became a legal obligation under the Maastricht Treaty[29]. Council Resolutions of 1990[30], 1993[31] and 1996[32] refer to the environment as a cross-cutting issue. The Resolution of 1990 notes the need to draw up guidelines enabling environmental considerations to be better integrated into external aid programmes. Chapter 11 and 12 of the 1993 Resolution deal with International Cooperation and emphasise that the Community is committed to 'assisting developing countries in addressing the increasingly grave environmental problems they face and in achieving sustainable development'. The subsequent 1996 Resolution addresses the question of integrating environmental issues, suggesting that Environmental Impact Assessment (EIA), is one of the most important instruments for promoting this aim. These were followed up by the Council Regulation (EC) No 722/97 of 22 April 1997 on environmental measures in developing countries in the context of sustainable development.

Research for Development: The role of scientific research in development was highlighted in March 1997 at a major conference on 'Research Partnerships for Sustainable Development', hosted by the Netherlands and organised jointly with the Commission. During the Conference, the EU was identified as a key-actor in support of development research. Within the Commission, work on development research is mainly concentrated in the Directorates General for Development, External Affairs (capacity building and knowledge transfer), and Research (research cooperation).

The Conference was the catalyst for the publication of a subsequent Communication (COM (97) 174 final) on: 'Scientific and technological research – a strategic part of the EU's development co-operation with developing countries'. This sets out the problems to be addressed by development research, and which range from broad social problems, to access to basic needs, to globalization and integration into the world trading system. It also sets out a strategy for the Commission, stressing in particular the importance of ensuring complementarity between the activities of the Development and External Affairs DGs and the specific development research programmes (INCO-DEV and INCO-MED) of the Research DG.

A subsequent Council Resolution (May 1997) draws attention to the importance of institution building and strengthening research capacities in developing countries, as well as to a research strategy for both

---

[28] This budget line for 'Women and Development' was already in place before the 1995 Council Resolution. It was created in 1990 by the European Parliament. In 1997 the Commission proposed a *'Council Regulation on integrating gender issues in development cooperation'* which contains clear political orientation with regard to this question and the use of the funds.

[29] Article 130r2.

[30] Council Resolution of 29 May 1990 on *Environment and Development.*

[31] Resolution of the Council and Representatives of the Government of the Member States, meeting within the Council of February 1993 on a *Community programme of policy and action in relation to the environment and sustainable development* (93/C 138/01).

[32] Council Resolution of 28 May 1996, *Environmental Assessment in Development Cooperation.*

problem-solving and strategic research. In addition it endorses the importance of research co-operation activities for sustainable development as an essential element of the strategy.

In October 1997 the European Parliament adopted an Opinion endorsing the findings of the Communication and supporting a reinforcement of activities in research for development particularly through capacity building with a larger proportion of funding allocated to this by the European Development Fund.

The Research DG's INCO programme, which encompasses development research for developing countries under two different activities, INCO-DEV and INCO-MED, was approved in January 1999 as part of the EU's Fifth Framework Programme for RTD. The second call for proposals for INCO-DEV will be published in March 2000, to support joint research projects between developing country scientists and European scientists. The total INCO budget for developing countries is 253 m euros for joint research projects involving developing country and European scientists.

Loans

EC aid is provided in loan form through the European Investment Bank (see Chapter 1). The aim of this aid, according to the EIB, is to encourage efficient management of the means available, and to tailor the type of financial assistance to, local economic conditions. EIB financing is only awarded to projects which are technically viable and economically justified. Long-term loans for industrial projects have a duration of about 10–12 years, while infrastructure and energy projects receive loans with a slightly longer repayment period of 12–15 years. Over one half of EIB lending went to the ACP countries, with 40% going to the Mediterranean and Middle East region. Just over 3% went to the CEECs and a negligible amount went to Latin America.

Infrastructure was the main sector to benefit from aid loans, with industry, mining and construction receiving 21% of loan finance, energy just under 18%, water supply 16% and transport and communications 12%. However, nearly a quarter of loans remained unallocable by sector (see Figure 2.3).

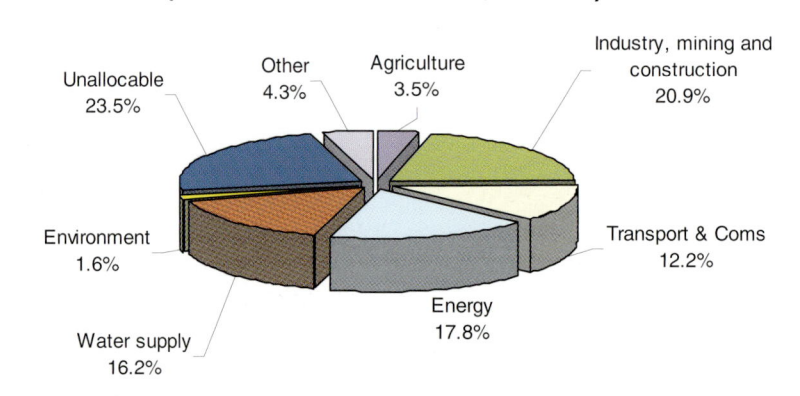

Figure 2.3: Sectoral Allocation Loans Managed by the EIB (1986–98, commitments, m euro)

- Unallocable 23.5%
- Other 4.3%
- Agriculture 3.5%
- Industry, mining and construction 20.9%
- Transport & Coms 12.2%
- Energy 17.8%
- Water supply 16.2%
- Environment 1.6%

Source: European Commission/ODI database 1999

3

EC External Cooperation with African, Caribbean and Pacific Countries

Trends and Distribution of EC External Cooperation to the ACP Countries[1]

Total EC aid committed to the ACP countries amounted to nearly 30 bn euro between 1986 and 1998, of which almost 77% was provided under the Lomé Conventions. It has grown significantly since 1986 with commitments rising from 1.1bn euro to over 2.8 bn euro in 1998, and disbursements increasing from 1 bn euro to nearly 2 bn euro (see Figure and Table 3.1) though commitments in particular have tended to rise then fall over the life of each European Development Fund (EDF). This can be seen most clearly in Fig 3.3.

This aid accounted for 40% of all aid committed by the EC and 45% of all disbursements between 1986 and 1998. The evolution of commitments and disbursements is dominated by the aid flows to sub-Saharan Africa, which is by far the biggest region in the group, both in terms of aid received and in terms of population. 2.4 bn euro was allocated to sub-Saharan Africa (78% of commitments made between 1986 and 1998), while the Caribbean and Pacific ACP countries and the Overseas Countries and Territories (OCTs) in those regions received 7% and 3% of all aid respectively.[2] Almost 6% of the ACP aid represented regional assistance (eg to West Africa, Southern Africa, Indian Ocean, etc) and the remaining 6% was unallocable by country or sub-region.

Total commitments to Africa varied considerably over the period again reflecting the cycle of the EDF. Assistance increased steeply from about 500 m euro in 1986 to 2400 m euro in 1988, falling back to 1000 m euro in 1990. Commitments rose again until a decline in 1993, reflecting a lack of agreement on Stabex disbursements, rising again in 1994 when Stabex funds for both 1993 and 1994 were committed (see section on Stabex below). Commitments in 1998, at nearly 2500 m euro, were quite close to their 1994 high. Disbursements have been somewhat lower but more stable, climbing more or less continuously between 1986 and 1992, when they reached 2100 m euro, before stabilising at around 1500 m euro in the late 1990s. The main recipients of EC aid to sub-Saharan Africa over the whole period are Ethiopia (consistently at the top), Côte d'Ivoire, Mozambique, Cameroon, Sudan and Tanzania, which together accounted for almost 30% of all aid to sub-Saharan Africa.

In the Caribbean annual commitments ranged between 49 m euro and 106 m euro up to 1991. After that flows rose significantly, up to 403 m euro in 1996 before dropping to 150 m euro in 1998. The steep increase can be explained by the inclusion of Haiti and the Dominican Republic in the ACP group during Lomé IV. The Dominican Republic accounted for 35% and 26% of all aid to the Caribbean in 1992 and 1993 respectively, while commitments to Haiti represented around 26% and 32% in 1994 and 1995 respectively. The main recipients in the Caribbean ACP region have been

---

[1] African countries in the ACP group are those benefiting from the Lomé Convention, ie all sub-Saharan African countries, and – since April 1997 – South Africa. Until then South Africa received financial assistance from the EC Budget and it is therefore discussed later in this chapter. Development cooperation with the Overseas Countries and Territories of the EC is also dealt with in this chapter as they are mainly in the Caribbean and Pacific regions and also benefit from the Lomé Convention.

[2] The OCTs in the Caribbean and Pacific accounted for 7.2% and 11.5% of commitments to each region respectively during 1986-98.

Jamaica, Haiti, the Dominican Republic and Trinidad and Tobago which together accounted for 59% of all aid to the region.

Figure 3.1: Regional Distribution of EC Cooperation with the ACP (1986-98, commitments and disbursements, m euro)

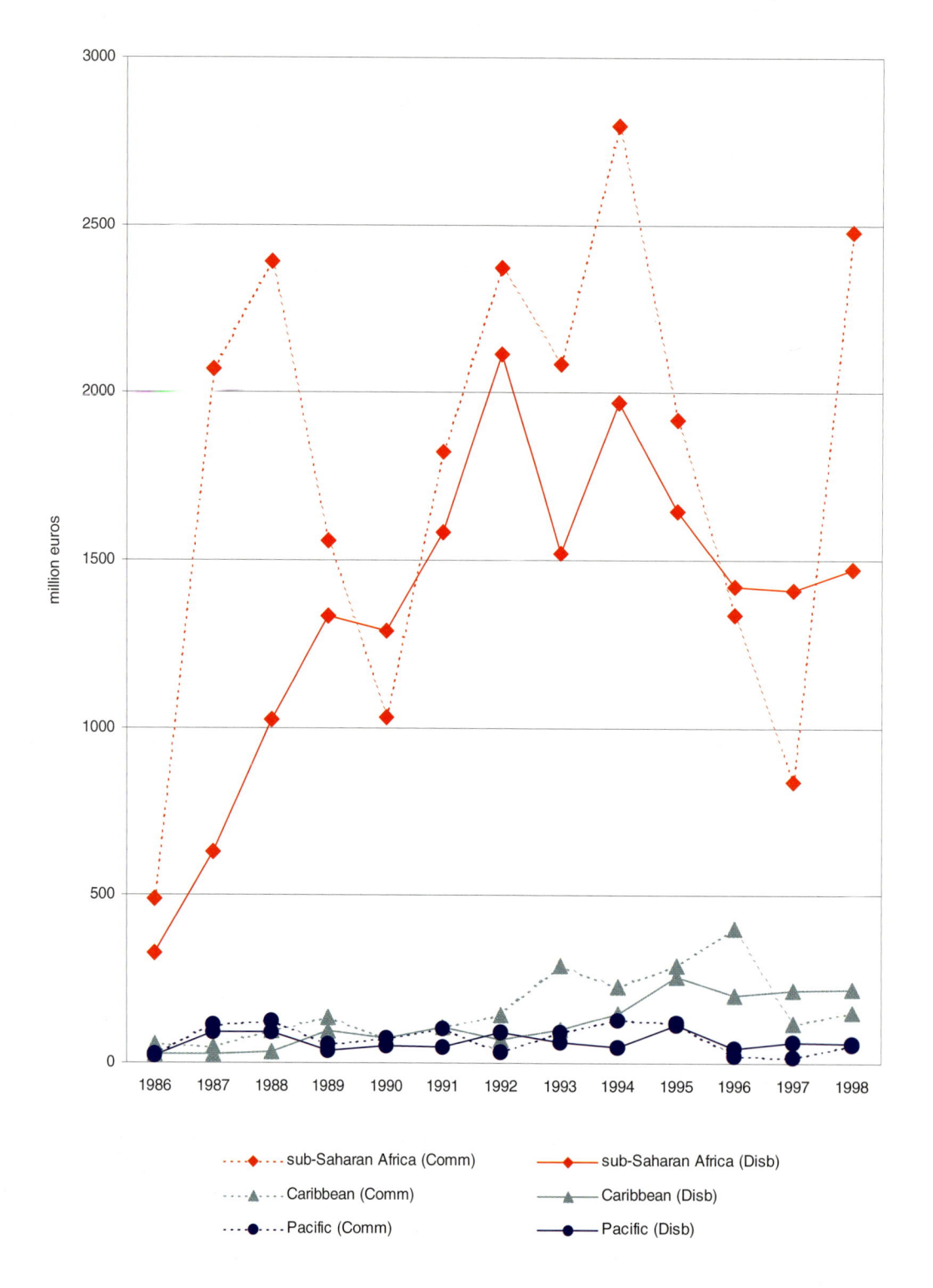

Source: European Commission/ODI database 1999; excludes the unallocable portion of ACP aid.

The pattern of commitments to the Pacific has also fluctuated considerably over ... (see Table 3.1). Papua New Guinea, the islands on which around 70% of the region's population lives, ... unted for more than half (56%) of total commitments to the Pacific, followed by Solomon Islands (9%).

The exact rate at which funds are disbursed is not easy to calculate from available data, since it would require the tracking of individual disbursements against their associated commitments. However, an approximate calculation shows some significant improvement over time for the ACP region. The ratio of total disbursements to total commitments for 1986-90 stood at 73.2%, rising to 78.0% for 1986-95, and again to 81.9% over the entire 1986-98 period. This is in part due to the introduction to fast-disbursing structural adjustment assistance in the early 1990s, and also to the drop in commitment levels in 1997 when commitments were outstripped by disbursements.

Table 3.1: Regional Distribution of EC Cooperation with the ACP (1986-98, commitments and disbursements, m euro)

	1986	1987	1988	1989	1990	1991	1992	1993	1994	1995	1996	1997	1998	Total
Commitments														
Total	1141	2632	2869	1994	1362	2123	2765	2774	3514	2599	1946	1127	2853	29698
sub-Sah Africa	491	2073	2390	1558	1031	1823	2374	2088	2798	1921	1337	841	2480	23204
Caribbean	55	49	94	137	74	106	145	292	230	291	403	119	150	2144
Pacific	27	115	127	54	73	104	35	92	128	121	22	19	56	974
Regional	4	44	128	173	149	126	182	264	258	266	4	141	-6	1732
Unallocable [a]	564	352	129	73	35	-36	31	38	100	1	180	6	173	1645
Disbursements														
Total	1057	1235	1542	1779	1703	2012	2592	1898	2445	2287	1899	1924	1952	24326
sub-Sah Africa	329	629	1025	1336	1289	1586	2117	1524	1971	1647	1421	1412	1476	17762
Caribbean	26	27	33	94	74	108	70	101	149	259	204	216	222	1583
Pacific	23	93	91	37	51	48	91	64	48	115	45	61	60	828
Regional	1	3	27	54	78	113	151	106	169	224	37	192	9	1164
Unallocable	680	482	366	258	210	157	163	103	107	41	192	44	185	2988

[a] The unallocable figures for 1986 and 1987 are relatively high as they include a large proportion of aid committed from EDF 5 (Lomé II: 1980-85) for which no accurate country breakdown was available. The negative commitment in 1991 is a decommitment from EDF 5 resulting from a transfer of a residual sum to EDF 6.

Source: European Commission/ODI database 1999

Recipients of EC Aid to the ACP

The main beneficiaries of EC aid to the ACP are all sub-Saharan African countries with the exception of Papua New Guinea, which ranks twenty-second over the whole time period, and Jamaica and Haiti which appear in the top 15 for 1996-98. The top 15 recipients account for 45% of all commitments made to the ACP between 1986 and 1998.

Shifts in the main beneficiaries among the ACP and Overseas Countries and Territories (OCTs) have been modest over the period (see Table 3.2). Food aid, humanitarian aid and project aid are relatively significant in the ranking for the second period. In the second period these sectors remain significant and aid to economic infrastructure and services also effects the rankings. Changes in the top 15 countries occur mainly because of a decrease in aid following suspension (eg Sudan) or an increase in aid as a result of a crisis (eg Rwanda) or rehabilitation (eg Mozambique and Angola).

In terms of aid *per capita* the Caribbean and Pacific island states, including most of the OCTs, rank highest among recipients in the 1990s. The top African states are Mauritania, Namibia, Botswana and Mauritius. Zaire and Nigeria, with high populations, are rather at the bottom of the league but Ethiopia, with one of the largest populations in the ACP group, has consistently been the leading recipient of EC aid (EDF and budget combined) both before and after the fall of the Mengistu Government.

Table 3.2: Top 15 Recipients of EC Cooperation – ACP (1986-98, share of total aid committed, %)

1986-90 (%)		1991-95 (%)		1996-98 (%)	
Ethiopia	5.7	Ethiopia	6.1	Ethiopia	10.4
Côte d'Ivoire	5.5	Rwanda[a]	4.1	Malawi	4.3
Nigeria	4.1	Mozambique	4.0	Zambia	3.3
Sudan	3.4	Côte d'Ivoire	3.6	Mali	3.1
Cameroon	3.2	Cameroon	3.4	Mozambique	3.1
Kenya	3.2	Zambia	3.2	Jamaica	2.8
Senegal	3.1	Uganda	3.1	Madagascar	2.8
Mozambique	3.0	Tanzania	3.0	Ghana	2.8
Guinea	2.6	Zimbabwe	2.7	Angola	2.5
Tanzania	2.5	Angola	2.7	Guinea	2.5
Zaire	2.4	Sudan	2.6	Tanzania	2.5
Mali	2.1	Nigeria	2.6	Uganda	2.3
Malawi	2.1	Burkina Faso	2.5	Haiti	2.3
Niger	2.0	Kenya	2.4	Sudan	2.3
Uganda	1.9	Guinea	2.4	Côte d'Ivoire	2.2
Top 15: % total EC aid to ACP	47.0	Top 15: % total EC aid to ACP	48.5	Top 15: % total EC aid to ACP	49.3

[a] In 1994–95, 259 m euro of emergency assistance went to the Rwandan crisis. Some of this aid may have benefited Burundi, but the data do not allow differentiation.

Source: European Commission/ODI database 1999

Sectoral Distribution of EC Aid to the ACP

The main instruments of EC aid (programme aid, food aid, humanitarian assistance and aid to NGOs) accounted for 43% of all aid to the ACP countries for 1986-98, with 51%, 15 bn euro, spent on project aid – mainly through the National and Regional Indicative Programmes and some smaller budget lines (see section on project aid below). The remainder, 6%, was unallocable by sector. Programme aid accounted for more than 7.5 bn euro, over a quarter of all aid to the ACP between 1986 and 1998, and food aid and humanitarian aid for about 9% and 7% respectively. Most project aid went to the transport and communications sector (12.1%), followed by the social infrastructure sectors (7.5%), the industry, mining and construction sector (6.7%), energy (5.6%), rural development (5.5%), and agriculture (5.1%).

Figure 3.2 compares the sectoral breakdown of aid to the ACP in the periods 1986–1990, 1991–95 and 1996-98 (as shares of total allocable aid in each period). Of the instruments, support for structural adjustment, humanitarian aid and aid to NGOs gained in importance, while Stabex and Sysmin transfers fell (due to falls in the % taken by Stabex). Food aid rose dramatically from the first to the second time period, before falling for the final period.

Table 3.3: Sectoral Allocation of EC Cooperation with the ACP
(1986-98, commitments, m euro and % of total aid)

Commitmnts (m euro)	1986	1987	1988	1989	1990	1991	1992	1993	1994	1995	1996	1997	1998	Total
Programme Aid	159	523	972	481	338	715	892	487	988	492	331	291	872	7543
Structural Adjustment	37	222	351	188	104	183	403	419	316	277	142	123	720	3484
Stabex	122	301	554	278	219	515	397	4	615	131	155	–	152	3444
Sysmin	–	–	66	16	15	18	92	64	57	84	34	168	1	616
Food Aid (development)	6	–	14	248	224	410	279	331	365	337	148	145	138	2643
Humanitarian Aid	18	36	61	83	72	79	117	144	348	417	435	167	179	2156
Humanit excl rehabilitation	18	33	55	76	57	62	104	127	316	187	328	101	132	1597
Rehabilitation	0	3	5	7	14	17	13	17	33	229	107	66	47	559
Aid to NGOs	13	22	23	27	29	34	29	36	36	41	70	63	65	487
Natural Resources	29	328	374	107	85	61	112	265	191	102	13	33	137	1835
Agriculture	27	302	352	86	54	43	70	220	146	87	-20	30	123	1521
Forestry	0	23	0	8	27	6	31	18	18	14	27	7	4	184
Fisheries	2	4	21	12	3	12	11	27	27	2	5	-5	9	129
Other Productive Services	149	242	299	233	76	250	252	295	166	258	85	3	95	2404
Industry, Mining & Construc	139	231	272	208	43	239	196	216	139	210	69	2	22	1987
Trade	7	10	13	16	12	10	43	52	21	25	1	-3	42	251
Tourism	3	1	14	9	21	1	12	27	5	21	15	4	30	163
Investment Promotion	–	–	–	–	–	–	–	–	1	2	–	–	–	3
Econ Infrastructure & Servs	126	578	313	354	229	411	388	462	653	533	535	169	847	5597
Transport & Comms	49	442	197	278	128	299	288	259	358	287	309	89	622	3605
Energy	77	135	114	75	98	104	99	187	262	206	131	65	98	1650
Banking, Finance & Bus Srvs	1	1	2	1	2	9	0	16	33	40	94	16	127	342
Social Infrastructure & Servs	38	142	174	111	106	57	268	393	235	226	135	10	321	2216
Education	7	48	48	38	41	4	67	96	86	24	26	1	69	556
Health & Population	0	27	43	14	9	12	108	143	40	78	69	2	92	636
Water Supply	30	40	78	49	51	37	77	108	62	88	28	0	141	789
Other Social Infra & Services	0	26	4	10	6	5	16	46	48	36	12	6	19	235
Governance & Civil Society	0	3	7	8	28	19	41	22	10	31	78	175	86	509
Multisector/Crosscutting	15	557	564	279	114	86	295	265	322	63	32	–	62	2653
Environment	3	4	6	20	8	13	20	66	14	19	2	5	7	186
Women in Development	–	–	–	–	–	–	1	0	0	0	2	1	0	5
Rural Development	4	529	516	239	77	52	145	47	18	7	10	–	11	1634
Other Multisector	8	24	43	20	29	21	128	152	289	37	18	14	44	828
Unallocable by Sector	587	201	69	63	63	1	94	74	199	99	84	72	51	1657
TOTAL	1141	2632	2869	1994	1362	2123	2765	2774	3514	2599	1946	1127	2853	29698

Commitments (%)	1986	1987	1988	1989	1990	1991	1992	1993	1994	1995	1996	1997	1998	Total
Programme Aid	13.9	19.9	33.9	24.1	24.8	33.7	32.3	17.6	28.1	18.9	17.0	25.8	30.6	25.4
Structural Adjustment	3.2	8.4	12.2	9.4	7.6	8.6	14.6	15.1	9.0	10.6	7.3	10.9	25.2	11.7
Stabex	10.7	11.5	19.3	13.9	16.1	24.3	14.4	0.2	17.5	5.0	8.0	0.0	5.3	11.6
Sysmin	–	–	2.3	0.8	1.1	0.8	3.3	2.3	1.6	3.3	1.7	14.9	–	2.1
Food Aid (development)	0.5	–	0.5	12.4	16.4	19.3	10.1	11.9	10.4	13.0	7.6	12.8	4.8	8.9
Humanitarian Aid	1.6	1.4	2.1	4.2	5.3	3.7	4.2	5.2	9.9	16.0	22.4	14.8	6.3	7.3
Humanit excl rehabilitation	1.6	1.3	1.9	3.8	4.2	2.9	3.8	4.6	9.0	7.2	16.8	9.0	4.6	5.4
Rehabilitation	–	0.1	0.2	0.3	1.1	0.8	0.5	0.6	0.9	8.8	5.5	5.9	1.7	1.9
Aid to NGOs	1.1	0.8	0.8	1.3	2.1	1.6	1.0	1.3	1.0	1.6	3.6	5.6	2.3	1.6
Natural Resources	2.5	12.5	13.0	5.4	6.2	2.9	4.0	9.5	5.4	3.9	0.6	2.9	4.8	6.2
Agriculture	2.4	11.5	12.3	4.3	4.0	2.0	2.5	7.9	4.1	3.3	-1.0	2.7	4.3	5.1
Forestry	–	0.9	–	0.4	2.0	0.3	1.1	0.6	0.5	0.5	1.4	0.6	0.1	0.6
Fisheries	0.2	0.1	0.7	0.6	0.2	0.6	0.4	1.0	0.8	0.1	0.3	-0.5	0.3	0.4
Other Productive Services	13.1	9.2	10.4	11.7	5.6	11.8	9.1	10.6	4.7	9.9	4.4	0.3	3.3	8.1
Industry, Mining & Construc	12.2	8.8	9.5	10.4	3.2	11.2	7.1	7.8	4.0	8.1	3.6	0.1	0.8	6.7
Trade	0.6	0.4	0.5	0.8	0.9	0.5	1.6	1.9	0.6	0.9	0.1	-0.2	1.5	0.8
Tourism	0.3	–	0.5	0.4	1.5	0.1	0.4	1.0	0.1	0.8	0.8	0.4	1.1	0.5
Investment Promotion	–	–	–	–	–	–	–	–	–	0.1	–	–	–	0.0
Econ Infrastructure & Servs	11.1	22.0	10.9	17.8	16.8	19.4	14.0	16.7	18.6	20.5	27.5	15.0	29.7	18.8
Transport & Comms	4.3	16.8	6.9	13.9	9.4	14.1	10.4	9.4	10.2	11.1	15.9	7.9	21.8	12.1
Energy	6.7	5.1	4.0	3.8	7.2	4.9	3.6	6.7	7.5	7.9	6.8	5.7	3.4	5.6
Banking, Finance & Bus Srvs	–	–	0.1	0.1	0.2	0.4	0.0	0.6	0.9	1.5	4.8	1.4	4.5	1.2
Social Infrastructure & Servs	3.3	5.4	6.1	5.6	7.8	2.7	9.7	14.2	6.7	8.7	6.9	0.8	11.2	7.5
Education	0.6	1.8	1.7	1.9	3.0	0.2	2.4	3.5	2.4	0.9	1.3	0.1	2.4	1.9
Health & Population	–	1.0	1.5	0.7	0.7	0.6	3.9	5.1	1.1	3.0	3.5	0.2	3.2	2.1
Water Supply	2.7	1.5	2.7	2.4	3.7	1.7	2.8	3.9	1.8	3.4	1.5	–	4.9	2.7
Other Social Infra & Services	–	1.0	0.1	0.5	0.4	0.2	0.6	1.7	1.4	1.4	0.6	0.5	0.7	0.8
Governance & Civil Society	–	0.1	0.2	0.4	2.0	0.9	1.5	0.8	0.3	1.2	4.0	15.5	3.0	1.7
Multisector/Crosscutting	1.3	21.2	19.7	14.0	8.3	4.0	10.7	9.5	9.2	2.4	1.6	0.0	2.2	8.9
Environment	0.2	0.1	0.2	1.0	0.6	0.6	0.7	2.4	0.4	0.7	0.1	0.5	0.2	0.6
Women in Development	–	–	–	–	–	–	0.1	–	–	–	0.1	–	–	0.0
Rural Development	0.3	20.1	18.0	12.0	5.6	2.4	5.2	1.7	0.5	0.3	0.5	-1.8	0.4	5.5
Other Multisector	0.7	0.9	1.5	1.0	2.2	1.0	4.6	5.5	8.2	1.4	0.9	1.2	1.5	2.8
Unallocable by Sector	51.5	7.6	2.4	3.2	4.6	0.1	3.4	2.7	5.7	3.8	4.3	6.4	1.8	5.6
TOTAL	100	100	100	100	100	100	100	100	100	100	100	100	100	100

Source: European Commission/ODI database 1999

In terms of project aid, support for rural development, the natural resources sector (agriculture, forestry and fisheries), and industry, mining and construction all declined. The high proportion for rural development in the earlier period can be explained by the Integrated Rural Development Programmes (IRDPs) implemented in those years. In the later period, support to rural development is more likely to be included in other sectors such as social and economic infrastructure, as individual projects were more common than the IRDPs. As a proportion of all allocable aid, assistance to the sectors of transport and communications, banking, finance and business services, and governance and civil society, increased significantly during the third period, while the share of aid to health and population almost tripled over the entire period. The section on project aid below provides more detail on the sectoral distribution of project aid within each of the sub-regions.

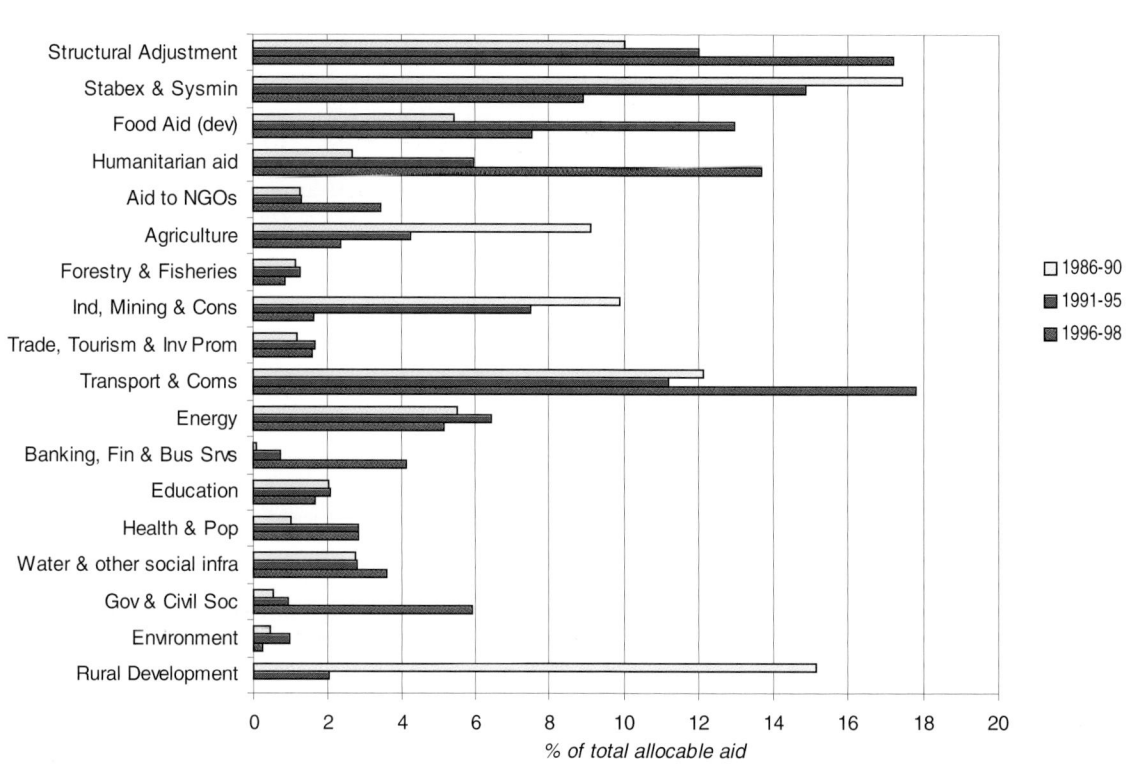

Figure 3.2: Sectoral Distribution of EC Cooperation with the ACP (1986-98, commitments, % of allocable aid)

Source: European Commission/ODI database 1999

Sources of EC External Cooperation with the ACP

The ACP countries received 22.8 bn euro over the 1986–98 period from the European Development Fund, which represents 77% of all EC aid to ACP countries. 16% of aid to the region, 4.9 bn euro, was allocated from the EC Budget, mainly from the lines for food aid and humanitarian aid (particularly in 1994 and 1995). The remaining 7% was provided from the 'own resources' of the European Investment Bank in the form of concessional loans. 7.6% of EDF flows are provided in the form of risk capital, and are managed by the European Investment Bank (see also Chapter 1). Figure 3.3 shows the trend in the sources of EC aid to the ACP, including grants and concessional loans.

Budget lines to assist ACP countries were established as a response to recipient needs (or EU concerns) not covered by the framework of the EDF. Compared with the EDF, the contribution from the EC Budget is substantially lower, though rising, at least until 1995. Between 1986 and 1998, 54% of this was committed as food aid (2.6 bn euro) and another 21% as humanitarian aid (1.0 bn euro). The remaining 1.2 bn euro, which accounted for only 4% of all aid to the ACP countries, was disbursed through other budget lines (see section on Financial and Technical Cooperation Instruments below).

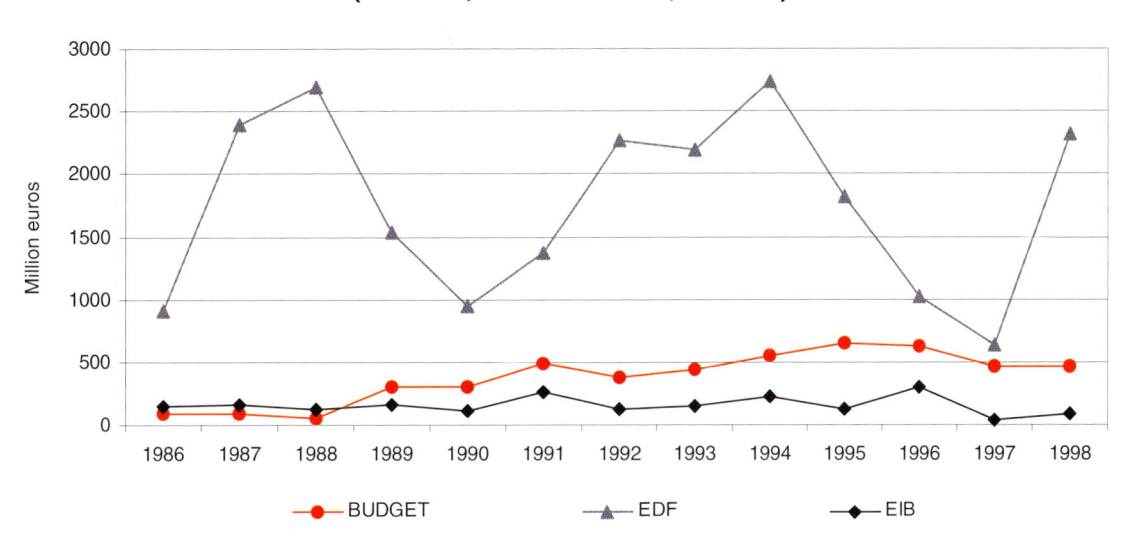

Figure 3.3: Trend in Sources of EC Cooperation with the ACP (1986-98, commitments, m euro)

Source: European Commission/ODI database 1999

The European Development Fund

Policies and Objectives of the Lomé Convention

The main objective of the Lomé Convention is 'to promote and expedite the economic, cultural and social development of the ACP states and to consolidate and diversify their (ACP and EU) relations in a spirit of solidarity and mutual interest', as stated in article 1 of Lomé III (1985–90) and repeated in Lomé IV and Lomé IVbis. Before 1985 this objective was less explicit, as the legal text of Lomé I and II focused more narrowly on trade and industrial and financial cooperation. The principles on which the Convention has been based from its inception are:

(i) equality between partners, and respect for sovereignty, mutual interests and interdependence;

(ii) the right of each state to determine its own political, social, cultural and economic policy options (although this is now partly in abeyance); and,

(iii) security of relations based on the achievements of the cooperation system (art. 2).

Box 3.1 Institutional framework of Lomé Convention

The Lomé Convention provides for a joint institutional framework established on a basis of parity between ACP States and the Member States of the European Union. According to the Convention:

The *Joint Council of Ministers* takes binding decisions and is responsible for resolving disputes relating to the application of the Convention. Under Lomé IV bis it has also provided a forum for 'enlarged political dialogue'. It meets at least once a year, and representation is formally at ministerial level.

The *Joint Committee of Ambassadors* is responsible to the Council of Ministers, and may propose recommendations, resolutions, etc, to the Council. In addition, the Council may delegate any of its powers to the Committee. The Committee meets at least twice a year, and membership is drawn from ACP Ambassadors and the Permanent Representations of Member States in Brussels.

The *Joint Assembly* considers the annual report issued by the Council of Ministers, and may adopt resolutions to be examined by the Council. It meets twice a year, and membership is drawn from the European Parliament and the parliaments of ACP countries.

The main distinguishing characteristics of the Lomé EU-ACP agreement are:

(i) the contractual relationship between the industrialised EU Member States and the ACP developing countries which contains obligations and rights for both partners;

(ii) the partnership principle, which attaches great importance to the equality of the partners, their sovereignty and the dialogue between them;[3]

(iii) the combination of trade and aid provisions in a single agreement, with the diversity of instruments that can be used alongside each other;

(iv) the long-term perspective brought to the Convention by its five-yearly duration (ten currently) and programmed allocation of funds, elements of which are unique in the donor community.

Lomé I and II concentrated heavily on the promotion of industrial development. During Lomé III this objective was overtaken by a more pressing concern: self-reliant development on the basis of self-sufficiency and food security. In addition to these priorities, Lomé IV put greater emphasis on the promotion of human rights, democracy and good governance (art. 5), strengthening of the position of women (art.4), the protection of the environment (art.6, 14), decentralised cooperation (art.20 22), diversification of ACP economies (art.18), and the promotion of the private sector (see also below). The Convention has consistently shown a commitment to regional cooperation.

With each Convention, the ACP group expanded, more 'areas' of cooperation were added (now twelve compared with four in Lomé I) and new instruments were introduced. The main provisions and instruments of the Convention can be divided into: (i) technical and financial cooperation (including cooperation in the field of commodities); (ii) trade cooperation including the special protocols; and (iii) other areas of cooperation. The level of funding available through each Convention and through the EIB is shown in Table 3.4.

Table 3.4: Evolution of the EDF and EIB Own Resources (m euro, current; and m euro constant, 1997 terms)

	1957 Rome Treaty EDF 1	1963 Yaoundé I EDF 2	1969 Yaoundé II EDF 3	75-80 Lomé I EDF 4	80-85 Lomé II EDF 5	85-90 Lomé III EDF 6	90-95 Lomé IV EDF 7	95-2000 Lomé IV EDF 8
EDF total	581	666	828	3 072	4 724	7 400	10 800	12 967
Grants[a]	581	620	748	2 150	2 999	4 860	7 995	9 592
Special Loans	–	–	–	446	525	600	–	–
STABEX	–	–	–	377	634	925	1 500	1 800
SYSMIN	–	–	–	–	282	415	480	575
Risk Capital	–	46	80	99	284	660	825	1 000
EIB own resources[b]	–	64	90	390	685	1 100	1 200	1 658
Total EDF + EIB	581	730	918	3 462	5 409	8 500	12 000	14 625
Per capita EDF: current (euro)[c]	10.7	9.7	10.5	12.3	13.5	17.9	21.9	23.6
p.c. constant (euro)[d]	62.9	50.3	41.2	31.5	22.6	24.2	24.3	23.6

[a] This includes assistance for regional cooperation, interest rate subsidies, structural adjustment assistance (Lomé IV), emergency and refugee assistance (Lomé IV) and other grants.
[b] This is a ceiling set by the board of the EIB which has never been reached.
[c] Total current value of EDF divided by associated country's population (millions) at the beginning of each convention period.
[d] EDF totals expressed in 1997 terms: current values deflated by the EC GDP deflator index centred in the mid-year of each convention (1961 for EDF 1; 1965 for EDF 2; 1971 for EDF 3).

Source: Grilli, Enzo R, *The European Community and the Developing Countries*, Cambridge: Cambridge University Press, 1993, p.99; and the ACP-EC *Courier*, January/February 1996

---

[3] This is evident in the co-management of EDF funds and the existence of joint institutions such as the EC–ACP Council of Ministers, and the Joint Assembly (for MPs).

Financial and Technical Cooperation

This is the aid component of the Convention financed from the EDF. Flows can be divided into programmable and non-programmable allocations. The *programmable* allocations are the National (NIP) and Regional (RIP) Indicative Programmes, that are allocated from each EDF to individual ACP countries and regions.[4] The allocation is effected every five years on the basis of a formula which captures objective criteria of a geographic, demographic and macroeconomic nature (GNP per capita, economic situation, external debt, etc.). The formula includes considerations of physical elements (landlocked and island states), the status of least developed countries (art.8 of the Convention), and other factors not precisely specified.

After notification by the Commission of the amount of programmable resources for each ACP country, the NIP is drawn up jointly by the recipient government and the Commission. It records priority areas for the spending of the NIP. The implementation of these country allocations differs by country, but commitments and especially disbursements can be subject to considerable delays. The implementation cycle of each Lomé Convention is therefore longer than the five years of the Convention itself, and the Commission thus manages several funds simultaneously.[5]

In June 1998, the Director General of DG VIII issued guidance for the setting up of Country Reviews, to be carried out at least annually. These are formal meetings that will bring together relevant staff from the different units of DG VIII, the Delegations, and where appropriate from other services. These reviews are to provide a compete and up-to-date overview of the Commission's actions, to examine the adequacy of the Commission's strategy, in particular with a view to facilitating complementarity with Member States and other donors. The Country Reviews will be followed by in-country meetings with ACP representatives.

The Convention attaches special importance to regional cooperation among the ACP countries and devotes a significant share of EDF funds to this purpose (see Box 3.2). RIPs are organised according to six geographic regions plus a linguistic grouping (for Portuguese-speaking countries). For RIPs 1000 m euro was available from Lomé III and 1250 m euro from Lomé IV, 9.3% and 9.6% respectively of all programmable resources.

The *non-programmable* funds from the EDF (ie those excluded from the NIPs and RIPs) are generally quick-disbursing instruments. Although their overall amount is fixed by each Convention, their allocations to the individual countries are not defined. These funds are granted to ACP countries case-by-case, depending on their eligibility for the particular non-programmable instrument. The main non-programmable resources of Lomé are the three categories within programme aid (support for structural adjustment,

> **Box 3.2: EC–ACP Regional Cooperation**
>
> Regional cooperation has formed an important component of Community assistance to the ACP countries. Regional programmes accounted for 10% of total EDF financing under Lomé I, rising to 14% under Lomé II and III, and falling to below 10% for Lomé IV. This recent dip probably reflects a dearth of good quality regional programmes suitable for funding, rather than a decline in the need for or relevance of regional cooperation itself.
>
> Evaluation of Community regional cooperation programmes in Africa indicate that political ownership is essential for success, and that cooperation is effective only where the mutual dependence of the participating countries is obvious.
>
> Regional projects serve national goals as well as bringing benefits to a region. Since governments have generally given greater weight to the former, the regional component of projects is usually the last one to receive support. Nonetheless, evaluation suggests that most regional projects have made some positive contribution towards an intensification of cooperation.

---

[4] Regions distinguished in the ACP group are Sahelian and Coastal West Africa, the Horn of Africa and East Africa, Southern Africa, the Indian Ocean, the Caribbean and the Pacific.

[5] EDF 5, for instance, of Lomé II (1980–85) was closed at the end of 1993. Outstanding balances which still existed then were transferred to EDF 7.

Stabex, and Sysmin) and humanitarian and rehabilitation assistance. The latter two are additional to the budget lines that exist in parallel for the same purpose. These will be included in the discussion of main instruments in the section below.

During Lomé I–III certain instruments were given as a loan (eg Sysmin, Stabex to a few countries), but since Lomé IV the EDF has become entirely concessional, with the exception of risk capital (8% of flows allocated to the ACP countries in EDF 7).

Trade Cooperation

Trade preferences: The EC offers duty and quota-free access, on a non-reciprocal basis, to exports from ACP countries. This excludes exports covered by the Common Agricultural Policy, which nonetheless receive better treatment than they would through the EU's Most Favoured Nation (MFN) regime. On the whole, since 1975, of all the Community's 'preferential' trading partners, ACP countries have enjoyed the greatest preferential market access to the EU: 92% of the products originating in the ACP countries enter the Community duty free, without quantitative limits. A further 7% are agricultural products subject to a tariff quota with zero duty. Four-fifths of the agricultural products covered by Chapters 1 to 24 of the Combined Nomenclature (CN) are completely liberalised, and all industrial products falling within Chapters 25 to 97 have a tariff exemption under Lomé. In 1997, imports originating in the ACP totaled 22 bn euro, with 62.5% of them consisting of industrial products (including commodities such as oil) and 37.5% of agricultural products. The preferential margin granted to the ACP countries above MFN tariffs (excluding protocols) is around 750 m euro, or 3.6% of the 1997 value of imports. The preferential margin over the Generalised System of Preferences (GSP) regime is 2.5% (500 m euro).

In addition, protocols exist for EC imports of beef/veal and for sugar[6], which grant selected ACP countries guaranteed import quota-type ceilings. Protocols for bananas[7] and rum also offer the beneficiaries a special import regime. These four commodity protocols account for 7.4% of all imports, and generated 1.6 bn euro in exports in 1997. The banana and sugar protocols have been particularly significant in boosting the export revenues of certain ACP countries, Mauritius being the best example.

It should be noted that the overall value of the Lomé trade regime, generous as it may be, has been declining over time. First, in the context of continuing trade liberalisation, both at the multilateral and regional levels, the value to the ACP of tariff preferences is bound to erode, although it may remain substantial for several years in specific products and for specific countries. For instance, in 2000, the preferential margin for manufactured goods over the GSP will be down to 1.6%. Sectors where the margin will remain relatively significant are chemicals, footwear, and textiles for clothing. As for agricultural products, in 2000, 50% of agricultural exports will no longer enjoy preferences (among which coffee and cocoa), while the other half will still have a margin of preference of some 10%.

Second, the four protocols also are threatened by the process of multilateral trade liberalisation, which is eroding the benefits they provide, and by the enforcement of WTO rules that seek to limit or ban such discriminating trade arrangements. Each also faces different challenges: the WTO panel ruling on the EU *banana* regime will probably negatively effect the capacity of the ACP to access the EU market.[8]

---

[6] The Sugar Protocol predates the Convention and has its origins in the Commonwealth Sugar Agreement. It forms a reciprocal agreement between the EC and the ACP under which the Commission undertakes to purchase and the ACP to supply certain quantities of ACP sugar each year at guaranteed threshold prices.

[7] The ACP banana producers have also been supported through Stabex which compensated them for the losses in export earnings from reduced prices in recent years and through a special budget line set up in 1994.

[8] The CAP reform (Agenda 2000) implies a progressive decline in *beef* prices, and the prospects of further liberalisation of trade in agriculture threaten to wipe out the benefits for the ACP over the next decade. The full liberalisation of imports of ACP rum effectively signals the end of the *rum* protocol in 2000. The EU *sugar* regime has not been affected yet by ongoing

EC Aid for Trade Development: In addition to the preferential treatment of ACP exports, the Lomé Convention provides support for trade promotion and trade development, including that of trade in services. EDF funds — in the form of programmable and non-programmable aid —have been traditionally used for participation in trade fairs and for technical assistance. The Lomé Conventions have also provided support for a number of special institutions benefiting ACP exporters, such as the Centres for Development of Industry (CDI) and Tropical Agriculture (CTA) and the ACP–EC institution APROMA (for soft commodities), as well as an all-ACP Trade Development Project (see Box 3.3).

> **Box 3.3: The Centre for the Development of Industry (CDI)**
>
> The CDI was set up by the EU and the ACP States in 1977 with the prime purpose of identifying, appraising, promoting, and assisting the creation of economically viable industrial projects in ACP countries. It also acts as an intermediary and facilitator between EU and ACP companies so as to promote joint ventures in the ACP countries and the transfer of industrial know-how and technology. It may provide expertise and financial assistance as well as technical support and training for ACP countries, operating generally at the level of the individual enterprise. It is decentralising its operations through the creation of local and regional service companies or consultants in the ACP countries.
>
> It is funded by the EDF budget receiving 60 million euro from the EDF under Lomé IV for the period 1990-5 and a further 73 million for the period 1995-2000.

Mid-term Review of Lomé IV

Although the fourth Lomé Convention was agreed for a period of ten years, the financial protocol was subject to a mandatory renewal after five years (art. 366 of Lomé IV). A mid-term review took place in 1994–95, in the context of changes in the economic and political situations of the ACP countries (democratisation process, structural adjustment), in Europe (enlargement, increasing attention to East European and Mediterranean partners) and in the international environment (Uruguay Round Agreement). Several amendments were approved:

- on political issues: respect for human rights, democratic principles and the rule of law became *essential elements* of the Convention;[9]

- on trade cooperation: *a small extension of preferential access* for ACP agricultural exports to the EU in a few areas; a minor relaxation of the *rules of origin*;

- on development finance and related procedures: *EDF 8 was agreed* at a level similar (in real terms) to the previous EDF —despite conflicts over the contributions of individual Member States to the new financial protocol. *Phased programming* was introduced, with an aim at 'building-in' additional flexibility.[10]

Post Lomé IV negotiations

Unlike the previous rounds, the post-Lomé IV negotiations foresaw a substantial transformation of ACP-EU cooperation and triggered a wide debate. After the publication of the Green Paper (November 1996), the EC invited written reactions and contributions by all Member States, and organised meetings in all EU countries, as well as in Africa, in the Caribbean and in the Pacific. The Commission's initiative to launch a broad-based consultation on the future of ACP-EU relations changed the very nature of the traditional negotiation process. Both in Europe and in the ACP, new constituencies emerged. An impressive number of analyses and positions were produced by bodies representing civil society, the research community, and the private sector. The formal EC negotiating mandate, based on a draft which the Commission circulated in January 1998, was approved by

---

CAP reforms and the binding of quotas in the GATT makes them less likely to be challenged. The reform of the sugar regime in 2001 may lead to lower internal prices. The enlargement of the EU to include countries that produce low-cost sugar, as well as the next multilateral Round, will probably increase the pressure to bring EU sugar prices into line with world market prices.

[9] Procedures were put in place which could lead to the *suspension* of the Convention (introduced as art. 366a), if these elements were violated (though this would be a measure of last resort).

[10] Funds are allocated to the ACP countries in two tranches: the first for 70% of the total allocation over the first three years; the second is performance-related, and is only earmarked for countries after an initial assessment of how the first tranche has been spent.

Member States under the UK Presidency in June. Negotiations with the ACP were opened in September 1998 and are due be closed on February 29, 2000.

While the EU is keen to preserve the main elements of the Lomé culture, it is not simply looking for a 'Lomé V'. Instead, the aim is to build a new, strengthened *partnership*, secured through deeper political dialogue geared towards poverty reduction, sustainable development and further integration of the ACP into the international economy. The need for 'differentiation' between ACP countries, especially through a strengthening of cooperation with the various ACP sub-regional groups (CARICOM, UEMOA, SADC, etc.) is also stressed. The EU sees an explicit linkage between development and broader political and economic agendas. While the principles of democracy, rule of law, respect for human rights and good governance are already set out in the existing Convention, the EU wants to go further and include a considerably strengthened good governance clause as a new essential element (article 5).[11]

More specifically, the EU's proposals for this new type of cooperation contract point to four major directions.

1. Giving a stronger **political foundation** to its cooperation with the ACP, characterised by more effective and open dialogue, performance-based aid allocations and adequate conflict prevention strategies. A broader, deeper and more effective political dialogue should be promoted —at the global, regional, sub-regional and national levels— on conflict prevention, post-conflict reconstruction, sustainable development, respect for human rights, democracy, drugs and organised crime, gender, etc. The EU also calls for flexible procedures and modalities, to be agreed according to efficiency criteria.

2. Establishing '**regionalised economic partnership agreements**', including the gradual introduction of reciprocity in trade arrangements, building on the ACP's regional integration initiatives. The approaching expiry of Lomé IV has triggered an intense debate on non-reciprocal trade preferences with regard to their *effectiveness*[12] and, maybe more pressingly, their *legality* vis-à-vis WTO rules.[13] Schematically, there are two ways to make Lomé WTO-compatible: either by taking the trade chapter out of the Convention and harmonising the regime with the existing Generalised System of Preferences, or transforming non-reciprocal preferences into GATT-compatible free trade agreements. The EU proposes a flexible, mixed arrangement, in the form of several free trade agreements to be signed with different ACP regions or countries, after several years of transition during which current preferences would be rolled over. This would preserve the principles of a comprehensive aid and trade agreement, covering an increasing number of areas, and of a specific ACP-EU trade link. One bilateral free trade agreement was signed with South Africa in October 1999.

3. **Extending partnership to a wider range of (non-state) actors** and 'mainstream' decentralised cooperation. A 'participatory partnership' is seen as a fundamental principle of future cooperation (the EU's negotiating mandate dedicates an entire chapter to the 'actors of partnership'). While recognising the primary role of national authorities in defining strategies and programmes for development, the EU wants to involve a wide range of actors in 'dialogue [...] on the policies and priorities of cooperation (especially in areas directly concerning them) and [...] in implementing cooperation projects and programmes'. The mandate also stresses the need for 'increasing decentralised cooperation'.

---

[11] Good governance is defined in the EU mandate as transparent and accountable management of resources, including 'effective action to prevent and combat bribery and corruption'.

[12] In the face of pervasive domestic supply constraints, with a few noticeable exceptions, preferences have not prevented ACP countries from losing market share in the EU.

[13] By providing special treatment to a group of countries (the ACP) without extending it to other developing countries at similar levels of development, the Lomé trade regime contravenes the Most Favoured Nation principle.

4. Undertaking a **'complete overhaul' of the procedures** for managing financial and technical cooperation, in favour of simplicity, rationalisation and differentiation.

Financial and Technical Cooperation Instruments

Support for Structural Adjustment

Structural Adjustment finance has been the most important Lomé instrument overall, closely followed by Stabex. EC support for structural adjustment started in the late 1980s, but has changed considerably in the last decade. Between 1986 and 1995, it took the form of Sectoral Import Programmes, General Import Programmes and the Structural Adjustment Facility. These support programmes (i) support the budget or a particular sector of the budget, through foreign currency transfers or counterpart funds; (ii) are quick-disbursing; and (iii) usually have conditionalities attached to them relating to economic and institutional reform (particularly in recent years).

On the basis of Article 188 in Lomé III the Community developed programmes for import support to ACP countries in 1986. The funds for this support were drawn from National Indicative Programmes (ie the programmable funds) allocated to individual countries and were targeted on specific sectors. General Import Programmes under the Special Debt Programme (established in 1987) were introduced to complement the Sectoral Import Programmes. Although the Special Debt Programme was officially linked to structural adjustment efforts by the ACP countries, interventions under the sectoral and general import programmes during Lomé III were not linked to specific reform objectives at a sectoral or macroeconomic level.

This changed radically with Lomé IV, under which the Community would provide import support only to those countries which had signed up to a structural adjustment programme agreed with the World Bank or IMF. A new emphasis was placed on specific Community concerns outlined in 1992 (Joint Report and Council Resolution of EC/ACP Council): namely the need: (i) to reconcile adjustment with long-term development, to adapt the pace of reform to country-specific situations, and to take into account the regional and social dimensions of structural adjustment; (ii) to maximise consistency with other Community instruments affecting a country's balance of payments and generating counterpart funds; (iii) to become more involved in the public finances of ACP states; and (iv) to improve coordination with other donors.

A special facility for structural adjustment support was introduced in Lomé IV and used alongside funds from the NIPs allocated for this purpose. The use of counterpart funds generated from structural adjustment support, as well as food aid, Stabex and Sysmin, is discussed in Box 3.4.

The trend in support for structural adjustment shows two steep increases;[14] one when the Special Debt Programme was introduced and Sectoral Import Programmes started to be implemented in 1987; the other when the Structural Adjustment Facility became operational in 1992.[15] The steep rise in commitments in 1998 to 872 m euro may be due to the long delay in the ratification of Member States of Lomé IV bis, which was resolved in time for a new Structural Adjustment Facility in 1998. Total structural adjustment support for the period 1986–98 amounted to approximately 3500 m euro.

---

[14] One Commission source (OLAS-FED) suggests somewhat different figures for 1997 and 1998 for structural adjustment commitments and disbursements from those indicated in Table 3.3. 1997: commitments (Structural Adjustment Facility (SAF) plus National Indicative Programme (NIP): 197.51 m euro; disbursements 175.15 m euro. 1998: commitments (SAF) 554.29 m euro; (NIP) 35.30 m euro; disbursements (SAF plus NIP) 325.79 m euro.

[15] As 89% of all structural adjustment support has gone to the ACP countries, the trend shown in Figure 2.2 gives a good impression of this trend.

53 ACP countries benefited from structural adjustment support (42 African, 9 Caribbean and 2 Pacific). The main recipients were Tanzania, Ethiopia, Zambia, Côte d'Ivoire, Ghana, Mali, Uganda and Burkina Faso, which each received more than 150 m euro between 1986 and 1998. It has not been possible to allocate all commitments for the earlier years, particularly the country breakdown for 1987–89 and the sectoral breakdown for the Sectoral Import Programmes. The relatively high proportion which is unallocable may therefore distort the picture for some countries. There are some moves to 'fold in' instruments such as Stabex and System into the programme of adjustment assistance when the Lomé Convention expires in 2000.

Stabex

Stabex was introduced in Lomé I to compensate ACP countries for the shortfall in export earnings due to fluctuations in the prices or supply of non-mineral – largely agricultural – commodities. The stabilisation of export earnings is intended to be a means of helping countries achieve the broader objective of economic and social progress by safeguarding purchasing power in the countries affected by losses (art. 186). The Stabex scheme is characterised by a product-by-product approach, and transfers are calculated on the basis of losses accrued on exports (art. 189). Transfers are made from a fixed allocation in each EDF to ACP governments.

The products eligible for Stabex transfers from the EDF and the criteria for losses are defined in articles 187 and 189 of the Lomé Convention respectively. The list of eligible products has gradually been expanded from 29 to 50 products. Originally an ACP country could request compensation but from Lomé IV onwards there are no ACP requests. ACP compensations are calculated solely by the Commission, the provisions of Articles 189, 196 and 197 in particular being taken into account. The freedom in utilisation of the transfer has also become more limited over time and is, since Lomé IV, determined by a 'framework of mutual obligations' for each transfer agreed between the EC and the ACP country. In the earlier Lomé Conventions a few of the more advanced ACP countries were liable to have to repay these transfers, but now they are all in the form of grants.

> **Box 3.4: Counterpart Funds generated by Structural Adjustment Assistance**
>
> Since Lomé IV an increasing share of EDF funds is provided in the form of counterpart funds from structural adjustment support, food aid, Stabex and Sysmin. Although strict rules for the use of counterpart funds did not exist before, since Lomé IV they have been targeted on financing local EDF projects and programmes, on social sector headings in the budget of ACP countries, and on mitigating the negative social consequences of structural adjustment (art. 226).
>
> Between 1991 and 1995 1349 m euro of counterpart funds were generated by structural adjustment finance provided under Lomé IV. More than three-quarters of this had been disbursed in the same period. Most of these funds (74%) came from the structural adjustment facility.
>
> A study undertaken by the DG VIII indicated that 15 countries absorbed about 80% of all counterpart funds generated. Most of these countries are in Africa with the exception of the Dominican Republic and Papua New Guinea. Counterpart funds mainly benefited the health and education sectors: the health sector received 602 m euro between 1990 and 1997 and the education sector 277 m euro between 1991 and September 1995. Other sectors receiving assistance through counterpart funds were road maintenance and public sector reform.
>
> ■ Public sector reform (3.2%)
> ■ Agriculture (3.6%)
> ■ Road maintenance (6.2%)
> ■ Education (28.5%)
> ■ Others (16.8%)
> ■ Projects (3.9%)
> ■ Health (37.9%)

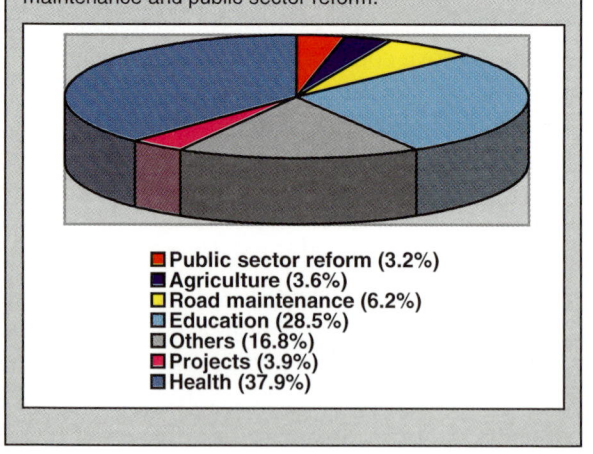

Stabex transfers usually account for a large share of the EDF. Fluctuations in transfers therefore have a significant impact on the trend in the EDF and subsequently in the aid to the ACP countries. A clear demonstration of this came in 1993 when no agreement could be reached on Stabex transfers. Hardly any commitments were made that year and aid from the EDF stagnated (see Figure 3.4).

Funding allocated to the system rose from 325 m euro for Lomé I, to 550 m euro for Lomé II, to 925 m euro for Lomé III and 1500 m for the first five years of application of Lomé IV. The second

Protocol to Lomé IV brought the allocation up to 1800 m euro, a 20% increase on the amount provided for by the first protocol.

During the period 1986–98 3.4 bn euro was committed through Stabex. With the exception of 1993, Stabex accounted annually for between 10% and 24% of all aid to the ACP until 1994, when it peaked at 24% making up for the near zero level in 1993 when there was no agreement on distribution. Since 1995 Stabex transfers have been relatively low and accounted for between 0% and 8% of all aid to the ACP.

Tropical beverages, coffee and cocoa, and cotton exports dominate and accounted for 88% of the transfers between 1990 and 1993. The main beneficiaries of Stabex have been Côte d'Ivoire, Cameroon, Ethiopia, Sudan, Papua New Guinea, Senegal, Kenya and Uganda. Together they represented 64% of all transfers between 1986 and 1998. For some of them Stabex is the most significant flow of aid from the Community. For instance, Côte d'Ivoire received 54% of its aid through Stabex, Cameroon 49%, and Papua New Guinea 36%.

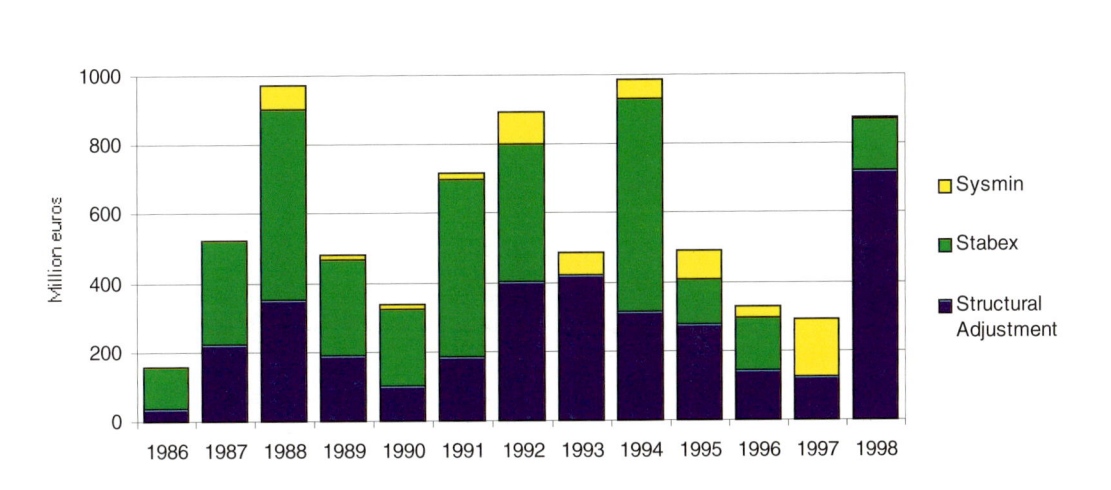

**Figure 3.4: Programme aid
(1986-98, commitments, m euro)**

Source: European Commission/ODI database 1999

In the process of the post-Lomé IV negotiations, the EU has proposed to significantly reform the allocation criteria and implementation mechanisms of Stabex and Sysmin. The aim is to grant additional support to a far greater number of ACP countries, when economic fluctuations cause losses of overall export earnings that threaten the financing of development requirements and the implementation of macroeconomic and sectoral reforms and policies. To that end, pre-programmed resources would be mobilised to be included in national budgets and in public investment programmes via budget aid.

Sysmin

From Lomé II onwards there has also been a scheme to help alleviate fluctuations in revenue arising from the production and sale of minerals (bauxite, alumina, copper, cobalt, iron, tin, phosphates, and manganese, and uranium since Lomé IV). The objective of the scheme is to 'contribute to establishing a more solid and wider basis for the development of the ACP states while supporting their efforts to safeguard their mining production and exports sector by remedial or preventive action, or for states heavily dependent on exports of one mining product to diversify and broaden the bases of their economic growth, notably by helping them complete development projects and programmes under way where these are seriously jeopardised owing to substantial falls in export earnings from that product' (art. 214).

ACP countries can request aid under Sysmin if they are dependent on mineral exports for a substantial part[16] of their export earnings, and if the viability of one or more enterprises in the mining sector has been or is about to be affected by temporary or unforeseeable difficulties that cause a fall in production or export capacity of around 10% and/or deterioration of the external balance (art. 215), or if those difficulties threaten the completion of development projects and programmes. During Lomé II and III the transfers took the form of special loans but since Lomé IV they are all grants. Sysmin funds may be 'on-lent' by the government to mining companies in need of restructuring, with a view to preventing difficulties in the future.

Procedures for decision-making on Sysmin projects are the same as for financial and technical cooperation (see above) and are subjected to thorough analysis. Utilisation of Sysmin funds for diversification has been emphasised in the current Convention.

For the period 1996-2000 an amount of 575 m euro is available, but may not all be used. This was due to the fact that Sysmin by its nature is an 'accident insurance' system, which only comes into operation when the eligibility criteria (such as a decline in mineral export prices) are met. The countries which have benefited most from Sysmin are Guinea, Mauritania, Jamaica, Zambia and Botswana.

For proposals to reform Sysmin under the post-Lomé agreements see previous section on Stabex.

Humanitarian Aid and Aid for Refugees

In addition to the main budget line for humanitarian assistance discussed in Chapter 2, some Lomé funds have been set aside for emergencies. For 1990–95 150 m euro had been allocated under art. 254 to emergency operations (such as in Rwanda, Sudan, Angola, Liberia and Sierra Leone).[17]

During the period 1986–1998 the ACP countries received 1.6 m euro in humanitarian assistance (excluding rehabilitation). Since becoming operational in 1993 ECHO has managed a high proportion of these funds rising from a third for 1993-95 to the vast majority of them for 1996-98. In 1994, 316 m euro of humanitarian assistance and 33% of all humanitarian aid allocations went to the ACP countries. 263 m euro came from the EDF, most of which went to the crisis in Burundi and Rwanda. In 1996 humanitarian aid to ACP countries peaked at 328 m though only 53 m euro of it came from the EDF. Over the entire period 1986–98 the main beneficiaries of EC humanitarian assistance were Rwanda and Burundi, Sudan, Angola, Somalia and Ethiopia, which together accounted for over half of the assistance.

Assistance for refugees also got special attention in EDF 7 (art. 255), and 100 m euro was set aside to assist refugees and returnees who are not covered by emergency aid. These funds are mainly used for post-conflict rehabilitation programmes. Other funds for rehabilitation are sourced from NIPs, Stabex and the special budget lines.

ACP (and other developing) countries have received rehabilitation assistance provided from two budget lines. The first, established in 1988, primarily targets the rehabilitation process of southern African countries recovering from war, including assistance for the return of refugees, displaced

---

[16] Countries can request aid under Sysmin if the relevant mining products have on average represented more than 15% of total exports for 4 years (10% for LLDCs) or 20% or more of their export earnings from all mining products (12% for LLDCs, landlocked and island countries).

[17] In 1994 this was topped up exceptionally with 150 m euro from Lomé funds for the Rwanda crisis.

people and demobilised soldiers (B7-3210, formerly B7-5071),[18] while the other, created in 1994, is global and focuses on the rehabilitation of productive sectors and infrastructure (B7-6410, formerly B7-5076). The major objectives of rehabilitation programmes are: the restoration of production, the repair of basic infrastructure, the resettlement and reintegration of displaced people and the re-establishment of local institutions. To be eligible for rehabilitation assistance countries have to meet criteria such as a minimum level of security, and the commitment of the government to democratic values.

Between 1986 and 1998 over 550 m euro was provided to the ACP for rehabilitation. 91 m euro went to Zaire in 1995 for the Rwanda crisis, 23% was committed to Angola since 1991 for its post-war rehabilitation programme and 13% to Mozambique since 1990 for the same purpose. According to European Commission estimates, approximately 30% of payments for rehabilitation are made to NGOs.

Food Aid

Food aid is the main instrument of EC aid to the ACP which is not paid from the EDF, but financed from the EC Budget, as explained in Chapter 2. The ACP countries received 2.6 bn euro of developmental food aid between 1986 and 1998, although this figure may be somewhat distorted due to the lack of data for the 1986–8 period which leaves a lot of the food aid in earlier years unallocable. Almost a quarter of food aid received by the ACP, 641 m euro, went to Ethiopia, followed by Sudan (293 m euro), Mozambique (262 m euro), Angola (207 m euro), Malawi (142 m euro) and Rwanda (127 m euro) between 1986 and 1998 (see table 2.2).

Aid to NGOs

As has been mentioned in Chapter 2, NGO co-financing is an important instrument for EC aid. ACP countries were allocated commitments of nearly 500 m euro from 1986-98 from the special budget line for NGO co-financing (B7-6000). This is a relatively small proportion of total aid to the ACP (about 1.6%), but it excludes EDF funds channelled *through* NGOs. Such NGO projects are accounted for under the appropriate sectoral heading, eg good governance. Over a third of the aid to NGOs went to six countries: Ethiopia (40 m euro); Kenya (34 m euro); Uganda; Congo (Zaire) and Burkina Faso (all at 25 m euro); and Tanzania (23 m euro).

Project Aid by Sub-region

Project aid accounts for 51% of all EC aid to the ACP countries and is mainly financed from the EDF through the National and Regional Indicative Programmes. In addition to this EDF financing, 342 m euro (1% of total aid to the ACP) was spent from the EC Budget on project aid. The main budget lines and relevant amounts committed between 1986 and 1998 are:

- Democratisation and human rights   82 m euro
- Tropical forestry   77 m euro
- Support for banana-producing countries   75 m euro
- Environment   61 m euro
- Support for the fight against AIDS   10 m euro
- Decentralised cooperation   10 m euro
- Common Foreign and Security Policy[19]   11 m euro

---

[18] Beneficiaries of this budget line include Angola, Botswana, Lesotho, Namibia, Malawi, Mozambique, Swaziland, Tanzania, Zambia and Zimbabwe. Initially this line was created to support the populations of the Front Line States and SADC countries, partly to counter South African destabilisation policies.

[19] Figures for 1996-98.

The late 1990s have seen the EC strategy and these instruments set to undergo substantial reforms. In February 1998, the EC reorganised its private sector and trade development units into a single department, shortly after issuing new guidelines for its trade development programmes. A reflection process should result in the formal adoption of a new approach in the course of 1999 (COM (98) 667, Final 20 November 1998). The new EC's approach to trade development focuses on increasing competitiveness and is very comprehensive in the means to be used. It is suggested that an integrated approach must simultaneously tackle bottlenecks at three levels: (i) government (to create an enabling environment, at the macro level); (ii) trade-related service providers (to increase and improve the supply of such services, at the meso level); and (iii) the firms themselves (to increase their overall competitiveness, at the micro level).

Sub-Saharan Africa: In Africa most of the project aid went to the *transport and communications* sector which received 2.6 bn euro between 1986 and 1998, or 11% of all aid to the sub-region. This proportion has not fluctuated much since 1989 until 1998 when it leapt to nearly a quarter of all aid to SSA. The most important beneficiaries are Ethiopia, which has more than 360 m euro of its aid allocated to this sector, followed by Tanzania, Burkina Faso, Mali, Madagascar and Cameroon, which each have commitments exceeding 100 m euro in this sector. Together they account for almost 40% of all transport projects in Sub-Saharan Africa.

Industry, mining and construction projects constituted the second biggest sector for EC aid to Africa. 1.6 bn euro was committed to these projects between 1986 and 1998, but there were considerable inter-year fluctuations. Mauritania, Nigeria and Guinea accounted for 29% of the commitments (466 m euro).

Rural development has also been significant, although this is mainly due to high commitments in 1987, 1988 and 1989, when rural development projects accounted for 26%, 21% and 18% of EC aid to Africa respectively. Since then commitments went down steadily and were in fact negative in 1997 and 1998 as sums were decommitted at the end of EDF 7.

Agricultural projects were allocated commitments totalling 1.2 bn euro for the 1986-98 periods and represented 5% of aid to Africa. The main countries benefiting from this aid were Ethiopia, Côte d'Ivoire and Kenya. *Energy* projects were of similar importance.

Commitments to the *social sectors* amounted to 1.5 bn euro – 7% of total funds to Africa. 1.3% went to *education and training*, 2.1% to the *health sector*, and 2.6% to *water and sanitation* projects (some being financed with loans managed by the EIB – see below). With the exception of 1997 (when commitments were zero) commitments to the health sector have been considerably higher in the 1990s compared to the 1980s. Commitments to the education and training sector have varied quite a lot from a maximum of 56 m euro in 1992 to a negative commitment for 1997. The Republic of Congo, Malawi, Angola, and Uganda were the main recipients of aid through the health sector, while for education it was Madagascar, Uganda and Zambia. Indirectly, the health and education sectors receive aid from counterpart funds (see section on structural adjustment above). NGO activities are particularly important in the provision of basic water and sanitation services, with NGO projects representing about 40% of the total EC investment in this sector in West Africa.

Aid for *governance and civil society*, which amounted to 350 m euro, was spread across a large number of African countries in small amounts. The Republic of Congo (Zaire), Namibia, Malawi and Mozambique all received over 30 m euro.

For *environmental conservation and protection,* Africa received 119 m euro from the EDF and a special budget line. Botswana and the Central African Republic received 16 and 15 m euro of this respectively. The special support for *gender* issues does not come out clearly in the statistics.[20]

---

[20] There is currently no way of assessing the size of flows directed at gender issues benefiting women through the channel of projects and programmes.

Caribbean: For the Caribbean the sectoral trends are somewhat different, and because of its smaller size fluctuations quickly occur following a big project in one of the sectors and/or countries. The share of *project aid* vis à vis the other instruments is larger (60%), though it has fallen in recent years. All instruments other than Sysmin account for a lower proportion of the aid. *Stabex transfers* have averaged 10% but peaked in 1995 and 1998 when they stood at 24% and 25% of Caribbean aid respectively. St Lucia and St Vincent received particularly high payouts in 1995 as compensation for the banana crisis, whereas most of the 1998 transfer went to St Vincent and the Grenadines and St Lucia. The main recipients of *support for structural adjustment* were Haiti, the Dominican Republic and Jamaica, which account for 65% of the total support to the Caribbean through this instrument. Sysmin, at 4% of total aid, is relatively more important than in SSA, accounting for 94 m euro for 1986-98, split between Jamaica (70 m euro) and Dominican Republic (23 m euro). Haiti received 80 m euro in food aid and 72 m euro in humanitarian assistance, accounting for 83% and 88% respectively of all aid to the Caribbean through these instruments.

For project aid, the main sector to receive support in the Caribbean, as in Africa, was the *transport and communications sector* which accounted for 311 m euro. Transport and communications projects were particularly significant in 1996 when they received 114 m euro, 67 m euro of which went to Jamaica and 40 m euro to Haiti. Overall the transport and communications sector has averaged 24% of project aid to the region.

Energy was the next most significant sector, receiving 19% of project aid to the region, compared to 11% in Africa. Again this was concentrated in 1996, when 122 out of the total 243 m euro were committed. Nearly half of this sum (53 m euro) went to Trinidad and Tobago.

Industry, mining and construction took the next largest amount, with 13% of project commitments or 170 m euro. This peaked in 1991, when Trinidad and Tobago received 38 m euro, and 1993 when Dominican Republic and Guyana each received over 20 m euro, bringing the share of industry projects to an exceptional 54 m euro, which was 24% of all project aid in that year.

The Caribbean receives a higher share of aid for *tourism* than does Africa. In 1990 an exceptionally high commitment was made, which accounted for more than 26% of all project aid to the Caribbean in that year, due largely to commitments made to the Netherlands Antilles (an OCT).

The high proportion of aid to the social sectors (15%) is mainly accounted for by big *water and sanitation* projects (some of which were financed by concessional loans) in Jamaica and Guyana in 1993 and 1995 respectively. *Health* issues have become more prominent in commitments to the Caribbean since 1992 and accounted for an exceptionally high 8% in 1993, mainly thanks to 9 m euro commitments to the Dominican Republic.

As a share of project aid, *rural development and agriculture* are less significant for the Caribbean than for Africa. *Rural development* represents 6% of all project aid to the Caribbean between 1986 and 1998, but this is mainly due to two years, 1988 and 1992, in which 21 m euro and 38 m euro were allocated to this sector. Only Dominican Republic, Guyana and Jamaica received substantial commitments in support of rural development. The agricultural sector, which got 59 m euro (5% of project aid) between 1986 and 1998, was only prominent in Jamaica, Surinam and Haiti. In the *environmental sector* there was only one significant commitment of 15 m euro (in 1993) to the Caribbean. Good governance and civil society, which totals 25 m euro, received 8 m euro of this in 1998; 4 m euro of this was a regional commitment.

Pacific: Aid flows to the Pacific up to 1996 have been highly influenced by *Stabex transfers* which accounted for 30% of all aid, but which were more than 60% in two of the years (1987 and 1992). 289 m euro was committed through Stabex, of which 195 m euro went to Papua New Guinea, 40 m euro to Solomon Islands, and 23 m euro to Vanuatu. For each, Stabex funds are the largest single component of EC aid (36%, 48%, and 49% of total commitments). For 1997 and 1998 Stabex flows have been negligible. The other instruments are not significant.

Project aid constituted 53% of the assistance to the Pacific islands. Again the main sectors are *transport and communications* (25% of project aid) and i*ndustry, mining and construction* (22%), followed by the *energy sector* (11%), with Papua New Guinea being the main beneficiary in each case. The *social sectors* accounted for 86 m euro, most of which went to education and training. Assistance to the Pacific islands in the *agriculture sector* has averaged 4% and support to the *Rural Development* sector up till 1998 was considerably lower than that to the African continent. In that year it was boosted by a commitment of 16 m euro to Western Samoa.

Sector Support: As a result of lessons learned in evaluation EC aid to ACP countries has increased its focus on policies, institutions and donor coordination. In some sectors there has been a shift away from stand-alone projects towards sector wide approaches, though the sums involved cannot currently easily be separated out from the data. In the health sector, for example, where EC activity has increased significantly over the last few years, there has been a move away from projects in specific areas to focus on coordinated action to reform the health sector. The shift to sectoral policies is also clear in the transport and education sectors.

Cross-cutting issues

A number of cross-cutting issues do not fully emerge from an analysis of the way funds have been committed. These are dealt with in this section.

Environment: Lomé IV placed the environment at the centre of EC/ACP cooperation, creating a special Title 1 to set out new environmental provisions. The general provisions of the Convention set the tone stating that cooperation shall 'help promote specific operations concerning the conservation of natural resources, renewable and non-renewable, the protection of ecosystems and the control of drought, desertification and deforestation' (Article 14). This commitment should continue in future agreements as environmental aspects are the third main horizontal axis in the mandate for the negotiation of the new development partnership agreement with ACP countries.

Gender: The importance of gender in EU-ACP development cooperation was first emphasised in Lomé IV. The EC's aid programme seeks to address gender issues through two main mechanisms. First by attempting to take account of gender issues and women's needs at each stage of the design of a project or programme. Secondly by projects with women's development as a specific goal

The Gender and Development desk covering ACP countries has for several years organised short-term missions of gender experts to individual ACP countries in order to assess the integration of gender issues in development interventions. A wider and more systematic approach has recently begun. It includes:
- an initial review; follow up and advice by gender experts available to all operational and technical services in Brussels;
- short term missions of gender experts to 13 different ACP countries; thematic studies;
- work to modify planning and monitoring tools;
- gender training;
- integration of gender in the project cycle management; improved account taken of gender perspectives in sectoral policy papers (health, education, environment, etc), and in briefing notes on human and social development.

By 1998, 80% of financial proposals put before the EDF committed included information on gender-specific aspects.

Human rights and democracy: References to human rights and democracy were first introduced in Lomé IV Article 5. Art 366 defines the procedure allowing the EU to interrupt aid where a country fails to fulfil elements of Article 5. In this context the Commission has introduced the evolution of human rights and democracy into the criteria used when considering the NIPs. The Common Position of 25 May 1998[21] states that the Union will consider increasing its support for African countries in which positive changes have or are taking place.

Poverty: Only in the last few years has poverty reduction become a more explicit objective of EC development cooperation with all countries, and was specifically emphasised in the Commission's Green Paper on the future of EU-ACP relations (1996) (see also Chapter 2). In particular:

- the Operational Manual published in 1998 (VIII/825/98) sets out the information needs with respect to country programming for meeting the objective of poverty reduction and suggests the actions to take at macro, sectoral and project levels;
- in the framework of the Lomé Convention, 8th EDF, the NIPs all identified poverty reduction as an important objective of development co-operation. In many African countries this was reflected in the choice of focal sectors, such as food security, rural development, or social sectors. In small island countries, specific poverty reduction programmes were often envisaged. It is too early to see if the objective has been reflected in all the projects presented to the 8th EDF;
- poverty assessments have been carried out in connection with poverty programmes in several small island countries; a major poverty-focused country programming exercise is underway in Nigeria;
- the Development DG has produced a draft Communication on Structural Adjustment assessing the results of past operations and setting out objectives for the future;
- in several sectors (health, education, food security, rural development, illicit drugs, transport and environment) there has been policy work to develop clear links with poverty reduction;
- at the level of project planning, improvements are being made to the identification sheet, to improve the monitoring of poverty issues; specific guidelines have been produced on planning microfinance projects;
- at the international level, the Commission has promoted awareness of the importance of dealing with the political and international dimensions of poverty. These issues are now recognised in the agendas of the SPA and DAC working groups on poverty, and the Development DG is actively engaged in this work;
- within the Development DG, there have been several staff training courses on poverty reduction; a series of briefing papers has been established.

Risk Capital and Loans from the EIB's Own Resources

From the first Yaoundé Convention the ACP countries and OCTs[22] have benefited from concessional loans financed from the EDF (as risk capital) and from the EIB's 'own resources' (see Table 3.5). Loans from the EIB's 'own resources' to the ACP countries receive subsidies from the EDF in order to maintain the interest rate level at between 3% and 6%.

Concessional loans amounted to 3.7 bn euro between 1986 and 1998, 2.0 bn euro from the EIB's own resources and the rest from the EDF. 77% of all loans went to sub-Saharan Africa, 15% to the Caribbean and 5% to the Pacific. The main beneficiaries of concessional loans were the more advanced countries in each of the sub-regions. In Africa, Nigeria took 350 m euro (9% of all loans),

---

[21] Common Position of 25 May 1998 defined by the Council on the basis of Article J.2 of the Treaty on European Union, concerning human rights, democratic principles, the rule of law and good governance in Africa 98/350/CFSP.

[22] A small proportion of the risk capital provided from the EDF (30 m euro for EDF 8) and loans from the EIB's own resources (up to 35 m euro for EDF 8) are committed to OCTs.

followed by Zimbabwe (6%), Kenya (5%) and Ghana and Ethiopia (both 4%). In the Caribbean, which received 559 m euro in concessional loans, Jamaica and Trinidad and Tobago were by far the biggest recipients of loans between 1986 and 1998 (4% and 3% of total loans or 27% and 22% of loans to that region respectively). Papua New Guinea accounted for more than half the loans to the Pacific, followed by Fiji and French Polynesia. For the period 1996-2000, the EIB has set aside 1.66 bn euro of its own resources for loans and will mange one billion euro of risk capital on behalf of the EDF.

Table 3.5: EIB-managed Loans from 'own resources' and Risk Capital (from the EDF) to the ACP 1986-98 (m euro)

	1986	1987	1988	1989	1990	1991	1992	1993	1994	1995	1996	1997	1998	Total
Total EIB Loans to ACP	210	343	293	280	154	384	248	223	462	348	395	57	353	3750
EIB Loans: ACP total	151	158	121	166	118	266	129	147	223	124	296	38	81	2017
Sub-Saharan Africa	109	137	94	107	109	204	121	101	137	80	105	34	69	1406
Caribbean	22	17	9	38	9	53	8	24	12	19	188	4	12	414
Pacific	21	4	18	21	–	9	–	22	4	25	4	–	–	128
Unallocable	–	–	–	–	–	–	–	–	70	–	–	–	–	70
Risk Capital: ACP total	59	185	172	114	36	119	119	75	239	225	99	19	272	1733
Sub-Saharan Africa	56	179	156	96	31	112	116	53	197	168	86	13	236	1500
Caribbean	2	4	6	15	3	4	3	8	36	35	12	4	12	145
Pacific	1	2	10	3	2	2	–	13	4	21	–	2	4	63
Unallocable	–	–	–	–	–	–	–	1	2	–	1	–	20	25

Source: European Commission/ODI database 1999

Most loans fall within the industry and energy sectors, which account for nearly half of all concessional loans. The transport and communications, water supply and banking, finance and business services sectors are also significant (see Figure 3.5). The large sum of loans which are unallocable by sector (a quarter) are mainly 'global loans', which indicates that the EIB provides the loans to a development bank in the region which then on-lends the funds.

Figure 3.5: EIB-managed Loans from 'own resources' and Risk Capital to ACP Countries (1986-98, commitments %)

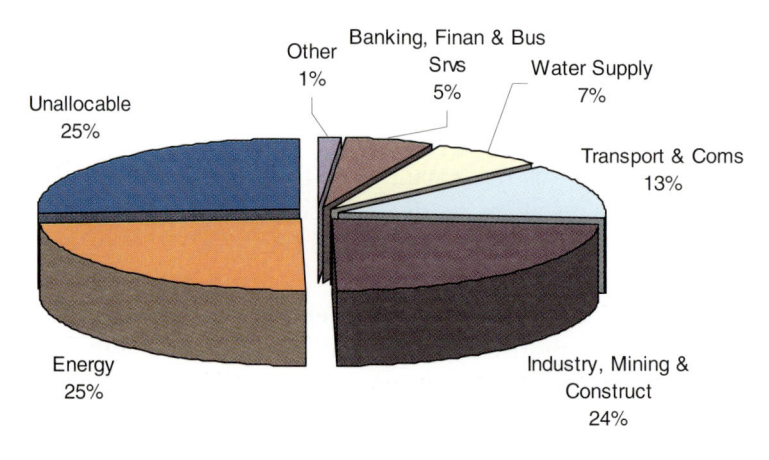

- Unallocable 25%
- Energy 25%
- Industry, Mining & Construct 24%
- Transport & Coms 13%
- Water Supply 7%
- Banking, Finan & Bus Srvs 5%
- Other 1%

Source: European Commission/ODI database 1999

Assistance to South Africa

The Community's relationship with South Africa was placed on a new footing when it formally became the 71st ACP country to be part in the Lomé Convention after Lomé-IV bis was ratified (April 1998). However, unlike the other 70 ACP countries, it neither benefits from the EDF nor from Lomé trade preferences. Instead, it has benefited since 1995 from a special financial facility – the European Programme for Reconstruction and Development – and should from January 2000 start to benefit from the 'Trade, Development and Co-operation Agreement', signed with the EU in October 1999, which also incorporates development and financial co-operation. Its qualified Lomé membership allows SA access to tenders for the 8th European Development Fund projects in all ACP countries and participation in Lomé Institutions. South Africa participates as a full partner in negotiations to establish the arrangements to succeed the Lomé IV convention.

From 1986 until 1994 EC aid to South Africa was provided through a specific budget line, the Special Programme for Assisting the Victims of Apartheid, channelled though NGOs and church organisations. With the advent of democracy, the Community's approach changed to a more usual channelling of aid through government, which was more clearly defined in a Council Regulation in November 1996.[23] However, the civil society channel was maintained, with the full agreement of the government, with a target of 25% of the annual EU aid budget to be administered through non-governmental partners. The EC programme was retitled the 'European Programme for Reconstruction and Development in South Africa', reflecting the intention that it should take account of the priorities set out in the South African Programme for Reconstruction and Development. The mandate of this programme is broad, covering support for democratisation and human rights; education and training; health; rural development; urban development and social housing; support of the private sector (particularly small and medium-sized enterprises); strengthening local institutions and organisations; regional cooperation and integration; and the environment. The legal base also prescribes that priority shall be given to the poorest sections of the population.

The European Council had agreed that resources necessary to support the South Africa Programme should be maintained at a substantial level during the transitional period. Over the period from 1986 to 1994, most of the assistance went to projects in education and training, governance and civil society, health and population, other social infrastructure and services, and agriculture, and was largely channelled through NGOs and church organisations. Since the 1994 election, the greater part of the available resources has gone to projects implemented in cooperation with the government.

Between 1986 and 1998 aid to South Africa from the EC budget amounted to 963 m euro, of which almost 65% was allocated since 1994. 33% of allocable aid went to education, which is the largest sector, 20% of allocable aid (160 m euro) went to other social infrastructure, and 21% went to the good governance and civil society sector to support the election process (see Figure 3.6).

In addition to the grant support described above, in June 1995 the EIB's Board of Governors authorised the Bank to commence operations in South Africa. A first framework agreement signed in September 1995 established a fund of 300 m euro for a period of two years. A second agreement was subsequently signed in March 1998 with an equal annual target amount of 150 m euro (total 375 m euro) for the period up to June 2000. The loans mainly target economic sectors such as industry, small and medium-sized enterprises (SMEs), energy, telecommunications and environmental protection. In 1995 45 m euro was made available in the form of global loans for SMEs in productive sectors and for smaller public infrastructure schemes, mainly water management..

---

[23] Council Regulation (EC) No. 2259/96 on Development Cooperation with South Africa, 22.11.96.

A new regulation on cooperation with South Africa is currently being discussed for the period 2000-06 which is intended to underpin a more tightly focused programme of assistance.

Figure 3.6: Sectoral Allocation of EC Cooperation with South Africa (1986-98, commitments, %)

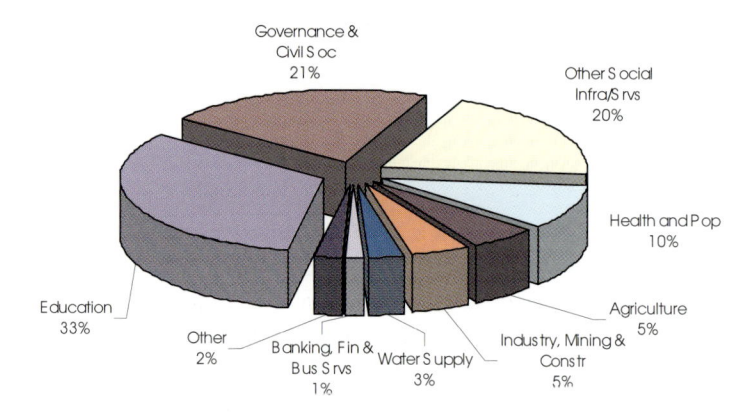

- Governance & Civil Soc 21%
- Other Social Infra/Srvs 20%
- Health and Pop 10%
- Agriculture 5%
- Industry, Mining & Constr 5%
- Water Supply 3%
- Banking, Fin & Bus Srvs 1%
- Other 2%
- Education 33%

Source: European Commission/ODI database 1999

4

EC External Cooperation with the Mediterranean and Middle East

Trends and Distribution

The Mediterranean and Middle East aid programme of the European Community has grown significantly in recent years.[1] As Figure 4.1 and Table 4.1 show, EC aid committed to the Mediterranean and Middle East has increased substantially, from 400 m euro in 1986 to over 1300 m euro in both 1997 and 1998. Aid flows to the East and Southern Mediterranean went up from around 280 m euro in 1986 to around 1 bn euro in 1997 and 1998. The steep increase in commitments in 1991 can be partly explained by the special support to the countries affected by the Gulf War. Another factor has been the introduction of the 'horizontal cooperation' element of the Med programme in 1992 (see below) aimed at benefiting the region as a whole or a number of partner countries in the region.

The Northern Mediterranean sub-region has seen its funds climb from 1994. There were high commitments in 1991 when special assistance was awarded to Turkey in particular, for the damage it faced as a result of the Gulf War. As a proportion of total aid to the region, aid to the Northern Mediterranean has averaged 10% and has maintained 13% for each of the years 1996–98. The

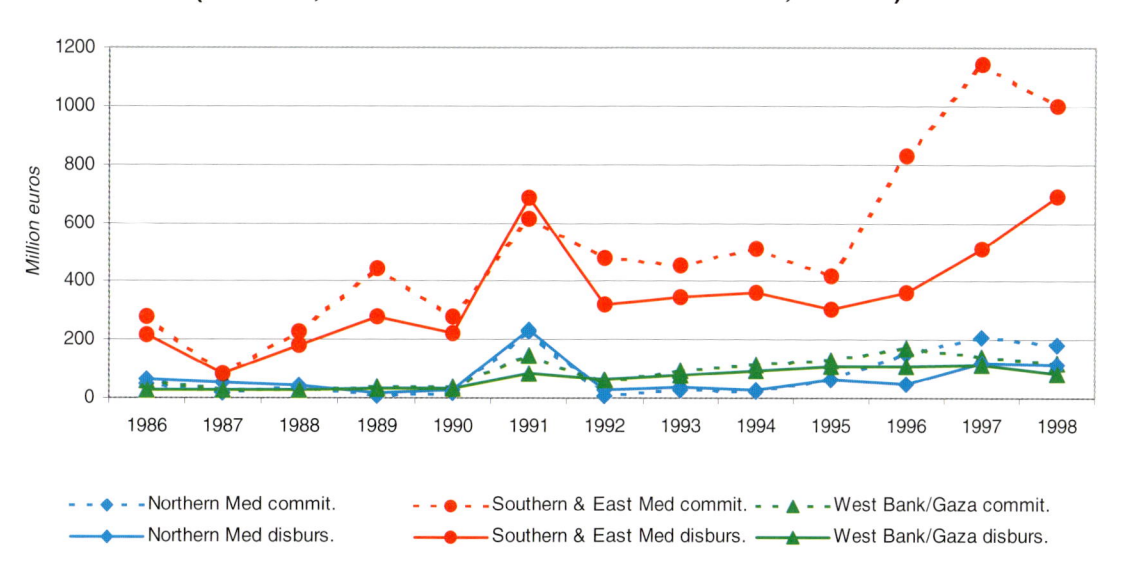

Figure 4.1: Regional Distribution of EC Cooperation with Med & Mid East (1986–98, commitments and disbursements, m euro)

Note: The main 'regions' in the Mediterranean & Middle East (as defined by the Commission) are: (i) Northern Mediterranean (Turkey, Malta, Cyprus, and initially Greece and Portugal); (ii) East and Southern Mediterranean (Morocco, Algeria, Tunisia and Egypt, Jordan, Syria and Lebanon); (iii) West Bank/Gaza; (iv) Other Middle East.

Source: European Commission/ODI database 1999

share of aid to the East and Southern Mediterranean, containing the biggest recipients in the region, declined from 75% in 1986–90 to 60% in 1991–95, before rising again to 72% for 1996–98. Aid to the West Bank/Gaza has almost quadrupled (from an annual average of 36 m euro for 1986–90 to 142 m euro for the years 1996–98). The commitments to Other Middle Eastern countries have gone up from almost nothing to over 36 m euro for all the years 1996-98. This went almost exclusively via Iraq (largely to Kurdish refugees) and Yemen.

In total 10 bn euro was committed to the region and 6.9 bn euro was disbursed. Disbursements have followed an upward trend over time, with exceptionally high payouts in 1991 (1012 m euro) due to the special support for countries affected by the Gulf War. Owing to a slow-down in commitments to the Northern Mediterranean countries from 1988–95, disbursements are higher than commitments during this time for this sub-region. On the other hand, it is clear from Table 4.1 that disbursements for the regional programmes lag behind commitments more than for other aid. This is a common feature of regional programmes involving more than one beneficiary country. (The ACP countries experience similar difficulties with their Regional Indicative Programmes.)

Table 4.1: Regional Distribution of EC Cooperation with Med & Middle East, 1986–98 (1986–98, commitments and disbursements, m euro)

	1986	1987	1988	1989	1990	1991	1992	1993	1994	1995	1996	1997	1998	Total
Commitments														
Total	401	149	309	511	386	1133	655	711	757	869	1189	1543	1368	9981
Northern Med	47	16	35	5	18	226	6	25	21	62	149	205	179	995
East & Sth Med	280	83	226	445	277	612	478	452	512	415	829	1142	999	6750
West Bank/Gaza	57	27	28	35	36	144	53	94	113	129	170	139	116	1141
Other Mid East	0	0	–	6	8	125	8	41	28	33	36	45	41	371
Regional	1	0	1	1	1	3	64	60	71	165	0	8	–	376
Unallocable	16	22	19	19	45	24	46	39	12	65	5	4	32	349
Disbursements														
Total	311	164	249	331	285	1012	468	594	581	578	601	794	943	6910
Northern Med	63	50	42	16	24	232	25	34	24	64	45	119	113	852
East & Sth Med	218	84	178	278	222	687	320	346	358	304	363	512	690	4559
West Bank/Gaza	25	25	26	30	30	80	61	78	92	108	106	113	81	856
Other Mid East	2	2	2	6	9	9	11	8	13	28	30	42	23	183
Regional	0	0	0	1	1	2	10	35	35	54	–	–	–	138
Unallocable	2	2	1	1	0	2	42	94	59	19	57	8	36	322

Source: European Commission/ODI database 1999

Recipients of EC Cooperation with the Mediterranean and Middle East

The main recipient in the region has consistently been Egypt, which has been allocated 25% of the total amount committed to the region (2479 m euro), mainly due to support to social infrastructure and services after 1996, and to other productive sectors which received a big commitment in 1998 (258 m euro, 250 m euro of which went to the Industrial Modernisation Programme which aims to support Egyptian SMEs by providing specialised technical assistance). The second biggest recipient was the West Bank/Gaza (1141 m euro), followed by Tunisia (1130 m euro) (see Table

---

[1] Since 1995 the main programme has been financed from one main MEDA budget line and is often referred to as the MEDA programme, however this chapter considers all aid flows to the Mediterranean and Middle East, not just those from the MEDA budget line, though this is by far the most significant.

4.2). Turkey receives most of the aid to the Northern Mediterranean, followed by Cyprus, while aid to Kurdish refugees brought Iraq into the top 10 recipients for 1991–95. In terms of per capita aid, Tunisia and Jordan ranked at the top of the list for the East and Southern Mediterranean sub-region.

A relatively high proportion of aid to the Mediterranean is unallocable by country, mainly due to commitments of 500 m euro in 1991 for countries immediately affected by the Gulf War. Commitments from that particular budget line, B7–700, accounted for 44% of total commitments for 1991 and 9% of all EC aid to the region for 1986–95.

Table 4.2: Top 10 Recipients of EC Cooperation from all budget lines Med & Mid East (1986–98, commitments, m euro)

Total 1986-90	%	Total 1991-95	%	Total 1996-98	%
Egypt	26.7	Egypt	23.5	Egypt	25.4
Tunisia	19.5	West Bank/Gaza	12.9	Morocco	12.8
Morocco	10.6	Jordan	10.4	West Bank/Gaza	10.4
West Bank/Gaza	10.4	Tunisia	9.3	Algeria	10.2
Algeria	8.2	Morocco	6.9	Turkey	10.0
Jordan	5.6	Algeria	5.8	Tunisia	9.9
Lebanon	2.8	Turkey	5.6	Lebanon	6.9
Portugal	2.5	Iraq	4.7	Jordan	5.8
Turkey	1.9	Lebanon	2.1	Cyprus	2.9
Malta	1.8	Cyprus	1.9	Yemen	1.6
Top 10: % of all Med	89.9	Top 10: % of all Med	83.2	Top 10: % of all Med	95.8

Source: European Commission/ODI database 1999

Sectoral Distribution of EC Cooperation with the Mediterranean and Middle East

Figure 4.2 shows the shift in the proportions of aid to the various sectors in three time periods from the late 1980s, 1991–5, and 1996–8. Most aid to the region (56%) has been provided through projects, mainly in the social infrastructure and services sector, with a further quarter going by the four main instruments, and the rest unallocable by sector.

Structural adjustment is the only instrument which has increased over the three time periods going from nothing to 8% to 11 % of all aid. More than 760 m euro of direct budgetary support for structural adjustment was committed after the introduction of the off-Protocol facility in 1992 and then the creation of the MEDA Programme for the East and Southern Mediterranean countries. It has gone mainly to Jordan, Morocco, Algeria and Tunisia. Food aid appears significantly from 1989 to 1995, but has dropped in importance since then, taking less than 1% of the total for the period 1996-98 (see Table 4.3). Humanitarian assistance increased in importance in the 1990s and was mainly provided to refugees in the West Bank/Gaza, to Kurdish refugees in Iraq and to Lebanon and Algeria. Humanitarian aid amounted to 900 m euro, around 9% of EC aid to the Mediterranean.

Since 1994 greater priority has recently been accorded to financing development NGOs to reach the poor, particularly in the Western Maghreb countries of Algeria, Tunisia, and Morocco, using decentralised cooperation funds to build partnerships between European NGOs and NGOs in the

Maghreb. The main objectives are to strengthen local institutions and support grassroots groups, and to encourage the exchange of experience of NGOs in the participating countries. This aid may not all show up as aid via NGOs, as some of it will fall under the sector of good governance and civil society.

As mentioned above, within project aid, social infrastructure and services dominate, accounting for 2.2 bn euro or 22% of total aid. All the sub sectors within this have also risen as a proportion of aid during the three time periods, with the largest being water supply, which has increased from 7%, to 12%, to 18% of all allocable aid. Nearly three-quarters of these funds were financed through loans managed by the EIB (see below). Aid to education has dramatically risen from less than 1% of allocable aid for 1986-90, to 4% for 1991-95 to 9% for 1996-98. Health has gone from a negligible in the second to 5% in the 3rd. The other sectors which have risen consistently in terms of share are that of banking, finance and business services and governance and civil society which both rose from nothing, to nearly 7% and 4% of allocable aid, respectively, in the final time period.

> **Box 4.1 The MEDA programme**
>
> The MEDA programme has been operating since 1995 (see MEDA Budget Line below).
>
> Over the period 1995-8 its commitments went to four main types of operations:
> - support to structural adjustment: 9% of total commitments;
> - support to economic transition and private sector development: 38% of total;
> - classical development projects: 42% of total;
> - regional projects: 11% of total.

Other sectors remained relatively stable or dipped before rising again. The agricultural sector on the other hand has declined sharply in terms of share of allocable aid (from 23% to 5%), and also in real terms of absolute amounts from an average of 55 m euro per year in 1986–90 to 49 m euro in 1996-98.

The focus on environmental conservation and protection in EC aid policy to the Mediterranean is reflected in the significance of aid to the environmental sector, especially in recent years. 290 m euro was committed to this sector between 1986 and 1998.

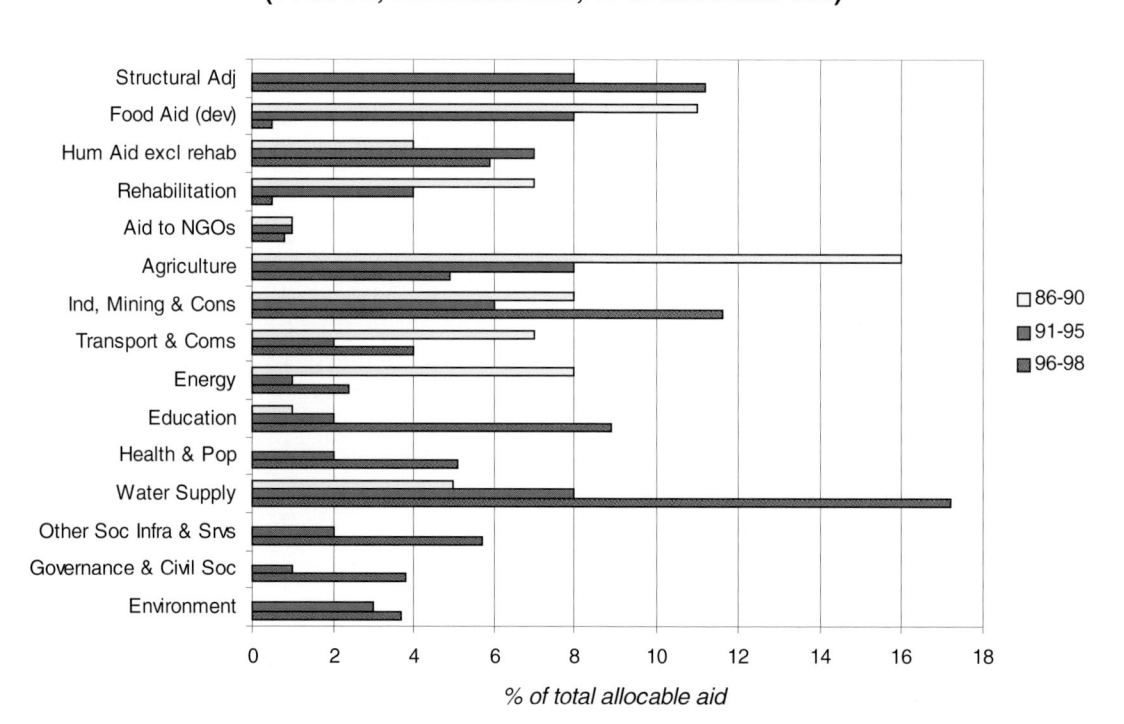

Figure 4.2: Sectoral Allocation of EC Cooperation with Med & Mid East (1986-98, commitments, % of allocable aid)

Source: European Commission/ODI database 1999

Table 4.3: Sectoral Allocation of EC Aid Cooperation with Med & Mid East 1986–98 (commitments, m euro and % of total aid)

COMMITMENTS (m euro)	1986	1987	1988	1989	1990	1991	1992	1993	1994	1995	1996	1997	1998	Total
Programme Aid	–	–	–	–	–	–	205	25	60	20	292	153	12	767
Structural Adjustment	–	–	–	–	0	0	205	25	60	20	292	153	12	767
Food Aid (development)	–	–	3	111	73	77	67	76	48	57	6	8	7	533
Humanitarian Aid	57	33	25	39	34	172	34	70	85	94	108	64	91	904
Humanit excl rehabilitation	36	9	1	15	9	145	6	40	51	52	94	60	89	605
Rehabilitation	21	24	24	24	25	27	28	30	35	42	14	4	2	299
Aid to NGOs	1	2	2	2	2	2	3	5	8	10	13	12	11	72
Natural Resources	90	4	17	92	73	43	22	74	109	75	31	41	156	827
Agriculture	90	4	16	92	72	31	22	74	109	75	26	41	132	784
Forestry	–	0	1	–	–	–	–	–	–	–	5	–	24	30
Fisheries	–	–	0	–	0	13	–	–	0	–	–	–	–	13
Other Productive Services	42	–	1	30	80	87	13	51	138	7	8	116	374	947
Industry, Mining & Construc	42	–	1	28	74	68	5	42	130	1	–	107	368	866
Trade	0	–	–	0	0	17	0	0	0	0	–	–	–	17
Investment Promotion	–	–	0	2	3	3	8	9	8	6	5	8	6	58
Econ Infrastructure & Servs	90	24	30	123	0	77	17	44	57	15	96	234	203	1010
Transport & Comms	60	–	22	43	–	62	4	0	4	1	47	105	10	359
Energy	30	24	8	80	0	15	13	0	12	0	35	35	30	282
Banking, Finance & Bus Srvs	–	–	–	–	–	0	0	43	41	14	13	94	163	370
Social Infrastructure & Servs	11	0	55	6	28	79	139	101	65	183	446	657	409	2179
Education	1	0	1	3	3	7	7	27	14	41	82	187	97	471
Health & Population	–	–	2	2	2	15	10	6	9	33	4	12	192	286
Water Supply	10	–	52	–	22	26	117	54	21	108	293	300	113	1116
Other Social Infra & Services	–	–	1	0	31	6	14	21	1	67	159	7	306
Governance & Civil Society	–	0	–	–	0	–	1	32	14	8	52	78	25	209
Multisector/Crosscutting	0	0	14	1	0	5	42	47	9	46	123	88	32	409
Environment	0	0	1	1	0	5	42	46	4	41	108	37	4	290
Rural Development	–	–	13	–	–	–	–	–	5	5	15	50	21	109
Unallocable by Sector	110	86	161	107	95	590	112	189	165	355	14	93	47	2123
TOTAL	401	149	309	511	386	1133	655	711	757	869	1189	1543	1368	9981

COMMITMENTS (%)	1986	1987	1988	1989	1990	1991	1992	1993	1994	1995	1996	1997	1998	Total
Programme Aid	–	–	–	–	–	–	31.3	3.5	7.9	2.3	24.6	9.9	0.8	7.7
Structural Adjustment	–	–	–	–	–	–	31.3	3.5	7.9	2.3	24.6	9.9	0.8	7.7
Food Aid (development)	–	–	1.1	21.7	19.0	6.8	10.2	10.7	6.3	6.5	0.5	0.5	0.5	5.3
Humanitarian Aid	14.3	21.9	8.0	7.6	8.9	15.2	5.2	9.8	11.3	10.8	9.1	4.1	6.6	9.1
Humanit excl rehabilitation	9.0	5.8	0.2	2.9	2.3	12.8	0.9	5.6	6.7	6.0	7.9	3.9	6.5	6.1
Rehabilitation	5.2	16.1	7.8	4.7	6.6	2.4	4.3	4.2	4.6	4.8	1.2	0.2	0.1	3.0
Aid to NGOs	0.2	1.2	0.7	0.4	0.6	0.2	0.4	0.7	1.0	1.1	1.1	0.8	0.8	0.7
Natural Resources	22.4	2.4	5.4	18.1	18.9	3.8	3.4	10.4	14.4	8.7	2.6	2.7	11.4	8.3
Agriculture	22.4	2.4	5.0	18.1	18.7	2.7	3.4	10.4	14.4	8.7	2.2	2.7	9.7	7.9
Forestry	–	–	0.3	–	–	–	–	–	–	–	0.4	–	1.8	0.3
Fisheries	–	–	–	–	0.1	1.1	–	–	–	–	–	–	–	0.1
Other Productive Services	10.5	0.0	0.2	5.8	20.6	7.7	2.0	7.1	18.2	0.8	0.6	7.5	27.4	9.5
Industry, Mining & Construc	10.5	–	0.2	5.4	19.3	6.0	0.8	5.9	17.2	0.1	–	6.9	26.9	8.7
Trade	–	–	–	–	–	1.5	–	–	–	–	–	–	–	0.2
Investment Promotion	–	–	–	0.4	0.8	0.2	1.2	1.2	1.1	0.7	0.4	0.5	0.4	0.6
Econ Infrastructure & Servs	22.4	15.8	9.9	24.1	0.0	6.8	2.6	6.2	7.6	1.7	8.0	15.2	14.9	10.1
Transport & Comms	15.0	–	7.1	8.5	–	5.5	0.6	0.1	0.6	0.1	4.0	6.8	0.7	3.6
Energy	7.5	15.8	2.8	15.7	–	1.3	1.9	–	1.5	–	2.9	2.3	2.2	2.8
Banking, Finance & Bus Srvs	–	–	–	–	–	–	0.1	6.1	5.4	1.6	1.1	6.1	11.9	3.7
Social Infrastructure & Servs	2.6	0.3	17.7	1.2	7.1	7.0	21.3	14.1	8.5	21.1	37.5	42.6	29.9	21.8
Education	0.2	0.3	0.4	0.6	0.8	0.6	1.0	3.9	1.8	4.7	6.9	12.1	7.1	4.7
Health & Population	–	–	0.6	0.4	0.5	1.3	1.5	0.8	1.1	3.8	0.3	0.8	14.1	2.9
Water Supply	2.4	–	16.8	–	5.7	2.3	17.9	7.6	2.8	12.4	24.6	19.4	8.3	11.2
Other Social Infra & Services	–	–	–	0.1	–	2.7	0.9	1.9	2.8	0.1	5.6	10.3	0.5	3.1
Governance & Civil Society	–	0.3	–	–	–	–	0.1	4.4	1.9	0.9	4.4	5.0	1.8	2.1
Multisector/Crosscutting	0.1	–	4.6	0.2	0.1	0.5	6.4	6.5	1.2	5.2	10.4	5.7	2.4	4.1
Environment	0.1	–	0.4	0.1	–	0.5	6.4	6.5	0.5	4.7	9.1	2.4	0.3	2.9
Rural Development	–	–	4.2	–	–	–	–	–	0.7	0.6	1.3	3.2	1.5	1.1
Unallocable by Sector	27.4	58.1	52.3	20.9	24.7	52.0	17.1	26.5	21.8	40.9	1.2	6.0	3.4	21.3
TOTAL	100	100	100	100	100	100	100	100	100	100	100	100	100	100.0

Source: European Commission/ODI database 1999

Northern Med: Turkey has benefited from commitments totalling 675 m euro. During the second and the third Protocols (1971–81), almost half the funds provided to Turkey (277 m euro) went to the *infrastructure sector*. A relatively large share was committed to *energy*, which accounted for 29% between 1963 and 1982. Between 1986 and 1995 Turkey received only 90 m euro (in addition to 175 m euro assistance after the Gulf War), mainly from horizontal budget lines, as the fourth Protocol was blocked for political reasons. Since 1996 Turkey has been receiving aid from the main MEDA budget line and commitments have risen to over 375 m euro over five years. Most of this has gone to the social sector, with water supply and sanitation taking most with 138 m euro, followed by education (76 m), and then health (59 m).

Cyprus received 207 m euro, over half of it committed since 1996, with water supply and sanitation and energy being the main sectors. 164 m euro of this was provided as concessionary loans. Malta received 58 m euro during 1986-98, with most of this going to water supply projects. In the most recent Protocols for Malta and Cyprus more funds were committed to prepare their economies for eventual accession to the Union.

East and Southern Mediterranean: During the first three Protocols for the East and Southern Mediterranean countries (1978–81; 1982–86; 1987–91) grants were disbursed mainly by way of financial and technical cooperation through project aid. Since Protocol 4, with the introduction of the New Mediterranean Policy, support for structural adjustment and regional cooperation has become more important.

From 1992 to 1998 753 m euro was allocated to countries in the East and South Mediterranean in the form of *support for structural adjustment* as follows, Jordan and Morocco (200 m euro), Algeria (192 m euro) and Tunisia (160 m euro). *Food aid* to the region amounted to 406 m euro between 1986 and 1998, with no commitments in 1998. Egypt received 188 m euro in food aid and Tunisia, the second biggest recipient of food aid in the region, 80 m euro. *Humanitarian assistance* to the East and Southern Mediterranean sub-region went mainly to Lebanon and Algeria. The former received 56 m euro of emergency assistance over the full period, including 42 m euro for rehabilitation since 1993.

In terms of project aid, which still accounted for nearly 77% of allocable aid to the sub-region between 1986 and 1998, most went to the *water supply and sanitation* and the *industry, mining and construction* sectors which both received just over 800 m euro, each accounting for 14% of allocable EC aid to the sub-region. This was closely followed by agriculture with over 700 m euro. All three sectors received significant loans as well as grants. Other important sectors were *transport and communication (5%), banking, finance and business services* (6% of allocable each) and *energy* (4%).

The Mediterranean countries received 2.7 bn euro in concessional loans between 1986 and 1998. Most went to the East and Southern Mediterranean (84%), with Egypt, Tunisia, Algeria and Jordan the main beneficiaries. The main sectors for lending were water supply and sanitation (31%), industry, mining and construction (16%). As in the case of the ACP, the large share of unallocable loans (almost a third) is mainly due to the proportion of 'global' loans which are lent to banks in the region rather than directly to projects (see Figure 4.3).

Figure 4.3: EIB-managed Loans from Own EIB Resources and Risk Capital to Med & Mid East 1986–98 (commitments, %)

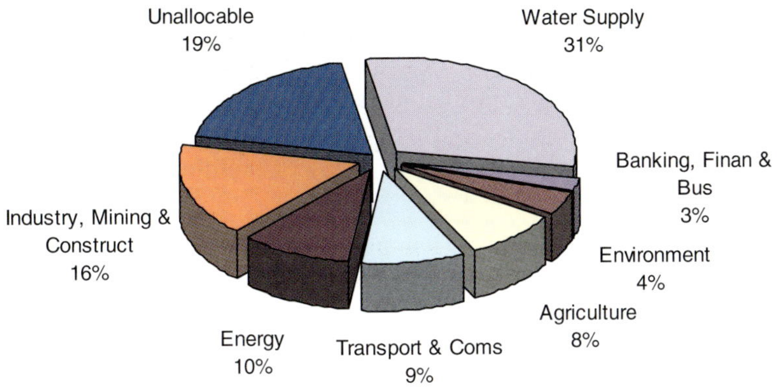

- Unallocable 19%
- Water Supply 31%
- Banking, Finan & Bus 3%
- Environment 4%
- Agriculture 8%
- Transport & Coms 9%
- Energy 10%
- Industry, Mining & Construct 16%

Source: European Commission/ODI database 1999

Sources of EC Cooperation with the Med and Middle East

Grants

The MEDA programme is now the principal financial instrument of the EU for the implementation of the Euro-Mediterranean Partnership. MEDA I accounted for 3425 m euro of the 4685 m euro of budgetary resources allocated for financial cooperation between the EU and its Mediterranean partners for the period 1995–1999. It is gradually replacing other forms of financial intervention carried out by the EU in the Mediterranean region. The Commission has, in October 1999, approved the proposals for a new MEDA Regulation, and has sent it for approval by the Member States.

The MEDA programme introduced an innovative approach for planning and implementing the EC assistance to the Mediterranean partner countries, notably by adopting a policy-led system where single projects are intended as measures to support the reforms in the economic and social structures embarked on by the Mediterranean partners. This new approach implied the adoption of multi-annual programming of the EC assistance (national and regional Indicative Programmes covering a three year period) based on the need to assist the reform process by supporting the 'transition' of the economies on the one hand, and by ensuring socially and environmentally sustainable development on the other hand.

The MEDA programme funds both national and regional activities. All 12 Mediterranean partners are eligible for regional activities within the MEDA Regional Indicative Programme which takes about 10% of resources. The remaining 90% are allocated to National Indicative Programmes which are restricted to nine of the partners: Algeria, Egypt, Jordan, Lebanon, Morocco, Syria, Tunisia, Turkey and the West Bank/Gaza. The indicative programme of the West Bank/Gaza is supplemented with an aid programme which falls under the support framework of the peace process. Aid to Cyprus and Malta is mainly funded outside of MEDA, while the programme in Turkey is supplemented with a pre-existing financial instrument. Israel is not entitled to bilateral aid on account of its high level of development, but can benefit from the regional programmes.

The MEDA programme was preceded by various protocols for the different sub-regions. The grants committed by the protocols for East and Southern Mediterranean steadily increased over the years:

Protocol 1 (1978–81) 307 million; Protocol 2 (1982–86) 415 million; Protocol 3 (1987–91) 615 million and Protocol 4 (1992–96) 775 million. In the northern Mediterranean Cyprus and Malta were covered by the same protocol until 1995, grants for which were as follows: Protocol 1 (1979–83) 20 million; Protocol 2 (1984–88) 29.5 million; Protocol 3 (1989–94) 33 million. Protocol 4 for Cyprus allocated 74 million and was to cover the period 1995–98, but was extended to the end of 1999 to allow all funds to be committed. Protocol 4 to Malta (45 million) covered the same time period and was likewise extended. Both Malta and Cyprus use the MEDA budget line for regional cooperation on water and the environment. Turkey was covered by its own protocol with grants: Protocol 1 (1963–70) 175 million; Protocol 2 (1971–76) 195 million and Protocol 3 (1977–81) 220 million, Protocol 4 was held up for political reasons.

The Mediterranean countries also benefit from several special budget lines. Two examples are the line created to provide support for countries immediately affected by the Gulf War, and the line to support democracy in the area. In 1991, 500 m euro from the Gulf War budget line went to Egypt (175 m euro), Jordan (150 m euro) and Turkey (175 m euro).

Loans

Grants from the Community budget are accompanied by substantial lending from the EIB. More than 27% of the Community's flows to the Mediterranean countries have been provided in the form of loans from the EIB's own resources or from the EC Budget. The level of concessionality of aid to the Mediterranean has gradually decreased and is significantly lower than in the case of the ACP countries. It also varies according to country, being zero for Israel, which only gets loans and no grant aid (and therefore does not feature in this analysis).

Under Protocols 1 and 2, the Maghreb and the Mashraq countries (East and Southern Mediterranean) received special loans granted for 40 years at 1% interest with a 10-year grace period. These were lent and managed by the Commission but recovered by the EIB. From Protocol 3 (1986) onwards, these special loans have been replaced by risk capital in order to benefit joint ventures, the industrial sector and SMEs in particular. Although the funds are still provided from the Budget, risk capital is lent and managed by the EIB and account for only 8% of all concessional loans to the sub-region. The Protocols for some Northern Mediterranean countries also included provisions for risk capital which came to 13 m euro, or 3% of loans to this sub-region. The Mediterranean countries also benefited from interest rate subsidies on loans from the EIB.

Although concessional loans have increased in absolute terms from an annual average of 137 m euro for 1986–90 to 398 m euro for 1996–98, they have decreased in importance from 33% in 1986–90 to 29% in 1996–98 as a share of total financial assistance to the Mediterranean. Under the Euro-Med Partnership arrangements, the EIB is committed to lend 2310 m euro between 1997 and the end of 1999 for investment projects in the region.

Policy and Objectives

Evolution of EC External Cooperation with the Mediterranean and Middle East

The EC-MED aid relationship has evolved over three phases: an emerging relationship, 1958–79; the Protocol period 1979–95, and the MEDA period from 1995. Before 1979, EC-MED aid was limited, consisting primarily of loans. With the Protocols and the signing of cooperation agreements, grant aid began. There were different agreements for various parts of the region all established on a country by country basis between 1961 and 1980 (see Table 4.4).

Table 4.4: Association and Cooperation Agreements between EC and Mediterranean Countries

	Special Association Agreements (under Art. 238) [a]		Cooperation afreements (unlimited duration) (under Art. 238)
1961-72	Turkey (1963) [b] Malta (1971) [d] Cyprus (1973) [d]	1975-1980	Israel III (1975) Algeria (1978) [c] Morocco (1978) Tunisia (1978) Egypt II (1978) Lebanon III (1978) Jordan (1978) Syria (1978) Yugoslavia III (1980)

[a] In addition, the EC established preferential (Spain, Egypt, & Portugal) and non-preferential trade agreements (Israel I (1964), Lebanon I (1965), and Yugoslavia II (1970)) between 1964 and 1972
[b] An additional protocol defining the rules for achieving a customs union and developing economic cooperation was signed in 1980.
[c] Algeria was originally eligible for EDF I in 1958
[d] Malta and Cyprus had agreements of limited duration

Source: European Commission

The Northern Mediterranean countries, Turkey, Cyprus, and Malta, have had an association agreement with the EC since 1963, 1970 and 1972 respectively, with a view to creating a customs union. Turkey has now proceeded to that stage, while Cyprus and Malta are awaiting accession to the Union in a future enlargement. A financial protocol was annexed to each of the association agreements in 1963 for Turkey, in 1978 for Cyprus, and in 1979 for Malta. These run for five years and regulate cooperation. The actual duration, however, of Protocol financing lasts longer than 5 years, because the commitments and disbursements of the Protocol allocations continue until exhausted (as in the case of the EDF).[2]

The East and Southern Mediterranean countries, the Mashraq (Egypt, Jordan, Lebanon and Syria) and the Maghreb (Algeria, Morocco, Tunisia), have had individual cooperation agreements with the EC since the late 1970s, some of which replaced trade agreements. The cooperation agreements offered economic cooperation in the form of trade preferences and conventional financial and technical cooperation. They were of unlimited duration, though their Financial Protocols were not. Israel has benefited from a free trade area agreement with the EC since 1989, rather than from concessional assistance.

In 1990 and 1991, when the fourth financial protocols for the East and Southern Mediterranean countries entered into force, the EC brought out its **'New Mediterranean Policy'**. This aimed at improving the economic and social stability of the region as a whole, and significantly increased aid to the largest Mediterranean countries (Algeria, Egypt, Morocco and Tunisia). The policy contained two innovations: greater support for economic reform and structural adjustment with a separate fund worth 300 m euro, and, the introduction of a special fund of 2030 m euro for horizontal cooperation (between non-governmental actors in the Mediterranean and the EU). In addition, trade cooperation was enhanced.

---

[2] The situation has changed since the introduction of the MEDA budget line by the European Parliament in 1995, and the allocation of 4685 m euro for the 1995–99 Mediterranean Policy by the Cannes Summit.

Assistance to Gaza/West Bank: This has been an important aid recipient in the region since the 1970s. Initially EC aid was mainly targeted at Palestinian refugees and channelled through the UN. From 1986 onwards a regular aid programme with preferential trade arrangements for exports from the Areas was established, its main focus being the strengthening of the economic, social and productive infrastructure. Between 1986 and 1998 around 1140 m euro of direct EC aid was committed and 855 m euro disbursed in Gaza/West Bank.

There are three components of financial and technical assistance to the Areas:

- *Financial support managed by UNRWA*, the United Nations Relief and Works Agency for Palestinian Refugees, established in 1949 after the Israel-Arab war had caused 726 000 Palestinians to flee to the West Bank of the River Jordan. It supports refugees in Gaza/West Bank and in Lebanon, Syria and Jordan. The EC started its contribution to the education, health and food aid programmes of UNRWA in 1971. Between 1971 and 1998 it has contributed more than 750 m euro.

- *NGO co-financing:* From 1979 onwards the EC financed NGO operations in Gaza/West Bank. Between 1979 and 1998 more than 29 m euro was spent in this way, 9 m euro of it in the last three years.

- *Direct aid managed by the European Commission*: After the European Council issued guidelines in 1986, a special budget line was introduced (B7–406 and B7–701, later B7–420) for direct aid to the West Bank/Gaza. This budget line has committed nearly 590 m euro since 1986. In 1991 an exceptional provision was granted to support recovery from the effects of the Gulf War. For the period 1994–98 the EC has set aside 500 m euro for the Palestine territories, half to be disbursed as grants (50 m euro per year) and half as loans from the European Investment Bank (from 1995 onwards). In 1997, an allocation of 20 m euro was agreed to support the recurrent costs of the Palestinian Ministry of Education to strengthen primary and secondary school provision. Since 1995 the Areas have also been eligible for funding from the main MEDA budget line.

> **Box 4.2: MEDA-Democracy**
>
> Following the Barcelona Conference, the European Parliament decided to create the MEDA-Democracy programme which was launched in 1996. It grants subsidies to non-profit-making associations, to support local or regional projects aimed at promoting:
> - Political rights relating to democracy and the rule of law;
> - Civil rights such as freedom of expression, meeting and association.

Euro-Mediterranean Partnership and the Barcelona Conference

A new stage in relations between the EU and the countries the Mediterranean began at the end of 1995 at a ministerial conference in Barcelona between the 15 Member States of the Union plus the Commission, 11 Mediterranean nations and the Palestinian Authorities.[3]

The Euro-Mediterranean partnership aims at a comprehensive form of cooperation between the two regions. Cooperation has now been agreed in a broad range of political, social and economic fields. The priorities for a work programme set out in the **Barcelona Declaration** are:

(i) Political and Security Partnership: The European and Mediterranean countries committed themselves to a Euro-Med zone of peace and stability (including issues of human rights, democracy, good governance and security) (see Box 4.2).

(ii) Economic and Financial Partnership: The main objectives of the Partnership are: to speed up progress towards lasting social and economic development; to improve living conditions by increasing employment and closing the development gap in the Euro-Mediterranean region; and to promote cooperation and regional integration. The gradual establishment of a free trade area

---

[3] The eleven Mediterranean countries plus the Palestinian Authorities are now known as the Med 12.

between the EC-15 and the Med-12 by 2010 is seen as the principal vehicle to achieve this (see section on trade below).

The Barcelona Declaration also refers to a 'substantial' increase in the financial assistance to be provided by the EC. In June 1995, the European Council in Cannes agreed that 4685 m euro should be provided from the EC Budget between 1995 and 1999. In addition, EIB loans will be available to the Med-12. The Barcelona conference agreed that a key factor in developing free trade will be cooperation and the growth of trade among the Med-12 themselves. In order to improve the effectiveness of private sector developments in the MED-partners, priority is given to three instruments: industrial cooperation; networks among economic EU-MED institutions; and business-to-business cooperation.

(iii) Partnership in Social, Cultural and Human Affairs: Aid has been allocated to provide support in the areas of culture, religion, education and the media, as well as between trade unions and public and private companies. The commitment to strengthen cooperation in order to reduce migratory pressures and illegal immigration is a further concern. Initiatives under consideration include: investment in human resources, decentralised cooperation (see Box 4.3), and cooperation between law and order authorities as part of the fight against terrorism, drug trafficking, organised crime and illegal immigration.

The MEDA Budget Line[4]

From 1997 the four Financial Protocols with the East and Southern Mediterranean, which expired in October 1996, were replaced by a single MEDA budget line (B7-410), which was introduced in 1995 with the aim of increasing the flexibility and speed of commitment and disbursement of funds. One of the main differences with the Financial Protocols in budgetary terms is that the MEDA line credits cannot be carried over from one financial year to another. The budgetary construction is therefore similar to that of Phare and Tacis. Programming of these funds will be undertaken on a three-year rolling basis with annual revisions (reflecting the way most EU bilateral donors undertake their programming exercises). There is a distinction between the regional indicative programme (which was first drawn up in 1997 for the 1997–99 period and is revised every 6 months) and the programming of national indicative programmes (first drawn up for the 1996–8 period and revised on an annual basis).

The Council of Ministers of the Union adopted, in compliance with the provisions of the MEDA Regulation, a series of general 'guidelines' describing the main principles for the use of MEDA funds on a bilateral and regional level.[5] Interventions under the MEDA programme cover four main sectors:

- **Support for structural adjustment:** budgetary support transferred to the government budget of partners implementing programmes of economic reform in collaboration with Bretton Woods institutions and the EC. The support aims to reduce the social impact of these reform programmes.

> **Box 4.3: Relaunch of Decentralised cooperation programmes in the Mediterranean**
>
> In April 1998 the Commission decided to relaunch the decentralised cooperation in the Mediterranean which had been temporarily suspended from the end of 1995. The relaunch involves three programmes:
> - MED URBS which aims to improve the living conditions of people in urban areas and to develop cooperation between local authorities;
> - MED CAMPUS which brings together, through networking, universities from the North and South of the Mediterranean in order to exchange experiences, and transfer technology and know-how;
> - MED MEDA which aims to develop networks in the media and journalistic fields.

---

[4] Council Regulation No 1488/96 of 26 July 1996, published in the Official Journal No L 189/1 of 30 July 1996.
[5] Decision 96/706/EC of 6 December 1996 published in OJ No L 325 of 14 December 1996.

- **Economic transition and private sector development:** to help ensure that the private sector, in particular SMEs, operates in a favourable economic policy environment and prepares for the planned Free Trade Area. Thus the MEDA programme funds activities such as the provision of technical support for privatisation, financial sector reforms, the modernisation of industry, and setting up business centres.
- **Strengthening the socio-economic balance:** funding sector support programmes and conventional cooperation projects e.g. health, basic education rural development, population programmes .
- **Strengthening civil society:** through the funding of activities run by non-governmental organisations, professional bodies and associations.

Trade Cooperation

Trade provisions were initially the main component of cooperation with the Mediterranean countries and remain important. Since the agreements of the 1960s and 1970s the Maghreb and Mashraq countries of the East and Southern Mediterranean have enjoyed duty-free access to the EU market for industrial products on a non-reciprocal basis (with some exceptions for certain textile and clothing exports in recent years). For agricultural exports, the Mediterranean countries enjoy preferential access which is stated in Additional Protocols to their agreements. The exports receive preferential rates and, for some products, tariff quotas within which the tariff is gradually reduced to zero.

The Euro-Mediterranean Partnership aims at gradually moving towards a free trade area between the European and South and East Mediterranean countries by the year 2010. This is to be achieved by means of Euro-Mediterranean Association Agreements negotiated between the EU and individual Mediterranean partners, to be complemented by Agreements between the partners themselves. Negotiations for Agreements have been concluded with Tunisia, Israel, Morocco, Jordan and the Palestinian Authority (see Table 4.5).

For each of the Mediterranean partners, the agreement provides that free trade shall gradually be implemented over a transitional period of 12 years maximum from the entry into force of the agreement. It will involve the progressive elimination of tariff and non-tariff barriers on manufactured products and a progressive liberalisation of trade in agricultural products and in services.

Table 4.5 Progress of negotiations on Euro-Mediterranean Association Agreements

Partner	Conclusion of negotiations	Signature of agreement	Entry into force
Tunisia	June 1995	July 1995	March 1998
Israel	September 1995	November 1995	–
Morocco	November 1995	February 1996	–
PLO for the benefit of the Palestinian Authority	December 1996	February 1997	July 1997
Jordan	April 1997	November 1997	–
Egypt, Lebanon, Algeria & Syria	in progress		–

Source: European Commission

In the case of industrial products originating from within the Union, Customs duties applicable to imports to the Mediterranean partner shall gradually be eliminated over the 12-year transitional period. Exports to the community of industrial products originating in the Mediterranean partners which are signatories to the agreements, continue to benefit form the pre-existing free trade regime.

For agricultural products the Agreement provides for a gradual implementation of a greater liberalisation of reciprocal trade through a widening of existing preferential measures and, as far as Morocco, Tunisia and Israel are concerned, a re-examination of the situation in the year 2000.

The benefits of free trade will be increased by taking further action on a number of accompanying measures. With this in mind the Commission issued a Communication on 30 September 1998 on the Euro-Mediterranean Partnership and the Single Market proposing that action be taken within the partnership to promote cooperation in such areas as: customs matters and taxation, free movement of goods, public procurement, intellectual property rights, financial services, data protection, competition rules and accounting and auditing. This proposal has been endorsed in principle by the partners.

5

EC External Cooperation to Asia and Latin America

Trends and Distribution

EC aid commitments to Asia and Latin America (usually known as the ALA programme) followed an upward trend till 1995, when they peaked at 1.2 bn euro or 17% of total allocable EC aid. Since then they have fallen somewhat (see Figure 5.1). Average annual commitments to Asia have more than doubled between 1986–90 and 1996–98 and those to Latin America have nearly tripled. As a proportion, ALA's share of total EC aid has risen slightly from 13.2% in 1986–90 to 14.6% in 1996–98. Both regions exhibit a similar pattern of growth of aid over the decade, and broad similarities in the type of aid committed.

There are two main budget lines for each region, one covering financial and technical cooperation, and the other economic cooperation. In addition both regions received support from various other budget lines, the main ones being for food aid, humanitarian aid and aid via NGOs. In the period 1996–98 financial and technical cooperation represented between a third and a half of all aid to each region (49% for Asia, 39% for Latin America), and economic cooperation 10% and 12% respectively. The peak in aid to Asia in 1989 was due to unusually large amounts of food aid to Bangladesh, China and India in that year, totalling over 130 m euro. The peak in 1995 was due to a combination of commitments including food aid to Bangladesh of 49 m euro, and a number of large projects in the forestry, banking finance and business services, women in development and environment sectors.

**Figure 5.1: EC Cooperation with Asia and Latin America
(1986–98, commitments and disbursements, m euro)**

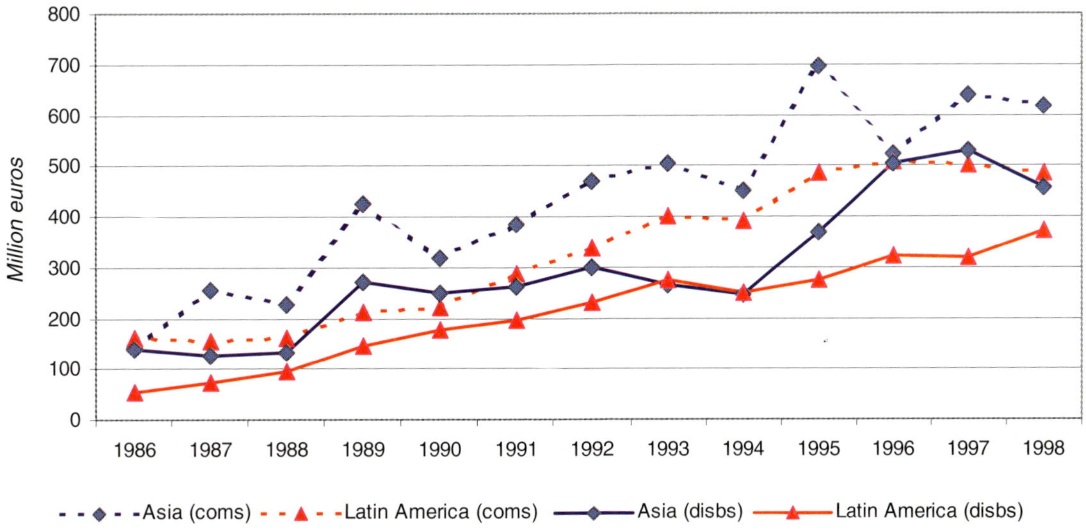

Source: European Commission/ODI database 1999

There has long been an informal understanding in the Commission that two-thirds of the EC aid programme to Asia and Latin America would be allocated to Asia, with the remaining third going to Latin America.[1] However, the balance between the two regions was 60:40 for the 1986–90 period, and Latin America further increased its share in the 1990s, with the split becoming 54:46 for 1996–98.

As with the ACP, the exact rate at which funds are disbursed is not easy to calculate from available data. However, an approximate calculation shows that EC programmes to both regions have slightly improved their disbursement rate over time. The ratio of total disbursements to total commitments for 1986–90 stood at 67% for Asia and 60% for Latin America, and rose to 68% and 65% respectively for 1986–98 as a whole.

Table 5.1: Regional Distribution of EC Cooperation with Asia and Latin America (1986–98, commitments and disbursements, m euro)

	1986	1987	1988	1989	1990	1991	1992	1993	1994	1995	1996	1997	1998	Total
Asia Commitments														
Total	140	257	226	426	317	383	470	504	451	696	522	639	617	5649
East Asia	5	12	29	54	26	21	11	21	40	62	80	142	125	627
South Asia	72	230	91	254	194	295	230	302	203	288	318	261	300	3040
South-East Asia	44	6	39	87	76	46	153	146	165	200	102	163	164	1391
Unallocable	19	9	67	31	21	21	76	35	44	146	21	73	27	592
Asia Disbursements														
Total	138	125	132	271	250	261	300	264	246	369	503	528	456	3843
East Asia	2	3	8	42	38	33	24	16	11	22	29	75	82	385
South Asia	75	78	80	171	146	135	174	144	132	189	237	238	190	1989
South-East Asia	37	27	31	37	37	66	75	53	76	112	137	125	123	936
Unallocable	23	17	14	21	29	26	28	50	27	46	100	89	61	533
Latin America Commitments														
Total	160	156	159	210	222	286	338	401	390	486	507	502	485	4301
South America	43	52	65	85	100	134	160	170	173	232	244	256	196	1910
Nth & Cent Am	16	66	25	46	59	73	129	140	182	212	180	143	154	1426
Regional	17	25	39	50	13	16	6	49	20	28	85	18	–	366
Unallocable	84	12	30	30	49	62	44	42	15	14	-2	85	134	599
Latin America Disbursements														
Total	53	72	94	146	176	196	231	273	247	275	323	319	370	2775
South America	8	25	25	62	77	78	88	100	108	100	133	111	186	1100
Nth & Cent Am	4	14	24	41	49	62	66	98	75	94	123	104	113	868
Regional	–	4	12	2	24	7	21	21	17	33	2	–	–	143
Unallocable	41	29	32	41	27	49	55	54	48	47	65	105	72	665

Source: Source: European Commission/ODI database 1999

Recipients of EC Cooperation with Asia and Latin America

Table 5.2 reveals a number of differences in the pattern of aid allocation between the two regions, as well as some continuity in the main recipients. The top ten Asian recipients received the vast bulk of all EC aid to Asia, but saw their share decline slightly from 86% to 84%. Aid was spread among more countries in the case of Latin America, but it became considerably more concentrated during the first part of the 1990s, with the share of the top ten rising from 54% to nearly 70%

---

[1] This has never been legally enshrined in EC regulations but is based on internal Commission instructions. The 18 countries which are generally taken to comprise Latin America and teh, based on the EC categorisation, are indicated in Appendix 4. The 23 countries which are taken to comprise Asia are likewise indicated in

before dropping again to 64%. Nonetheless, both programmes embraced a rapidly growing number of recipients over the time period, with the number of recipients receiving an average of 5 m euro a year rising from eight to sixteen for Asia, and from ten to sixteen for Latin America. Although Asia as a region received considerably more aid than Latin America, Asian countries received far less on a *per capita* basis. Nicaragua was allocated a total of 111 euro per person between 1986 and 1998, with Bolivia committed over 60 and El Salvador over 45 euro, and a total of 13 Latin America countries receiving a total of over 10 euro per person. In contrast, the highest ranking Asian country in *per capita* terms was Cambodia, which received 30 euro, and only four Asian countries received over 10 euro per person. Thus while Asia received more aid overall than Latin America, this did not compensate for its far greater population.

India and Bangladesh remained the largest Asian recipients, but both saw their share of total Asian aid drop over the time period, for India it halved from 34% to 17%, and Bangladesh's share dropped from 17% to 14%. By 1996–98 Indonesia, Sri Lanka and Laos had slipped out of the top ten to be replaced by Vietnam, North Korea and Cambodia. The ten largest Latin American recipients remained almost static over the period, but with Honduras temporarily replaced by Cuba during the second time period, and Chile losing its place to Paraguay for 1996–98.

Table 5.2: Top 10 Recipients of EC Cooperation – Asia and Latin America (1986–98, commitments, %)

Asia Total 1986–90	%	Asia Total 1991–95	%	Asia Total 1996–98	%
India	34.4	India	18.4	India	16.6
Bangladesh	16.6	Bangladesh	18.3	Bangladesh	14.0
China	8.7	Philippines	7.3	China	11.0
Philippines	6.3	Pakistan	7.0	Afghanistan	8.4
Thailand	6.2	China	5.8	Korea DPR (North Korea)	8.3
Pakistan	6.2	Cambodia	5.8	Viet Nam	7.8
Indonesia	3.2	Vietnam	5.5	Cambodia	6.5
Sri Lanka	2.0	Indonesia	5.1	Pakistan	6.0
Laos	1.4	Afghanistan	4.9	Philippines	3.0
Afghanistan	1.0	Nepal	2.2	Thailand	2.8
Top 10: % of all Asia	86.1	Top 10: % of all Asia	80.4	Top 10: % of all Asia	84.4
Latin Am Total 1986–90	%	Latin Am Total 1991–95	%	Latin Am Total 1996–98	%
Bolivia	11.8	Peru	12.2	Peru	10.9
Peru	10.5	Nicaragua	10.1	Nicaragua	10.1
Nicaragua	7.3	El Salvador	8.0	Bolivia	10.0
Chile	4.5	Guatemala	7.9	Guatemala	8.8
Guatemala	4.1	Bolivia	7.3	Brazil	6.9
El Salvador	3.9	Brazil	5.9	Colombia	3.9
Columbia	3.2	Chile	5.0	Paraguay	3.7
Ecuador	3.2	Cuba	4.1	El Salvador	3.3
Honduras	2.9	Columbia	4.0	Honduras	3.1
Brazil	2.8	Ecuador	3.7	Ecuador	3.0
Top 10: % total Latin Am	54.2	Top 10: % total Latin Am	68.3	Top 10: % of all Latin Am	63.8

Source: European Commission/ODI database 1999

Sectoral Distribution of EC External Cooperation with Asia and Latin America

Although both regions receive broadly similar types of aid – financial and technical, and economic cooperation – the precise sectoral composition of this aid differs significantly.

Both regions have been major beneficiaries of three of the four aid instruments, food aid, humanitarian assistance and aid to NGOs. South Asia alone received *food aid* commitments worth nearly 600 m euro between 1988 and 1998, and the total to Asia as a whole stood at nearly 860 m euro. The main Asian recipients were Bangladesh (364 m euro), China (128 m euro) and India (101 m euro). Food aid to Latin America totalled over 450 m euro, and the major beneficiaries were Peru (157 m euro), Nicaragua (76 m euro), and Bolivia and Cuba each with around 50 m euro (see Figures 5.2 and 5.3). However food aid has fallen dramatically in Latin America since 1996 partly as a result of the new Food Aid Regulation of 1996 which allows money from B7–20 to be spent on a wider range of food security operations. In Latin America this has taken the form of commitments to agriculture and programme aid for the years 1997–98.

Humanitarian aid (including rehabilitation) to both regions was only very slightly lower, with Asia receiving nearly 820 m euro and Latin America 430 m euro, and, in contrast to food aid, this sector has been growing. Humanitarian assistance went beyond providing relief aid or food supplies, and encompassed finance for reconstruction, rehabilitation, and disaster prevention. ECHO has, for example, helped establish a number of disaster early warning systems throughout Asia, including India, Burma, the Philippines, Vietnam, Nepal and Bangladesh. In 1992 the Commission established a programme to support the reintegration of Vietnamese returnees. This funded advice centres and over 100 000 information kits, as well as contributing to economic reconstruction. In 1995 emergency relief was provided to North Korea following exceptional floods in many provinces. Overall the largest Asian recipients over the 1986–98 period were Afghanistan (244 m euro), Bangladesh (112 m euro), Cambodia (91 m euro), Vietnam (74 m euro), and Pakistan (58 m euro). In Latin America the main recipients were Nicaragua (86 m euro) and Guatemala (80 m euro) followed by Cuba (65 m euro) and El Salvador (50 m euro).

Asia and Latin America also benefit from a budget line for humanitarian aid to refugees and displaced persons (B7–2120 during 1996–98, becoming B7–3020 for Asia and B7–3120 for Latin America in 1999). These are managed by DG External Relations and have committed between 50–60 m euro per year to the two regions for the period 1996–98.

Aid to NGOs has been consistently high in Latin America with total commitments for 1986–98 of over 500 m euro or nearly 12% of aid. The sector is growing in Asia, having nearly doubled as a proportion of allocable aid from 4% to 7% between 1986–90 and 1996–98 (see Fig 5.2). Programme aid has been much lower and less consistent with some *Stabex* funds to Asia in the late 1980s, and since 1997 *structural adjustment* funds to Bolivia (30 m euro), Nicaragua and Honduras (both less than 10 m euro).

Project aid to Asia has risen steadily as a proportion of allocable aid from 58% to 65%, while for Latin America it dipped slightly during 1991–95 before regaining its earlier percentage (70%). The *social infrastructure and services* sector is the most significant sector for project aid and both regions show increased commitments to it over 1996–98, though the earlier patterns were quite different. Asia saw aid in this sector dramatically increase as a share of all aid, from 2% of allocable aid in 1986–90, to 14% for 1991–95, and further to 30% in 1996–98. Latin America, in contrast, started out with a high level of social aid (17%), but its share of total aid fell in the 1990s to 14% of allocable aid, before climbing again to 26% (see also Tables 5.3 and 5.4).[2] Within this sector *education* accounted for 8% of all aid to Asia in the 1990s, and rose from less than 1% Latin America in the early 1990s to 11% for 1996–98, largely due to programmes in Guatemala, Nicaragua and El Salvador.

Asia experienced a dramatic growth in the aid committed to the *health and population* sub-sector, whereas for Latin America the proportion of aid to this sector rose from 6% to 9% before dropping to 4%. The EC programme in Asia has placed emphasis on improving health centres in poor, rural areas by upgrading existing facilities and developing district hospitals. In 1994 a pilot programme promoting action against cancer was launched in Latin America. Initially it was limited to Costa Rica, Colombia and Paraguay with a budget of nearly 1 m euro, but in 1996 it was extended to all of Latin America with a budget of over 13 m euro. Both regions have benefited from a budget line created in 1995 to combat drug abuse and trafficking.

Another growth area in Asia is *rural development*, which, in contrast to all other regional programmes, saw its sectoral share increase to over 10% of allocable aid to the region in the 1996–98 period. In Latin America it remains significant at 8%, though it has dropped from a peak of 12% for 1991–95.

For Latin America the *natural resources* sector is of considerable significance, taking 12% of allocations for 1991–95 and 1996–98, slightly down from 15% for 1986–90. Agriculture is still the main subsector, though quickly being taken over by forestry aid which grew from nothing in the 1980s to 76 m euro for Latin America in 1996–98. The natural resources sector has dropped considerably for Asia from 32% of allocable aid in 1986–90 to 11% for 1991–95 to 3% for the final time period. The growth in the forestry sector reflects a new commitment to the conservation of tropical forests enshrined in Council Regulation 443/92 of February 1992, which allocated 10% of financial and technical cooperation credits for both regions to the environmental and forestry sectors.

The sector of *economic infrastructure* took 6% of allocable aid for Asia and 3% for Latin America. In Asia banking, finance and business was the most significant sub-sector at 3%, followed by energy. In Latin America the banking, finance and business sector has only been significant since 1995.

Within other productive sectors *investment promotion* is the most important sub-sector in both regions at 4% during 1996–98. The European Community Investment Partners *(ECIP)* scheme described in Chapter 2 has been of considerable significance. In the period 1988–98 over 40% of all ECIP finance, or over 132 m euro, was concentrated in Asia, while 30%, or 87 m euro, was allocated to Latin America.

Figure 5.3 illustrates the steady growth in importance of EC support for *good governance* in the 1990s in Latin America, rising to 5% in the period 1996–98. This reflects the introduction of a clause on human rights and democratisation in the 'third-generation' accords with Latin American countries, which sets out the universality of human rights and support for vulnerable groups, such as children, women and indigenous people. In Asia it fell from 1% to almost zero for 1991–95 before picking up again to over 2% for the final time period

---

[2] As in Chapter 2, the text refers to sectoral shares of *allocable* EC aid to each region, while Tables 5.3 and 5.4 indicate shares of *all* aid (including the unallocable portion).

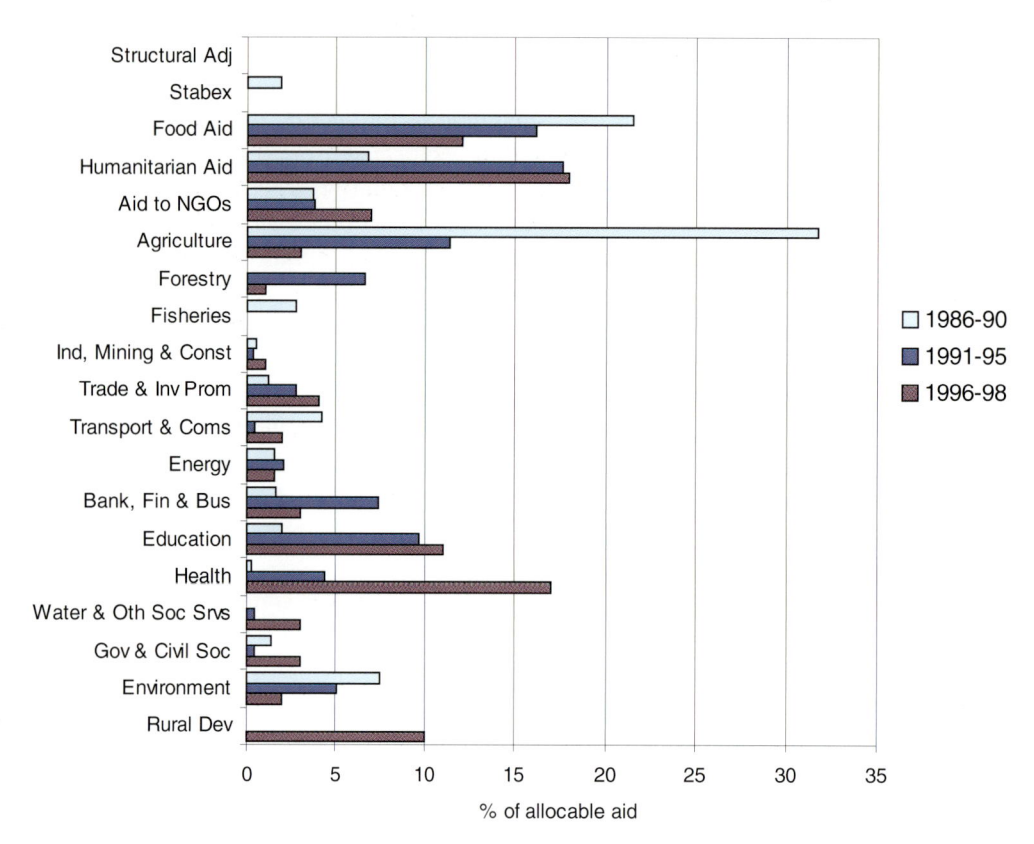

**Figure 5.2: Sectoral Allocation of EC Cooperation with Asia
(1986–98, commitments, % of allocable aid)**

**Figure 5.3: Sectoral Allocation of EC Cooperation with Latin America
(1986–98, commitments, % of allocable aid)**

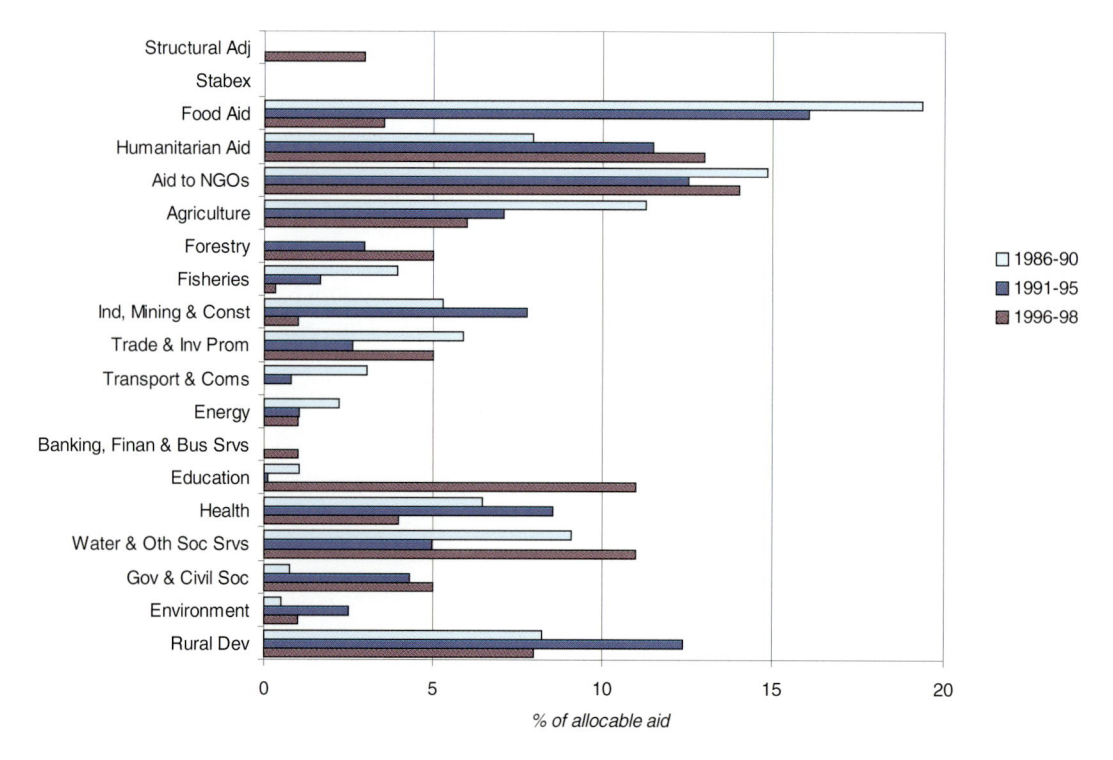

Source: European Commission/ODI database 1999

Revised guidelines on ALA assistance drawn up in 1991 appear to have had an initial impact with respect to *environmental* aid. Aid specifically targeted on the environment grew significantly in the early 1990s, in Latin America from almost zero during 1986–90 to an annual average of 8 m euro in 1991–95, and in Asia from an annual average of 19 m euro to 24 m euro (though this represents a falling share of total aid). However since 1996 they have dropped significantly in both regions. These totals arguably underestimate the increase in environmentally focused aid, since aid to the *forestry* sector, much of which has an important environmental content, falls under 'natural resources' in the ODI/DAC categorisation.

Relative to other regional programmes, EC aid to Asia included substantial sums in support of the role of *women in development* totalling 20 m euro for Latin America and 54 m euro for Asia since 1992. Although, as noted in Chapter 2, precise quantification is difficult in the absence of a reliable marker system. Promoting the concept of savings and helping women to open savings accounts has been a strategy followed in a number of EC-funded projects, as a way of helping rural women to improve their welfare and status. Credit schemes for women have been implemented by the Community in both South and South-East Asia, often combined with technical and business training.

Finally, *regional* assistance forms an important part of EC aid to Latin America, and accounted for over 360 m euro, or nearly 8.4% of all aid to the region over the 1986–98 period (see Table 5.1). The regional approach is seen as particularly appropriate in the sectors of transport and communications, intra-regional trade promotion, strengthening regional institutions and the environment. Conferences and studies are also often funded on a regional basis.

Loans

The European Investment Bank was authorised to finance projects in Asia and Latin America in 1993 for a limited amount on a trial basis, using its own resources and at market rates. The facility was subsequently renewed for an additional three years (1997–99). As these are not concessional loans they are not covered in this report.

Table 5.3: Sectoral Allocation of EC Cooperation with Asia
(1986–98, commitments, m euro and % of total aid)

	1986	1987	1988	1989	1990	1991	1992	1993	1994	1995	1996	1997	1998	Total
Commitments (m euro)														
Programme Aid	–	6	11	6	2	0	–	–	–	–	–	–	–	25
Stabex	–	6	11	5	2	0	–	–	–	–	–	–	–	24
Food Aid (development)	–	–	19	173	81	69	100	56	63	98	39	80	81	859
Humanitarian Aid	2	17	10	37	20	65	84	88	90	95	95	93	123	819
Humanitarian excl rehabilitation	2	17	10	37	20	65	84	88	81	83	90	84	120	780
Rehabilitation	–	–	–	–	–	–	–	–	9	12	5	9	3	39
Aid to NGOs	5	7	11	9	14	13	14	20	20	23	48	38	31	253
Natural Resources	28	178	47	104	79	141	47	42	86	115	18	26	33	944
Agriculture	21	176	25	100	79	141	15	14	49	53	16	17	25	732
Forestry	–	–	–	–	–	–	32	29	37	61	2	9	7	176
Fisheries	7	3	22	4	–	–	–	–	–	–	–	–	–	35
Other Productive Sectors	–	1	3	10	8	6	8	14	22	24	37	27	20	179
Industry, Mining & Construct	–	1	1	4	1	2	–	2	3	1	2	1	6	24
Trade	–	0	2	4	1	0	1	1	0	–	0	4	–	14
Investment Promotion	–	–	0	2	6	4	7	11	18	23	34	22	13	140
Economic Infrastructure & Servs	33	9	27	16	8	31	44	35	33	94	3	70	37	438
Transport & Communications	21	3	17	10	2	9	–	2	–	1	1	11	15	92
Energy	5	5	5	3	1	6	31	2	9	0	1	15	15	99
Banking, Finan & Bus Srvs	7	0	5	3	5	16	13	31	24	93	1	44	6	247
Social Infrastructure & Services	–	15	12	1	3	51	16	160	62	54	186	172	159	892
Education	–	15	10	–	–	6	5	150	50	19	27	28	132	442
Health & Population	–	0	1	1	2	45	8	5	12	34	140	137	10	395
Governance & Civil Society	–	2	6	0	8	0	0	4	4	3	13	14	23	77
Multisector/Crosscutting	71	13	19	45	88	4	108	71	58	154	51	119	99	901
Environment	0	–	8	28	58	4	33	17	1	65	20	4	3	242
Women in Development	–	–	–	–	–	–	0	–	0	37	3	0	13	54
Rural development	–	–	–	–	–	–	–	–	–	–	18	74	80	171
Unallocable by Sector	2	7	61	25	7	2	48	13	14	37	32	2	11	261
Total volume, m euro	140	257	226	426	317	383	470	504	451	696	522	639	617	5649
Commitments (%)														
Programme Aid	–	2.4	4.9	1.4	0.5	–	–	–	–	–	–	–	–	0.4
Stabex	–	2.4	4.9	1.2	0.5	–	–	–	–	–	–	–	–	0.4
Food Aid (development)	–	–	8.2	40.5	25.6	18.0	21.4	11.0	14.0	14.1	7.4	12.6	13.2	15.2
Humanitarian Aid	1.1	6.8	4.3	8.7	6.4	16.9	17.9	17.5	20.0	13.7	18.2	14.5	20.0	14.5
Humanitarian excl rehabilitation	1.1	6.8	4.3	8.7	6.4	16.9	17.9	17.5	17.9	11.9	17.2	13.1	19.5	13.8
Rehabilitation	–	–	–	–	–	–	–	–	2.0	1.8	1.0	1.4	0.5	0.7
Aid to NGOs	3.4	2.8	5.0	2.2	4.5	3.3	3.0	4.0	4.4	3.2	9.1	5.9	5.0	4.5
Natural Resources	19.8	69.5	20.9	24.4	25.0	36.9	9.9	8.4	19.0	16.5	3.5	4.0	5.3	16.7
Agriculture	15.0	68.5	11.1	23.5	25.0	36.9	3.2	2.7	10.8	7.7	3.1	2.7	4.1	13.0
Forestry	–	–	–	–	–	–	6.7	5.7	8.2	8.8	0.4	1.4	1.2	3.1
Fisheries	4.8	1.0	9.8	0.9	–	–	–	–	–	–	–	–	–	0.6
Other Productive Sectors	–	0.3	1.4	2.4	2.4	1.5	1.7	2.8	4.8	3.5	7.0	4.1	3.2	3.2
Industry, Mining & Construct	–	0.3	0.4	1.0	0.2	0.4	–	0.4	0.7	0.2	0.5	0.1	1.0	0.4
Trade	–	–	0.9	1.0	0.4	0.1	0.2	0.1	0.1	–	0.1	0.6	–	0.3
Investment Promotion	–	–	0.2	0.4	1.8	1.0	1.5	2.3	4.1	3.3	6.4	3.4	2.0	2.5
Economic Infrastructure & Servs	23.8	3.4	11.9	3.7	2.5	8.1	9.4	6.9	7.3	13.4	0.5	10.9	5.9	7.8
Transport & Communications	15.1	1.3	7.6	2.4	0.5	2.3	–	0.3	–	0.1	0.2	1.7	2.5	1.6
Energy	3.6	2.1	2.1	0.6	0.5	1.5	6.6	0.5	2.1	–	0.2	2.3	2.4	1.7
Banking, Finan & Bus Srvs	5.1	–	2.3	0.7	1.5	4.3	2.8	6.1	5.2	13.4	0.1	6.9	1.0	4.4
Social Infrastructure & Services	–	6.0	5.1	0.2	0.8	13.4	3.4	31.8	13.8	7.8	35.7	26.8	25.9	15.8
Education	–	5.8	4.6	–	–	1.4	1.1	29.8	11.0	2.8	5.2	4.3	21.4	7.8
Health & Population	–	0.1	0.4	0.1	0.6	11.7	1.7	1.1	2.6	4.9	26.8	21.5	1.6	7.0
Governance & Civil Society	–	1.0	2.8	0.1	2.5	0.0	0.1	0.7	0.8	0.4	2.5	2.2	3.7	1.4
Multisector/Crosscutting	50.2	5.3	8.6	10.5	27.6	1.1	23.0	14.1	12.9	22.1	9.8	18.7	16.1	16.0
Environment	–	–	3.7	6.7	18.4	1.1	7.1	3.4	0.2	9.3	3.9	0.5	0.4	4.3
Women in Development	–	–	–	–	–	–	–	–	–	5.3	0.7	–	2.1	1.0
Rural development	–	–	–	–	–	–	–	–	–	–	3.4	11.6	12.9	3.0
Unallocable by Sector	1.7	2.6	26.8	5.8	2.2	0.6	10.2	2.7	3.0	5.4	6.2	0.3	1.8	4.6
Total volume, m euro	100	100	100	100	100	100	100	100	100	100	100	100	100	100

Source: European Commission/ODI database 1999

Table 5.4: Sectoral Allocation of EC Cooperation wtih Latin America (1986–98, commitments, m euro and % of total aid)

	1986	1987	1988	1989	1990	1991	1992	1993	1994	1995	1996	1997	1998	Total
Commitments (m euro)														
Programme Aid	–	–	–	–	–	–	–	–	–	–	–	18	28	46
Structural	–	–	–	–	–	–	–	–	–	–	–	18	28	46
Food Aid (development)	–	–	6	67	58	55	48	56	50	52	51	9	0	453
Humanitarian Aid	3	1	9	29	12	16	22	32	59	59	56	61	73	432
Humanitarian excl rehabilitation	3	1	9	29	12	16	22	32	49	47	40	61	65	385
Rehabilitation	–	–	–	–	–	–	–	–	10	12	16	0	8	47
Aid to NGOs	12	15	25	24	25	34	37	39	51	43	63	58	78	504
Natural Resources	6	35	21	11	31	16	68	70	12	25	57	62	52	466
Agriculture	6	35	15	3	17	9	35	41	8	22	25	35	31	283
Forestry	–	–	–	–	–	–	20	21	5	2	31	24	21	125
Fisheries	–	–	6	8	13	7	13	7	–	–	1	3	–	57
Other Productive Sectors	22	2	3	1	48	36	17	18	43	56	34	45	10	335
Industry, Mining & Construct	22	–	2	–	12	31	10	9	31	45	5	12	–	180
Trade	0	2	0	–	32	–	–	–	–	–	3	4	0	42
Tourism	–	–	–	–	–	–	–	–	–	–	1	1	–	2
Investment Promotion	–	–	1	1	3	5	7	9	12	10	25	28	10	110
Economic Infrastructure & Servs	–	3	26	4	3	6	6	–	7	10	5	14	22	108
Transport & Communications	–	–	21	–	–	3	–	–	7	3	2	1	1	38
Energy	–	3	5	4	3	4	6	–	–	7	3	10	6	51
Banking, Finan & Bus Srvs	–	–	–	–	–	–	–	–	–	–	0	3	16	19
Social Infrastructure & Services	34	36	15	8	20	25	35	40	20	103	119	162	86	702
Education	3	–	–	4	–	–	–	–	2		54	73	27	162
Health & Population	22	16	1	3	2	24	17	15	16	68	20	29	2	235
Water	9	20	13	0	17	1	16	20		24	6	37	12	175
Other Soc Infra & Srvs	–	1	1	1	1	1	1	6	2	11	38	23	46	131
Governance & Civil Society	–	–	–	–	5	10	10	15	14	21	32	27	16	150
Multisector/Crosscutting	3	50	–	1	5	49	53	65	66	58	51	35	105	541
Environment	0	0	0	1	2	4	2	6	16	14	4	6	3	57
Women in Development	–	–	–	–	–	–	0	4	5	0	11	–	–	20
Rural development	3	50	–	–	3	39	50	48	44	21	28	29	51	365
Other Multisector	–	–	–	–	–	6	1	8	1	23	8	0	51	98
Unallocable by Sector	80	13	53	65	16	38	42	66	69	58	39	9	14	565
Total volume, m euro	160	156	159	210	222	286	338	401	390	486	507	502	485	4301
Commitments (%)														
Programme Aid	–	–	–	–	–	–	–	–	–	–	–	3.6	5.7	1.1
Structural	–	–	–	–	–	–	–	–	–	–	–	3.6	5.7	1.1
Food Aid (development)	–	–	4.1	31.9	26.1	19.1	14.3	13.9	12.8	10.8	10.0	1.9	0.1	10.5
Humanitarian Aid	1.7	0.6	5.8	14.0	5.3	5.6	6.4	8.0	15.0	12.2	11.1	12.2	15.1	10.0
Humanitarian excl rehabilitation	1.7	0.6	5.8	14.0	5.3	5.6	6.4	8.0	12.5	9.6	7.8	12.2	13.4	8.9
Rehabilitation	–	–	–	–	–	–	–	–	2.5	2.6	3.2	–	1.7	1.1
Aid to NGOs	7.5	9.7	15.9	11.3	11.1	12.0	10.8	9.7	13.1	8.9	12.4	11.6	16.1	11.7
Natural Resources	3.6	22.5	13.0	5.2	13.9	5.7	20.2	17.3	3.1	5.1	11.3	12.3	10.8	10.8
Agriculture	3.6	22.5	9.2	1.6	7.9	3.2	10.4	10.2	1.9	4.6	4.9	7.0	6.4	6.6
Forestry	–	–	–	–	–	–	6.0	5.3	1.2	0.5	6.2	4.8	4.4	2.9
Fisheries	–	–	3.8	3.6	6.0	2.4	3.8	1.8	–	–	0.2	0.5	–	1.3
Other Productive Sectors	13.8	1.4	1.8	0.4	21.6	12.7	5.1	4.4	11.1	11.5	6.7	8.9	2.0	7.8
Industry, Mining & Construct	13.8	–	1.2	–	5.4	11.0	3.0	2.2	8.0	9.3	1.1	2.3	–	4.2
Trade	–	1.4	0.3	–	14.6	–	–	–	–	–	0.6	0.8	0.1	1.0
Tourism	–	–	–	–	–	–	–	–	–	–	0.3	0.2	–	–
Investment Promotion	–	–	0.4	0.4	1.6	1.8	2.0	2.2	3.0	2.2	4.8	5.7	2.0	2.6
Economic Infrastructure & Servs	–	1.9	16.2	2.1	1.2	2.2	1.8	0.0	1.8	2.1	1.1	2.8	4.6	2.5
Transport & Communications	–	–	13.0	–	–	0.9	–	–	1.8	0.7	0.4	0.3	0.2	0.9
Energy	–	1.9	3.2	2.1	1.2	1.3	1.8	–	–	1.4	0.6	2.0	1.2	1.2
Banking, Finan & Bus Srvs	–	–	–	–	–	–	–	–	–	–	0.1	0.5	3.3	0.4
Social Infrastructure & Services	21.3	23.3	9.4	3.7	8.9	8.8	10.3	10.1	5.0	21.2	23.4	32.3	17.8	16.3
Education	2.1	–	–	1.8	–	–	–	–	0.5		10.6	14.5	5.5	3.8
Health & Population	13.6	10.4	0.6	1.6	0.8	8.3	5.1	3.8	4.1	14.0	4.0	5.8	0.4	5.5
Water	5.6	12.5	8.5	0.0	7.9	0.2	4.8	4.9	–	4.9	1.3	7.4	2.4	4.1
Other Soc Infra & Srvs	–	0.4	0.3	0.4	0.2	0.3	0.4	1.4	0.5	2.3	7.5	4.6	9.5	3.0
Governance & Civil Society	–	–	–	–	2.3	3.5	3.0	3.8	3.5	4.3	6.3	5.3	3.2	3.5
Multisector/Crosscutting	1.8	32.1	0.2	0.4	2.4	17.0	15.7	16.2	16.8	12.0	10.0	7.0	21.6	12.6
Environment	–	–	0.2	0.4	0.9	1.2	0.6	1.4	4.1	2.9	0.8	1.2	0.6	1.3
Women in Development	–	–	–	–	–	–	–	0.9	1.3	0.1	2.1	–	–	0.5
Rural development	1.8	32.1	–	–	1.5	13.6	14.8	11.9	11.2	4.3	5.5	5.8	10.4	8.5
Other Multisector	–	–	–	–	–	2.2	0.3	2.0	0.2	4.7	1.6	–	10.6	2.3
Unallocable by Sector	50.3	8.4	33.5	30.9	7.2	13.4	12.4	16.6	17.8	12.0	7.8	1.9	3.0	13.1
Total volume, m euro	100	100	100	100	100	100	100	100	100	100	100	100	100	100

Source: European Commission/ODI database 1999

Policy and Objectives

Evolution of EC External Cooperation with Asia and Latin America

Whereas development cooperation between the European Community and sub-Saharan Africa and thus the ACP countries dates back to the late 1950s, the Community's aid relationship with Latin America and Asia is considerably more recent. EC relations with Latin America came first, when an arrangement called 'the Brussels Dialogue' began and the EC established official relations with members of the Andean Pact as a regional organisation, later the 'Andean Group'.[3] Bilateral trade agreements were established with a number of countries in the early 1970s, but cooperation was quite limited in scope and volume relative to the ACP countries. Soon after Denmark, Ireland and the United Kingdom joined the Community in 1973, a formal proposal was made to extend cooperation to the Asian and Latin American (ALA) developing countries. A programme of financial and technical cooperation followed in 1976, since which time the scope of EC aid has broadened considerably.

> **Box 5.1: EC–Latin American Regional Cooperation**
>
> EC cooperation with Latin America operates at three levels:
>
> i) at the regional level the Community has been conducting formal political dialogue with the Rio Group (South America and Mexico) since 1990;
>
> ii) at the sub-regional level the San José dialogue has been under way since 1984 with the Central American countries;
>
> iii) at the bilateral level the Commission has concluded 'third-generation' agreements with various countries and groups of countries, including the Andean Pact which benefits from higher levels of aid and also special trading advantages (GSP arrangements).
>
> In addition, in line with its commitment to regional integration, the Community is supporting Mercosur, the Southern Cone common market whose agreement was signed in 1991 with Argentina, Brazil, Paraguay and Uruguay. Chile and Bolivia are associate members enjoying free trade but not imposing the Common External Tariff.

Initially the emphasis was firmly on financial and technical cooperation, as set out in Council Regulation 442/81 of 1981. This established an overall framework and guiding principles for cooperation, and set out five objectives: i) to assist the poorest countries; ii) to improve the living standards of the most marginalised strata of the population; iii) to promote rural development and agricultural production; iv) to promote a regional approach to development; and v) to meet humanitarian needs in cases of natural disaster.

The initial 'first' and 'second' generation bilateral agreements with Latin American countries were less favourable than the assistance offered to the ACP countries, as budgets were set by the Commission annually (rather than the multi-annual financial programmes under Lomé), and there was no contractual commitment as there was under Lomé. The cooperation agreements of the 1990s, however, have strengthened and deepened EC-Latin American relations. These 'third-generation' framework agreements were designed to provide an appropriate legal framework for developing more extensive and in-depth economic cooperation. A growing emphasis on regional cooperation has also been a feature of the Community's relations with the continent. This is reflected in the Council Resolution of 1 June 1995, which concluded that support for regional cooperation and integration was a major component of the Union's development policy and could contribute to 'the smooth and gradual integration of the developing countries into the world economy', as stated in the Maastricht Treaty (art. 130u) (see Box 5.1).

Both the increased depth and the stress on economic development apparent in the third-generation agreements are characteristic of the broad trend in the Community's relationship with both Asia and Latin America. The 1992 Council Regulation (443/92) on financial and technical assistance to

---

[3] The Andean Group, formalised in 1983, comprises Bolivia, Colombia, Ecuador, Peru and Venezuela.

and economic cooperation with the ALA countries was an important element in this evolution. It recommended that five-year programming should be established for each objective, country or region, where possible. Furthermore, in elevating economic cooperation as a second axis, alongside financial and technical assistance, it stated that the former would target those countries or regions enjoying strong growth while the latter was aimed at the poorest countries and groups. Economic cooperation is to be directed at executives and decision-makers in particular, and seeks to render the economic, legislative and administrative institutional structures more conducive to development. Such cooperation is appropriate at a regional level as well, in support of intra-regional trade, regional institutions for economic integration, and telecommunications, *inter alia*.

In 1994 the Commission formulated an Asia Strategy (COM(94)314), which reaffirms the Community's commitment to raise the European profile in Asia. The strengthening of ties between the Community and Asia is reflected in recent Council Decisions approving Cooperation Agreements with Vietnam and Nepal, for example.[4] These agreements represent a commitment to enhance the level of Community cooperation (both economic and development), which should be targeted on poorer groups. Both agreements emphasise employment generation, primary health care, the role of women and, in the case of Nepal, the role of NGOs in development. By 1997 all developing Asian countries but the smallest[5] had signed cooperation agreements of some kind with the Community, either bilaterally as a group. The only large exceptions are Afghanistan and Burma/Myanmar.

China was covered by a different Directorate General than the rest of Asia. The Communication from the Commission of March 1998[6] sets out a proposal for a new EU-China partnership which promotes cooperation as a tool to meet the EU strategic objectives, these including:

- engaging China further in the international community though an upgraded political dialogue;
- supporting China's transition to an open society based upon the rule of law and the respect for human rights;
- integrating China further in the world economy by bringing it more fully into the world trading system and by supporting the process of economic and social reform underway in the country; and
- raising the EU's profile in China.

Cooperation instruments

Programme aid

A few least developed ALA (mainly Asian) countries have benefited from *Stabex-type* flows, an instrument which is otherwise confined to ACP countries. In 1987 the Community agreed to introduce a similar compensation scheme for developing countries which were not signatories to the Lomé Convention. The scheme provided financial resources for projects, programmes and operations, largely in the agricultural sector, where a loss of export revenue occurred between 1986 and 1990. The countries eligible for the scheme were Bangladesh, Bhutan, Yemen, Haiti, Nepal and Burma, though the Burma scheme was later suspended for political reasons.

---

[4] Council Decision of 14 May 1996 Concerning the Conclusion of the Cooperation Agreement between the European Community and the Socialist Republic of Vietnam (96/351/EC), and Council Decision of 20 May 1996 regarding Nepal (96/354/EC).

[5] Bhutan and the Maldives.

[6] Building a Comprehensive Partnership with China: Communication from the Commission March 1998

The humanitarian aid received by ALA countries has been described earlier. Rehabilitation programmes have been a feature of aid to the ALA as the community recognises that the needs of refugees, returnees and demobilised soldiers may not be met by humanitarian or development aid alone. The framework for such assistance was clarified in a Council Regulation in March 1997, which stated that the Community will support projects for the subsistence and self-sufficiency of uprooted people and their reinsertion into the socio-economic fabric.[7] More specifically, operations will cover mine clearance, combating sexual violence, recovery of property, judicial review where human rights have been violated, and support to host communities into which refugees are integrated.

Project Aid

Social infrastructure and services is likely to remain a priority area for ALA cooperation. A Commission report of 1995 outlined how the EC's partnership with the Latin American region might develop between 1996 and 2000 emphasised the importance of *education and training*.[8] This is likely to build on the so-called ALFA programme of university exchanges (of students and know-how) between the EU and Latin America. Other schemes that are put forward include basic education, literacy, vocational training and technical education, with an emphasis on access for disadvantaged groups and on teacher training.

Rural development has been a growth sector in Asia and remains significant in Latin America. This is because the Community recognises that, despite considerable economic growth in the region in the 1990s, not all sections of the population have benefited from this.[9] Four priority areas have been identified: i) supporting effective and coherent economic and agricultural policies; ii) institutional strengthening of marketing organisations; iii) rural credit; and iv) technological innovation and increasing productivity. These are broad and ambitious objectives, and a 1994 Commission evaluation has indicated considerable difficulties in implementing EC rural development assistance policies in practice.[10]

A number of *decentralised programmes* of regional scope in Latin America form a distinct strand of community economic cooperation:

- AL-Invest and ECIP aim to increase mutual awareness among the bi-regional partners by establishing contact between businesses in the private sector, and eventually to boost trade and create joint ventures if possible (see Box 5.2);

Box 5.2 AL-invest

AL-invest aims to promote direct investment, joint ventures and strategic alliances between Latin America and European small and medium-sized enterprises. It seeks to achieve theses objectives through the setting up of a net of Eurocentros (European Business Cooperation Centres) in Latin America and a similar 'Coopecos' in Europe, together with the co-funding of periodical sectorial meetings. Over the 1995–2000 period 175 of such meetings have already taken place under the AL-INVEST umbrella with a total funding of 41m euro. In return, it is estimated that private enterprises on both sides of the Atlantic have generated business twice the value of the Commission's financial aid. The objective set for the 2000–04 period are as follows:

- the consolidation of the two networks of Eurocentros and Coopecos, in Latin America and Europe respectively;
- the realisation of 200 sectorial meetings scheduled to take place by 2004;
- the organisation of, at least, four AL-PARTENARIAT conferences;
- the promotion of 20 ARIEL projects aimed at assisting individually 500 SMEs to sign up joint ventures and other economic collaboration agreements

---

[7] Council Regulation (EC) No. 443/97 of 3 March 1997, on Operations to Aid Uprooted People in Asian and Latin American Developing Countries.

[8] Communication from the Commission to the Council and the European Parliament, *The European Union and Latin America: the present situation and prospects for closer partnership 1996–2000*, Brussels, 23.10.1995, COM(95) 495.

[9] See European Community DG IB, 1995, *La Coopération entre l'Union Europeene et l'Amérique Latine dans le domaine du Développement rural*.

[10] European Commission, 1994, *Evaulation Sectorielle: développement rural; note de synthèse*.

- ALFA is a programme of inter-university exchanges of students and research workers;
- URB-AL aims to encourage the exchange of experience among cities, regions and other administrative entities in areas such as local resource management, the rehabilitation of marginal or inner-city areas, the provision of social and health services, and operations against drug abuse. The programme was established in 1996 with a budget of nearly 22 m euro over four years;
- ALURE aims to assist with the drafting of energy policies and the restructuring of the energy sector (see Box 5.3).

> **Box 5.3: Energy aid in Latin America (ALURE)**
>
> The main objectives of the ALURE programme are to:
> i) support states in reforming energy policy and the institutional framework;
> ii) promote the distribution of natural gas;
> iii) use environmentally sound technologies;
> iv) support rural electrification initiatives providing energy to excluded groups;
> v) encourage the participation of the private sector.

The *energy sector* is seen as particularly important in Latin America as the region faces considerable challenges in its provision in view of the current and forecast rates of economic growth. The Community thus seeks to contribute to more efficient and rational energy use and to assist in the development of renewable energy resources.

Asia benefits from a similar investment scheme. Here the *Asia-Invest* programme promotes business linkages between the EU and Asia. The mechanisms for this include the Asia Enterprise and Partnership programme to co-finance EU-Asian business meetings; the Business Priming Fund, to support groups of European and Asian companies preparing for collaboration; and the Asia Invest Facility, which will fund research into investment opportunities in Asia. Asia-Invest has a budget of 45 m euro for 5 years.

Cross-cutting issues

Environment: Revised guidelines on ALA assistance drawn up in 1991 specifically require that environmental considerations be taken into account in all aid activities and that a portion of the cooperation budget be exclusively reserved for environmental measures. Thus, the environmental dimension went from being practically non-existent in bilateral agreements, to becoming one of the core features.[11] This is also mentioned in the Council Regulation of 1992 which states that cooperation with countries in Asia and Latin America has the long term aim of 'protection of the environment and natural resources, and sustainable development'.[12]

Gender: A number pilot countries were identified in 1996 for efforts on integrating gender issues. Reports from these pilot schemes are intended to lay the basis for a detailed gender action plan.

Poverty: Over the last few years poverty reduction has become a more explicit objective of EC development cooperation with all countries (see Chapter 2).

Coordination: In Asia considerable emphasis has been placed on coordinating EC aid with Member State aid as a means of increasing its impact and profile. Similarly, the Commission has recommended that the EC Latin America programme identify during the 1996–2000 period the priority areas for coordination with the EU Member States, and thereby increase the effectiveness and visibility of all EU cooperation.

---

[11] See *Europe Information*, DE 73, June 1992, 'Environment in Development: European Community Policy and Action', Brussels.

[12] Council Regulation EEC No 443/92 of 25 February 1992 on financial and technical assistance to, and cooperation with, the developing countries in Asia and Latin America.

Trade Cooperation

Asia: There are no regional or bilateral preferential agreements applicable to Asian developing countries. Asian countries are therefore covered by the GSP, which has been annually renewed since it was first created in 1971. The present revised scheme, more development oriented than the previous one, and of longer duration, applies to industrial products since January 1995, and to an enlarged list of agricultural products since January 1997. The new scheme provides for preferential tariffs modulated according to the sensitivity of products and for graduation of countries in the sectors where they have already reached a sufficient level of export penetration. It foresees the granting of additional preferences to countries applying certain International Labour Organisation conventions and standards laid down by the International Tropical Timber organisation.

Latin America: EU imports from LA in 1997 came to $38.1 bn and its exports to the region were worth $52.4 bn. The EU is the second-largest extra-regional trading partners for LA and the first for Mercosur. EU exports to LA have doubled in 10 years, but the structure of trade between the two regions remains traditional: EU imports mainly constitute raw material and European exports are predominately manufactured products.

The trade structure of the LA subcontinent is marked by the rise in power of strong regional groups, and by the aim of a vast free-trade are in the America for 2005 under the impetus of the US. The prospect of a new stage in trade relations between the EU and LA is being explored with the possibility of launching new negotiations in view of the liberalisation of mutual exchanges.

To encourage access to the European market by LA exports, especially those of less developed countries the EU has granted LA preferential conditions of access for industrial and agricultural products under the generalised system of preferences (GSP). This has been accompanied by special schemes for the Andean countries since 1990 and for Central America (for agricultural products) since 1992 to encourage them in their fight against drugs. In December 1998 this 'drug' GSP was extended to central American industrial products. However, this unilateral instrument of the Community, renewed for three years (until end 2001), is not permanent in nature. The decision as to whether to extend the GSP, or to amend it, lies with the members of the EU.

6

EC External Cooperation with Central and Eastern Europe

Trends and Distribution of EC Cooperation with the CEECs

Although there were occasional and small flows to a number of Central and East European countries (CEECs) in the 1980s, the start of the Phare programme in 1990 marks the beginning of significant EC cooperation with the region (see Table 6.1). In the 1990s the vast bulk (75%) of EC cooperation was provided by Phare, though three other sources have also been significant.

Commitments to the CEECs increased very rapidly from nearly 700 m euro in 1990 to 1.5 bn euro in 1993 and then levelled off. The fact that EC *disbursements* also grew very rapidly from 1990, reaching a new height of nearly 2 bn euro in 1998, underlines the responsiveness of the Phare programme to the increasing political and hence financial demands that were made on it over this period (see Figure 6.1).

**Figure 6.1: EC Cooperation with CEECs
(1989– 98, commitments and disbursements, m euro)**

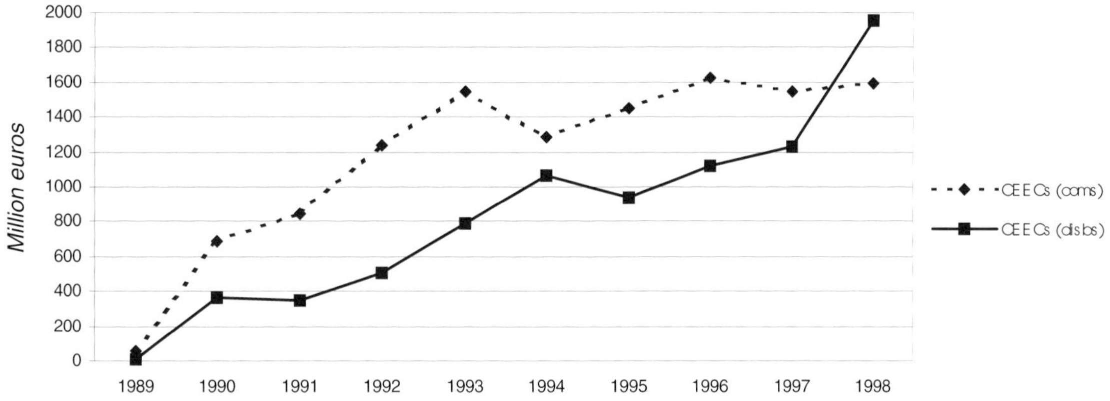

Source: European Commission/ODI database 1999

Recipients of EC External Cooperation with the CEECs

The countries that used to form Yugoslavia are the main recipients of EC cooperation to the CEECs, with ex-Yugoslavia[1] receiving 14%, and Bosnia-Herzegovina a further 11% for the period 1996– 98 (see Table 6.2). The top five recipients (being the two countries above plus Poland 13%; Romania 8%; Bulgaria 6%) jointly received just over half of total flows over the 1996– 98 period. This is down from 59% during 1990– 95. However when interpreting these figures it should be

---

[1] It is often difficult from the available data to identify which countries are concerned when the former Yugoslavia is referred to. Where the data does allow this detail, the sum is allocated to the specific country. Otherwise it is included under the heading Yugoslavia (ex).

Table 6.1: Top 10 Recipients of EC Cooperation with the CEECs
(1990– 95 and 1996– 98, % total cooperation)

1990– 1995		1996– 1998	
Yugoslavia (ex)	18.3	Yugoslavia (ex)	13.7
Poland	16.9	Poland	12.5
Romania	8.6	Bosnia-Herzegovina	11.3
Hungary	8.3	Romania	7.9
Bulgaria	6.8	Bulgaria	6.0
Albania	6.5	Hungary	6.0
Czechoslovakia (ex)	3.3	Albania	4.4
Czech Republic	3.3	Czech Republic	3.7
Slovenia	2.3	Macedonia	3.3
Lithuania	1.8	Lithuania	3.1
Top 10:% of total CEEC	**76.0**	**Top 10:% of total CEEC**	**71.9**

Source: European Commission/ODI database 1999

remembered that the sums that would formerly have all been recorded as going to ex-Yugoslavia are increasingly instead being recorded as allocations to specific countries: Bosnia and Herzegovina, Croatia, Macedonia, Serbia and Montenegro and Slovenia. This has the automatic effect of making the cooperation appear less concentrated in the latter time period.

Table 6.2: Regional Distribution of EC Cooperation with CEECs
(1986– 98, commitments and disbursements, m euro)

	1986	1987	1988	1989	1990	1991	1992	1993	1994	1995	1996	1997	1998	Total
Commitments														
Total	–	2	1	52	683	845	1238	1541	1281	1446	1618	1541	1587	11835
CEECs	–	2	1	44	409	683	1059	1358	1065	1096	1329	1195	1356	9599
Regional	–	–	–	7	274	162	180	183	216	349	285	327	213	2195
Unallocable	–	–	–	–	–	–	–	–	–	1	4	19	17	41
Disbursements														
Total	3	0	0	12	360	348	501	789	1063	941	1118	1226	1951	8312
CEECs	3	–	–	4	110	249	435	550	645	800	990	1058	1642	6495
Regional	–	–	–	7	250	99	66	73	101	141	7	0	–	738
Unallocable	–	–	–	–	–	–	–	165	317	–	120	169	309	1080

Source: European Commission/ODI database 1999

Sectoral Distribution of EC External Cooperation with the CEECs

The Phare programme was created with two overriding objectives in mind: to consolidate the reform process of the economies in transition, and to promote the closer integration of CEECs with the European Union. Phare assistance, therefore, bears only limited resemblance to what is usually understood by the term development aid. As a result Phare activities are not readily classifiable according to 'traditional' development cooperation categories, including the ODI categorisation which is based on DAC codes. To take account of this, the largest programme, Phare, is broken down according to sectors used by the Phare programme itself. However, cooperation with the CEECs is also categorised according to the instruments and sectors used elsewhere in this study in order to allow some comparison to be made with flows to other regions.

The Phare programme has given particular emphasis to co-financing infrastructure, in line with the decision of the Essen Council that improving infrastructure is a major element in preparing the CEECs for accession to the European Union (see Table 6.3). The aim is both to improve physical links and to promote economic growth.

Phare sectors which do not readily fit into the ODI/DAC classification are those of public administration reform, consumer protection, and harmonisation of legislation, and are reflected in Table 6.3. The Essen strategy stresses the importance of preparing countries to join the EU internal market, which involves the adoption and implementation of a body of legislation and practices known as the 'acquis communautaire'. Phare cooperation seeks to facilitate this by supporting the necessary reform in the public administrations of Central and East European countries by providing know-how to strengthen their administrative capacity, and by funding programmes in all Phare countries to develop and harmonise legislation.

Table 6.3: Sectoral Allocation of the Phare Programme (commitments, m euro)

	1990	1991	1992	1993	1994	1995	1996	1997	Total
Infrastructure (Energy, Transport, Telecom)	7	42	97	115	326	457	424	371	1045
Private Sector, Restructuring, Privatisation	64	181	192	195	93	139	186	159	863
Education, Training & Research	37	90	141	162	170	147	126	94	746
Multisector/Other	27	56	135	181	56	88	77	88	543
Environment & Nuclear Safety	103	93	90	39	78	82	56	76	483
Agricultural Restructuring	136	89	80	79	17	41	28	32	441
Humanitarian, Food & Critical Aid	102	71	120	45	30	25	125	20	393
Financial Sector	7	40	45	61	56	41	–	–	249
Administration & Public Institutions	10	27	25	66	82	25	159	199	234
Social Development & Employment	3	36	48	15	29	47	18	88	178
Public Health	–	45	15	27	13	2	–	–	102
Integrated Regional Measures	–	4	17	10	4	47	–	–	82
Civil Society & Democratisation (incl. NGOs)	–	1	9	10	16	10	24	20	46
Consumer Protection	–	–	–	5	4	2	–	–	11
Harmonisation of Legislation	–	–	–	–	–	2	–	–	2
TOTAL	**495**	**774**	**1012**	**1008**	**973**	**1155**	**1223**	**1147**	**5418**

Note: The most recent Phare annual reports contain a slightly different sectoral classification, which may explain apparently zero figures for 1996 and 1997 for some sectors.

Source: European Commission: Phare Annual Report 1997

Table 6.4 and Figure 6.2 reflect the ODI/DAC categorisation. From this it can be seen that cooperation with CEECs prioritises *economic infrastructure*, representing 29% (1990–98), with over half of this concentrated in transport and communications.

Phare has provided over 300 m euro for the development of small and medium-sized industries, given their perceived role in job creation, mobilising investment and spreading the enterprise culture. Banking sector reform, the break up of central monopoly banks and the creation of central and commercial banks, have also been supported. The value of EC cooperation in the economic infrastructure sector cannot be measured by the gross volume alone, since although it may finance only a small percentage of a project's final costs it may fill the gap between the amount that international financing institutions can lend and the contribution provided from government.

Humanitarian assistance ranked close second at 22% of commitments, 54% of this funded by ECHO. Up till 1995 a further 40% was funded by Phare. From 1996– 98 the Obnova programme has funded 53% of humanitarian assistance, with the Phare contribution dropping to 2%. The countries of the former Yugoslavia taken together, took 88% of humanitarian aid commitments. The remaining 12% was designed to meet basic human needs at a time when enormous economic and social transition brought deprivation to sections of the CEEC population, most notably in Albania and Romania.

Table 6.4: Sectoral Allocation of EC Cooperation with CEECs
(1987–98, commitments, m euro and share, %)

VOLUME OF COMMITMENTS, m euro	1987	1988	1989	1990	1991	1992	1993	1994	1995	1996	1997	1998	Total
Programme Aid	–	–	–	–	–	–	–	–	–	–	10	–	10
Food Aid (development)	–	–	43	183	63	64	94	8	–	–	–	–	456
Humanitarian Aid	2	–	8	105	80	282	441	310	272	294	432	383	2608
Humanitarian Aid excl rehabilitation	2	–	8	105	80	282	441	307	267	190	185	137	2003
Rehabilitation	–	–	–	–	–	–	–	3	4	105	247	246	606
Aid to NGOs	–	–	–	–	3	8	25	21	32	10	0	0	100
Natural Resources Productive Sectors	–	–	–	136	89	80	79	18	45	28	23	33	529
Agriculture	–	–	–	136	89	80	79	18	45	28	23	33	529
Other Productive Sectors	0	–	–	1	–	5	8	2	9	2	35	–	62
Industry, Mining & Construct	–	–	–	1	–	5	–	–	8	–	35	–	50
Trade	0	–	–	0	–	0	8	2	1	2	–	–	11
Economic Infrastructure & Services	–	–	–	77	278	332	389	426	496	569	326	525	3416
Transport, Coms & Energy	–	–	–	6	57	100	129	272	314	445	227	395	1945
Banking, Finan & Bus Srvs	–	–	–	71	221	232	261	153	182	124	99	130	1471
Social Infrastructure & Services	–	–	–	40	170	196	193	216	193	153	159	85	1404
Education	–	–	–	37	90	141	162	170	147	110	82	49	988
Health & Population	–	–	–	–	45	17	27	13	3	–	11	–	115
Water Supply	–	–	–	–	–	–	–	7	26	10	6	–	48
Other Soc Infra & Srvs	–	–	–	3	36	39	4	27	17	33	60	36	254
Governance & Civil Society	–	–	–	10	27	26	66	82	26	212	221	271	940
Multisector/Crosscutting	–	0	–	130	131	197	183	140	172	80	23	81	1136
Environment	–	0	–	103	78	62	17	89	96	49	22	80	594
Other Multisector	–	–	–	27	54	135	166	51	77	31	–	1	541
Unallocable by Sector	–	1	1	1	5	49	64	59	202	271	313	209	1174
CEECs total	2	1	52	683	845	1238	1541	1281	1446	1618	1541	1587	11836

SHARE (%)	1987	1988	1989	1990	1991	1992	1993	1994	1995	1996	1997	1998	Total
Programme Aid	–	–	–	–	–	–	–	–	–	–	0.6	–	0.1
Food Aid (development)	–	–	83.3	26.9	7.5	5.2	6.1	0.6	–	–	–	–	3.8
Humanitarian Aid	98.4	–	15.2	15.3	9.4	22.8	28.6	24.2	18.8	18.2	28.0	24.2	22.0
Humanitarian Aid excl rehabilitation	98.4	–	15.2	15.3	9.4	22.8	28.6	24.0	18.5	11.7	12.0	8.6	16.9
Rehabilitation	–	–	–	–	–	–	–	0.2	0.3	6.5	16.0	15.5	5.1
Aid to NGOs	–	–	–	–	0.4	0.7	1.6	1.6	2.2	0.6	–	–	0.8
Natural Resources Productive Sectors	–	–	–	19.9	10.5	6.5	5.1	1.4	3.1	1.7	1.5	2.1	4.5
Agriculture	–	–	–	19.9	10.5	6.5	5.1	1.4	3.1	1.7	1.5	2.1	4.5
Other Productive Sectors	0.2	–	–	0.2	–	0.4	0.5	0.2	0.6	0.1	2.3	–	0.5
Industry, Mining & Construct	–	–	–	0.2	–	0.4	–	–	0.6	–	2.3	–	0.4
Trade	0.2	–	–	–	–	–	0.5	0.2	0.1	–	–	–	0.1
Economic Infrastructure & Services	–	–	–	11.3	32.8	26.8	25.3	33.2	34.3	35.2	21.1	33.1	28.9
Transport, Coms & Energy	–	–	–	0.9	6.7	8.1	8.4	21.3	21.7	27.5	14.7	24.9	16.4
Banking, Finan & Bus Srvs	–	–	–	10.4	26.1	18.7	16.9	12.0	12.6	7.6	6.4	8.2	12.4
Social Infrastructure & Services	–	–	–	5.8	20.2	15.8	12.5	16.9	13.3	9.5	10.3	5.4	11.9
Education	–	–	–	5.4	10.6	11.3	10.5	13.3	10.2	6.8	5.3	3.1	8.3
Health & Population	–	–	–	–	5.3	1.3	1.7	1.0	0.2	–	0.7	–	1.0
Water Supply	–	–	–	–	–	–	–	0.5	1.8	0.6	0.4	–	0.4
Other Soc Infra & Srvs	–	–	–	0.4	4.2	3.2	0.3	2.1	1.1	2.1	3.9	2.3	2.1
Governance & Civil Society	–	–	–	1.5	3.1	2.1	4.3	6.4	1.8	13.1	14.4	17.0	7.9
Multisector/Crosscutting	–	19.8	–	19.0	15.5	15.9	11.9	10.9	11.9	4.9	1.5	5.1	9.6
Environment	–	19.8	–	15.0	9.2	5.0	1.1	6.9	6.6	3.0	1.5	5.0	5.0
Other Multisector	–	–	–	4.0	6.3	10.9	10.8	3.9	5.3	–	–	0.1	4.6
Unallocable by Sector	1.4	80.2	1.4	0.1	0.6	4.0	4.2	4.6	14.0	16.7	20.3	13.2	9.9
CEECs total	100	100	100	100	100	100	100	100	100	100	100	100	100

Source: European Commission/ODI database 1999

Social infrastructure and services (principally education) also emerges as a major sector, as is clearly shown in Figure 6.2. The social infrastructure and governance sectors are probably best considered as a whole, since much of the assistance in these two sectors does not concern traditional support to primary or secondary schooling or even tertiary education, but covers technical assistance designed to strengthen public administration, harmonise standards or reform legal systems, for example, though there has been some support for primary health and preventative care. To this end Phare contains a *'democracy programme'*, based on an initiative of the European Parliament which became operational in 1994. The Phare Democracy programme, worth 15 m euro in 1998, seeks to strengthen civil society and democracy, mainly through supporting non-governmental organisations.

The countries supported under Phare also benefit from the Tempus programme, which works to develop and restructure higher education institution. This is approached through Joint European Projects, whereby higher education institutions from two or three EU Member States cooperate with similar institutions from the CEECs to adapt teaching methods and degrees to the needs of the market.

The new phase of the Tempus programme for the years 2000 to 2006 will however exclusively target the non-associated Phare countries eligible for Tempus support (in 1999: Albania, Bosnia-Herzegovina and Former Yugoslav Republic of Macedonia) and the 13 countries supported under TACIS. The associated countries will no longer be eligible for Tempus support as they have joined the Community programme in the areas of education, training and youth, in the context of the pre-accession strategy.

Phare social programmes also include significant support for the fight against *drugs*, which seeks to control illegal trafficking and money-laundering, and demand-reduction. Phare has worked with central and local governments to seek to provide adequate social protection during the period of economic reform. Technical assistance has been provided in the areas of employment policy, pension reform and retraining schemes for the unemployed, among others.

Table 6.4 indicates that Phare provides significant resources in support of *environmental* objectives (some 5% of all cooperation with the CEECs between 1990 and 1998). Initially, Phare funded interventions in a somewhat *ad hoc* manner, supplying equipment to monitor air and water pollution, and funding studies of specific problems. More recently a more strategic approach has been developed, including policies for specific sectors such as waste treatment.

Phare has also financed *NGO* activities, though much of this has been for Commission-directed activities counting as cooperation *through* rather than *to* NGOs, and is therefore not identified separately in this analysis. Commission estimates indicate that EC commitments to NGOs reached some 500 NGOs in the CEECs and NIS or European NGOs operating in these regions. Table 6.4 reveals that some 100 m euro of EC cooperation with the CEECs was committed *to* NGOs, mainly in the areas of civil society and democratisation. Emphasis has been placed on promoting NGOs working in the social sector with disadvantaged groups, as well as on developing exchanges and cooperation between sister organisations from different Phare countries, or with NGOs based in EU countries. The main source of funding for NGO activities in Phare countries is through the so-called 'Lien Programme' (Link Inter European NGOs).

A programme has also been developed to facilitate productive *investment* in the CEECs, particularly through the creation and development of joint ventures. A network of financial intermediaries provides the link between the European Commission and the beneficiaries. Over 120 m euro were allocated to its programme between 1991 and 1995. With respect to small and medium-sized businesses, Phare assistance is designed to reduce investment risks, thereby obtaining a multiplier effect which unlocks funds from other sources.

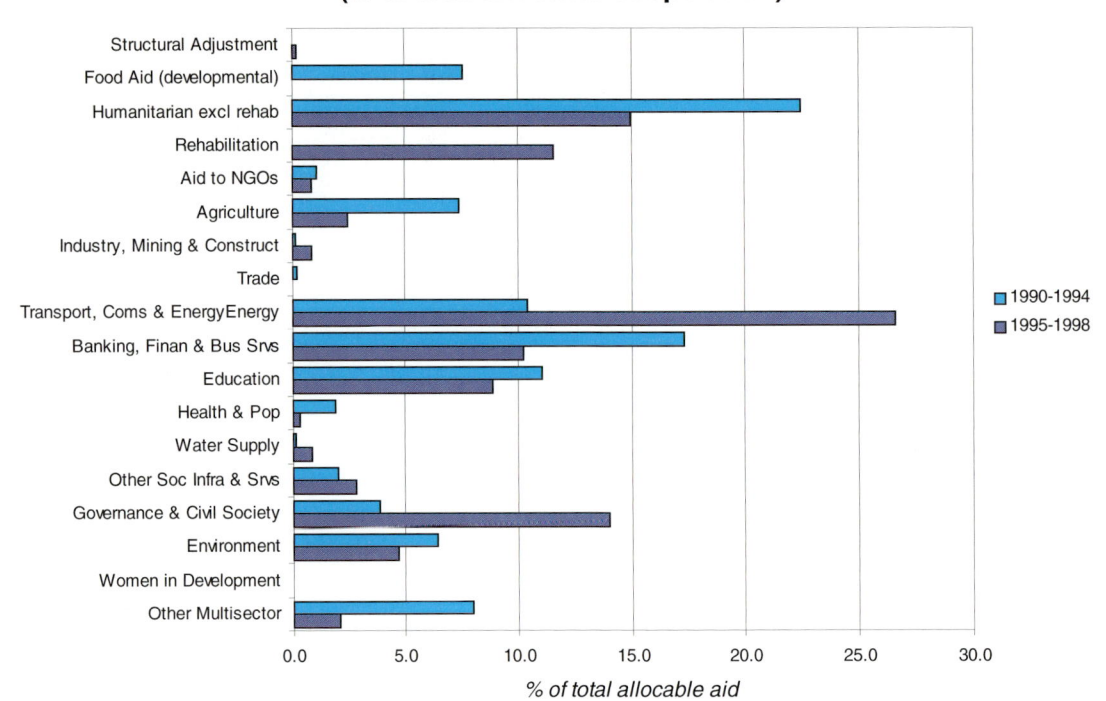

Figure 6.2: Sectoral Allocation of EC cooperation with CEECs 1990–98 (% of total allocable cooperation)

Source: European Commission/ODI database 1999

Table 6.1 indicates the importance of multi-country or intra-regional cooperation which since 1989 has varied between 12 and 40% of funds committed. Most of this (about 75% in 1994) formed part of Phare's cross-border programme, which seeks to promote regional integration through the development of infrastructure, principally transport, utilities, environment, economic development and human resources. Multi-country programmes have also financed nuclear safety, the fight against the illegal drug trade, customs and transit modernisation, and telecommunications. The scope of these programmes reflects the emphasis of the Essen strategy not only on developing closer economic ties but also in safeguarding democratic reform. Phare is in line with the Pact on Stability in Europe, signed in Paris in March 1995, which backed 'good neighbourliness' between the countries of eastern and western Europe.

Sources of EC Cooperation with the CEECs

As can be seen from Table 6.5, the vast majority of cooperation with the CEECs comes from the Phare budget line, though three other sources have also been significant. For the years 1990 to 1994 food aid funded through the European Agricultural Guidance and Guarantee Fund (EAGGF), represented 6% of flows to the region. From 1993 large flows of humanitarian aid managed by ECHO totalling some 1400 m euro have gone almost exclusively to the former republics of Yugoslavia (see Table 6.2). In addition the Obnova programme for reconstruction in former Yugoslavia has committed 587 m euro for the three years from 1996.

Table 6.5: Sources of EC Cooperation with the CEECs (1990–98[a], commitments, m euro)

	1990	1991	1992	1993	1994	1995	1996	1997	1998	Total
CEECs Commitments:	683	845	1238	1588	1294	1446	1618	1541	1587	11840
Phare Programme	495	774	1012	1008	973	1155	1249	1073	1132	8871
Obnova Programme	–	–	–	–	–	–	98	247	243	588
Humanitarian Aid through ECHO	–	–	–	396	272	237	189	165	137	1396
ex-republics of Yugoslavia	–	–	–	395	269	235	187	133	123	1342
EAGGF	183	63	64	94	8	0	–	–	–	412
Regional	183	53	20	–	–	–	–	–	–	256
Albania	–	–	44	75	5	–	–	–	–	124
ex-republics of Yugoslavia	–	–	–	19	3	–	–	–	–	22
EIB[b]	–	–	–	47	–	32	135	1376	200	1743
CEEC Disbursements:	360	348	501	836	1076	941	1118	1226	1951	8357
Phare Programme	171	284	436	521	723	762	804	782	972	5455
Obnova Programme	–	–	–	–	–	–	13	42	122	177
Humanitarian Aid through ECHO	–	–	–	166	317	168	163	194	156	1164
EAGGF	183	53	54	94	8	0	–	–	–	392
EIB	–	–	–	47	–	32	98	203	693	1073

a Commitments to the CEECs totalled 55 m euro (1986–89).
b The precise amounts which qualify as OA for 1996-98 could not be determined, and thus only a portion are included in the overall total for commitments to the CEECs.

Source: European Commission/ODI database 1999

Policy and Objectives

Phare's aim is twofold: for the ten countries that have applied to join the EU[2], it is to prepare them for accession. For the other three countries, Phare's aim is to support their transition to democracy and a market economy.

Phare has formally adopted guidelines for 1998–99 which apply to all programmes. These indicate that Phare will focus on two main priorities: institution building and investment support. A range of measures and mechanisms was foreseen in both these areas. Preparations for twinning, a key instrument of institution building, got under way during 1998, while the Large-Scale Infrastructure Facility, a new investment support mechanism, was also launched during the year.

Enlargement

The formal launch of the accession process was in 1998 with the adoption of the Accession Partnerships which set out the priorities to be tackled in preparation for membership and the framework for all pre-accession assistance. This enlargement is a comprehensive, inclusive and ongoing process. Each of the applicant states will proceed at its own pace, depending on its degree of preparedness.

The enlargement process has three components:

1) The European Conference
The European Conference provides a multilateral framework which brings together all the countries that wish to accede to the Union and share its values and aims. The fifteen Member States of the EU and twelve candidate countries are invited to the Conference, which met first in London on 12 March 1998.

2) The Accession Process
On 30 March 1998, the accession process, comprising the ten central and eastern European

---

[2] Hungary, Poland, Romania, Slovakia, Latvia, Estonia, Lithuania, Bulgaria, the Czech Republic and Slovenia.

countries plus Cyprus, was launched. It involves the reinforcement of the Pre-Accession Strategy, which will enable the applicant countries to align themselves as far as possible on the 'acquis' (the body of EC legislation) of the Union before accession.

A key element of the reinforced Pre-Accession Strategy is the Accession Partnerships which have been drawn up for the ten central and eastern European countries setting out a series of short- and medium-term priorities for further work in preparing for accession. They are designed to mobilise all forms of assistance to the countries of central Europe in a single framework. In response to the Accession Partnership, each candidate country has prepared a National Programme for the Adoption of the Acquis, which sets out the ways in which the priorities of the Accession Partnership will be implemented, including timetables and human and financial resource allocations. They are updated regularly.

A second element is the proposed doubling of financial cooperation targeted on accession priorities. The financial assistance will come from a reoriented Phare Programme, new programmes for environment and transport as well as agricultural and rural development. For those countries not yet ready for the opening of negotiations, an additional 'catch-up facility' has been set up. A wide range of Community programmes will be progressively opened to candidates, covering such fields as education and training, environment, customs and taxation, research and culture, which will help accustom many different groups in the candidate countries to the working methods of the EU.

3) Accession Negotiations
Negotiations were launched on 31 March 1998 with the six countries recommended by the Commission (Hungary, Poland, Estonia, the Czech Republic, Slovenia, Cyprus). Negotiations with these countries are being conducted in bilateral accession conferences between the Member States and each of the applicants. Since then, and at the 1999 Helsinki Summit, it was decided to give equal opportunity to apply for accession to the other Central and Eastern European Countries, recognising that each would need to proceed at its own pace.

Future directions: Phare, ISPA and SAPARD

Phare will continue beyond 2000, and will be complemented by two new pre-accession instruments, called ISPA and SAPARD. Investments in major transport and environmental infrastructure will be financed from ISPA, and those in agriculture and rural development from SAPARD. In November 1998 the Council approved in principle the Regulations on these two instruments and a coordination Regulation. The latter ensures coherence between the three instruments; it stipulates that Phare, ISPA and SAPARD should be coordinated within the framework of the Phare Management Committee.

Pre-accession cooperation will more than double after 2000, to over 3 bn euro per year (1.5 bn euro for Phare, 1 bn euro for ISPA, and 520 m euro for SAPARD).

Preparations for ISPA were supported during 1998, under the Large-Scale Infrastructure Facility, while the Special Preparatory Programme (see Box 6.1), a component of the national programmes, was continued to assist the candidates in setting up the structures and policies for eventual participation in the Structural Funds.

Box 6.1: Special Preparatory Programme

After accession, the candidate countries will be eligible for support from the EU Structural Funds. To help ensure a smooth transition to the new system, the Special Preparatory Programme was set up. This programme aims to help the candidate countries put in place the institutions and strategies necessary for the successful implementation of activities financed from the Structural Funds after accession. The Special Preparatory Programme should prepare the candidate countries to design and implement programmes similar to those in EU Objective 1 regions.

Cooperation Instruments

Phare has recently been reorientated from a 'demand-driven' programme (in which the partner countries requested funding for priorities which they established) to an 'accession-driven' programme based on the Accession Partnerships.

Within this two clear priorities have been fixed: institution building and investment support. These two priorities were set out in the 'Guidelines for Phare programme implementation in candidate countries, 1998–1999', which were adopted in June 1998 and cover the Phare budgets for 1998 and 1999.

Institution building

Institution building covers a number of areas such as twinning, participation in Community programmes and technical assistance (see Box 6.2). It involves programmes such as Leonardo da Vinci, Youth for Europe, Raphael, Media, Save, Life, Combating cancer, Equal opportunities, SMEs, Tempus. The candidate countries were also given the possibility to become fully associated with the Fifth Research and Development Framework Programme (1998–2002).

Investment support

Adoption of the 'acquis communautaire' not only means approximating legislation and strengthening institutional and administrative structures. It also means adapting infrastructures and enterprises in the candidate countries to meet EC standards, which requires considerable investment. Accounting for around 70 per cent of the Phare budget in the candidate countries, investment support thus entails mobilising the investments needed to help the candidate countries bring their industries and major infrastructure up to EC standards.

> **Box 6.2: Twinning**
>
> The aim of twinning is to make available the expertise of Member State practitioners to help the candidate countries implement the acquis. The core of twinning is the secondment of EU practitioners, known as Pre-Accession Advisors, to the institutions in the candidate countries responsible for implementing the acquis.
>
> At the very end of 1997 the Commission took the first steps to launch twinning. A network of National Contact Points was established to work with the Commission in the twinning process.
>
> In 1998 the twinning projects under development focused on the same four key areas of the acquis in each candidate country: agriculture, environment, finance, and justice and home affairs. The candidates had the option of including an additional area to meet individual needs. Preparatory measures for the implementation of the Structural Funds was added as a topic later in the year.

Alongside continued support under the Phare national programmes in the areas of transport, energy and environment, Phare's investment support activities focused on three new areas in 1998:

- increased coordination with the international financial institutions
- the launch of the Large-Scale Infrastructure Facility
- Preparation for the Instrument for Structural Pre-Accession Assistance (ISPA).

Evaluations of the Phare Programme

In response to the Commission's Sound and Efficient Management initiative (SEM 2000), DG IA set up an Evaluation Unit for the Phare, Tacis and Obnova Programmes in January 1997. Mid-1998, this Unit has been integrated into the SCR Evaluation Unit.

Within the framework of the Phare Programme, the Evaluation Unit has undertaken the following types of evaluations: sectoral evaluations, to provide input for policy and strategy development; country evaluations, to provide inputs for the annual planning exercise; and evaluations of Phare cooperation instruments, to provide input for the future revision of the Phare Regulation as well as for the Accession process.

7

EC External Cooperation with the New Independent States

Trends and Distribution of EC Cooperation with the NIS

Significant EC aid commitments to the New Independent States began with the establishment of the Tacis programme in 1991 which has contributed 67% of all commitments since then. The NIS have also received significant flows of food aid since 1990 funded by the Aid flows through the European Agricultural Guidance and Guarantee Fund (EAGGF), and from 1993 large flows of humanitarian aid managed by ECHO (see Table 7.2).

Figure 7.1 shows the evolution of aid to the NIS. Tacis commitments increased quite rapidly, but for the first years disbursements lagged considerably behind. The implementation performance of the Tacis programme, particularly its disbursement rate, has come under heavy criticism. Procedures have been simplified and internal coordination improved since 1996, resulting in a marked increase in the number of contracts agreed for projects. This is reflected in the improved disbursement rates revealed in Figure 7.1.

In order to promote cooperation between the New Independent States, which are closely interdependent, multi-country and regional programmes are an important aspect of the Tacis programme. Such aid represents close to one-third of all commitments.

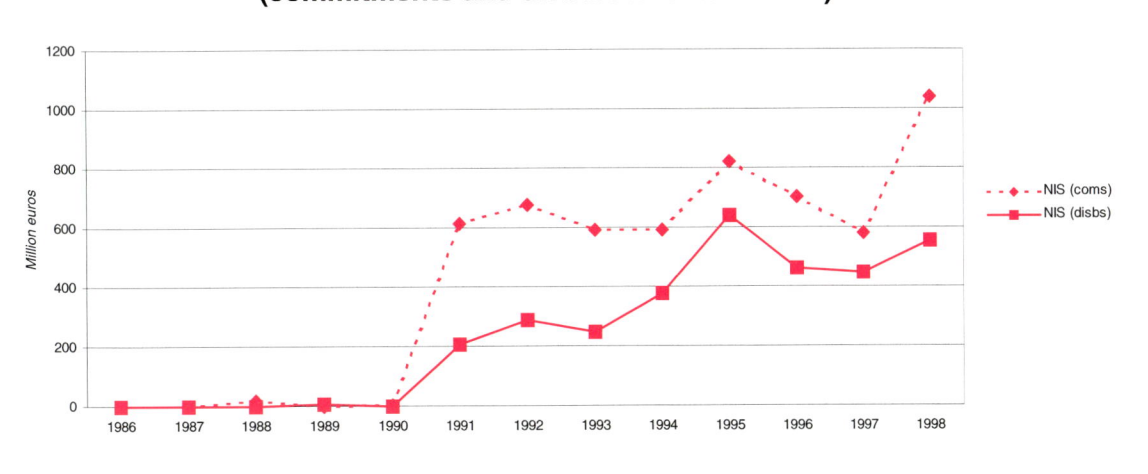

Figure 7.1: EC Cooperation with the NIS: Tacis dates from 1991 (commitments and disbursements m euro)

Source: European Commission/ODI database 1999

Recipients of EC External Cooperation with the NIS

Table 7.2 reveals that aid to the NIS is heavily concentrated in a limited number of countries. One-third of all aid went to Russia, 9% to Ukraine, while one third went to regional programmes for the 1996–98 period. This is partially explained by the fact that Russia has 52% of the NIS population and Ukraine a further 19%. Population is one of the criteria stated as determining Tacis aid flows, the others are gross domestic product, commitment to reform process, and the success of earlier programmes in the respective countries.

Table 7.1: Regional Distribution of EC Aid to the NIS (m euro)

	1986	1987	1988	1989	1990	1991	1992	1993	1994	1995	1996	1997	1998	Total
Commitments														
Total	0	0	20	0	5	615	679	592	593	821	702	583	1041	5652
NIS countries	–	–	20	–	5	503	531	366	389	410	481	308	802	3815
Regional	–	–	–	–	–	106	109	194	149	335	218	269	234	1614
Unallocable	–	–	–	–	–	6	39	32	56	76	3	6	4	222
Disbursements [a]														
Total	–	0	0	6	0	209	289	248	377	642	462	449	555	3237
NIS countries	–	–	–	6	–	208	258	87	132	290	374	250	315	1922
Regional	–	–	–	–	–	–	–	9	63	254	–	–	–	325
Unallocable	–	–	–	–	0	0	31	152	182	98	88	199	240	990

[a] It appears that some of the unallocable disbursements for 1996-98 are for regional aid, but the data we have received does not allow us to differentiate this.

Source: European Commission/ODI database 1999

Sectoral Distribution of EC External Cooperation with the NIS

Table 7.3 and Figure 7.2 show the sectoral breakdown of the programme and how this has altered over time. These illustrate that Tacis's main objective is to support transition to market economy and democracy. Therefore an important part of cooperation concern the reform of existing economic structures and the creation of new ones.

The primary sector is *economic infrastructure*, representing 30% of commitments for 1986–98. Of this, over 60% is allocated to energy (including nuclear safety) projects and programmes which dominate the programme (see Figure 7.2). Since 1995 Tacis allocated over 340 m euro to its nuclear safety programme, to improve the safety of nuclear plants and waste management, to strengthen the regulatory framework, and to promote regional cooperation on nuclear safety among countries operating Soviet-built reactors.

Table 7.2: Top 10 Recipients of EC Cooperation with the NIS (1990-95 and 1996-98, commitments, % total aid)

1990–1995		1996–1998	
Russian Federation	26.0	Russian Federation	34.0
Soviet Union (former)	15.5	Ukraine	9.8
Ukraine	6.3	Georgia	5.4
Baltic States	3.1	Azerbaijan	5.2
Kazakhstan	2.4	Armenia	3.8
Azerbaijan	2.2	Tajikistan	3.2
Georgia	2.2	Kyrgyz Rep.	2.0
Armenia	2.1	Uzbekistan	2.0
Belarus	1.7	Kazakhstan	0.9
Uzbekistan	1.3	Mongolia	0.7
Top 10:% of total NIS	62.9	Top 10:% of total NIS	98.1

Source: European Commission/ODI database 1999

Food aid is the next most significant sector for the NIS with commitments of nearly 1.3 bn euro since 1991, or 22% of the programme, though much of this was provided out of the European Agricultural Guidance and Guarantee Fund, rather than from the main external cooperation budget lines (see Tables 7.3 and 7.4). In 1998, in response to the Russian crisis, the Russian Federation received a commitment of 400 m euro (from EAGGF), with the aim of allowing scarce budget resources to used for outstanding wages and pensions instead of for importing food at commercial rates.

Social infrastructure and services (principally education) also emerges as a major sector within Tacis, however Figure 7.2 shows that commitments to education have dropped for the period 1995–98 as compared to 1990–94 (5% as opposed to 12% of allocable aid). The social infrastructure and governance sectors are probably best considered as a whole, since much of the assistance in these two sectors does two sectors does not concern traditional support to primary or secondary schooling or even tertiary education.[1] Much of this support covers technical assistance designed to strengthen public administration, harmonise standards or reform legal systems, for example, though there has been some support for primary health and preventative care. In addition Tacis, like Phare, contains a '*democracy programme*', based on an initiative of the European Parliament which became operational in 1994. The Tacis Democracy programme has operated in the NIS since 1992. It has concentrated on the transfer of parliamentary mechanisms and know-how to politicians on the strengthening of NGOs, and the transfer of skills to professional groups on democratic practices.

Humanitarian assistance ranked fourth for the NIS, totalling 482 m euro or 9% for 1991–98. This was mainly through ECHO which provided 85% of this.

Tacis established an Environmental Support Facility in 1994, which aims to fund short-term, high-profile and replicable environmental projects. The fact that environmental assistance does not feature in Tacis data before 1996 results from the statistical categorisation employed by Tacis, since in 1995 Tacis committed 12 m euro to environmental interventions, notably assisting the development of national environmental strategies and developing an inter-state capacity to tackle the environmental problems in the Caspian Sea.

Tacis has also financed *NGO* activities. Commission estimates indicate that EC aid to NGOs reached some 500 NGOs in the CEECs and NIS or European NGOs operating in these regions. The main source of funding for NGO activities in Phare and Tacis countries is through the so-called 'Lien Programme' (Link Inter-European NGOs). In addition, considerable amounts of aid have been channelled through NGOs in the form of activities initiated by the Commission and executed by NGOs. These activities are not identified separately in this analysis.

Programme Aid includes, for the first time in 199, 18 m euro provided to Armenia and Georgia from a new budget line (B7–531) for macro-economic assistance to the NIS. This included a mix of budgetary grants and long-term loans.

---

[1] Tacis countries do, however, benefit from the Tempus programme, which committed nearly 50 m euro over the 1993-95 period to develop and restructure higher education institutions in the NIS. This is approached through Joint European Projects, in which higher education institutions from two or three EU Member States cooperate with similar institutions from the NIS to adapt teaching methods and degrees to the needs of the market.

Table 7.3: Sectoral Allocation of EC Cooperation with the NIS (1986-98, commitments, m euro and share, %)

VOLUME OF COMMITMENTS, m euro	1986	1987	1988	1989	1990	1991	1992	1993	1994	1995	1996	1997	1998	Total
Programme Aid	–	–	–	–	–	–	–	–	–	–	–	22	64	86
Food Aid (development)	–	–	–	–	–	207	254	64	29	167	112	35	400	1269
Humanitarian Aid	–	–	19	–	5	11	4	75	92	137	54	36	49	482
Humanitarian Aid excl rehabilitation	–	–	19	–	5	11	4	75	92	137	54	36	39	473
Aid to NGOs	–	–	0	0	0	–	–	0	0	1	0	1	3	6
Natural Resources Productive Sectors	–	–	–	–	–	80	63	32	42	51	6	10	6	290
Agriculture	–	–	–	–	–	80	63	32	42	51	6	10	6	290
Other Productive Sectors	–	–	–	–	–	–	18	15	16	8	58	65	82	261
Industry, Mining & Construct	–	–	–	–	–	–	18	15	16	8	58	65	82	261
Economic Infrastructure & Services	–	–	–	–	–	205	206	248	220	218	211	182	187	1677
Transport & Communications	–	–	–	–	–	50	40	39	27	29	20	39	41	284
Energy	–	–	–	–	–	118	119	138	141	152	149	108	123	1048
Banking, Finan & Bus Srvs	–	–	–	–	–	38	47	71	52	37	33	24	23	325
Social Infrastructure & Services	–	–	–	–	–	103	42	80	60	99	48	65	110	607
Education	–	–	–	–	–	103	42	80	60	99	0	3	26	413
Governance & Civil Society	–	–	–	–	–	–	38	8	51	10	17	28	8	160
Multisector/Crosscutting	–	–	–	–	–	6	24	30	42	40	24	31	35	232
Environment	–	–	–	–	–	–	–	–	–	–	24	31	35	90
Other Multisector	–	–	–	–	–	6	24	30	42	40	–	0	–	142
Unallocable by Sector	0	0	–	–	0	2	30	40	42	90	171	109	97	582
NISs total	–	–	20	–	5	615	679	592	593	821	702	583	1041	5652

SHARE (%)	1986	1987	1988	1989	1990	1991	1992	1993	1994	1995	1996	1997	1998	Total
Programme Aid	–	–	–	–	–	–	–	–	–	–	–	3.8	6.1	1.5
Food Aid (development)	–	–	–	–	–	33.7	37.4	10.9	5.0	20.4	15.9	5.9	38.5	22.5
Humanitarian Aid	–	–	98.7	–	96.0	1.8	0.6	12.7	15.5	16.7	7.6	6.2	4.7	8.5
Humanitarian Aid excl rehabilitation	–	–	98.7	–	96.0	1.8	0.6	12.7	15.5	16.7	7.7	6.2	3.8	8.4
Aid to NGOs	–	–	1.3	10–	1.6	–	–	–	–	0.1	–	0.1	0.3	0.1
Natural Resources Productive Sectors	–	–	–	–	–	13.0	9.3	5.4	7.0	6.2	0.9	1.8	0.6	5.1
Agriculture	–	–	–	–	–	13.0	9.3	5.4	7.0	6.2	0.9	1.8	0.6	5.1
Other Productive Sectors	–	–	–	–	–	–	2.7	2.5	2.7	0.9	8.3	11.2	7.8	4.6
Industry, Mining & Construct	–	–	–	–	–	–	2.7	2.5	2.7	0.9	8.3	11.2	7.8	4.6
Economic Infrastructure & Services	–	–	–	–	–	33.4	30.4	41.8	37.0	26.5	30.0	31.2	18.0	29.7
Transport & Communications	–	–	–	–	–	8.1	5.9	6.6	4.5	3.5	2.8	6.7	3.9	5.0
Energy	–	–	–	–	–	19.2	17.5	23.3	23.7	18.5	21.2	18.5	11.9	18.5
Banking, Finan & Bus Srvs	–	–	–	–	–	6.1	7.0	12.0	8.8	4.5	4.7	4.2	2.2	5.7
Social Infrastructure & Services	–	–	–	–	–	16.8	6.2	13.5	10.1	12.1	6.9	11.1	10.5	10.7
Education	–	–	–	–	–	16.8	6.2	13.5	10.1	12.1	–	0.4	2.5	7.3
Governance & Civil Society	–	–	–	–	–	–	5.6	1.4	8.6	1.2	2.5	4.7	0.8	2.8
Multisector/Crosscutting	–	–	–	–	–	1.0	3.5	5.1	7.0	4.9	3.5	5.3	3.4	4.1
Environment	–	–	–	–	–	–	–	–	–	–	3.4	5.3	3.4	1.6
Other Multisector	–	–	–	–	–	1.0	3.5	5.1	7.0	4.9	–	0.1	–	2.5
Unallocable by Sector	–	–	–	–	2.4	0.4	4.4	6.8	7.1	10.9	24.4	18.8	9.3	10.3
NISs total	100	100	100	100	100	100	100	100	100	100	100	100	100	100

Source: European Commission/ODI database 1999

Sources of EC aid to the NIS

Since 1991 the main source of aid to the NIS has been the Tacis programme which has contributed 67% of all subsequent commitments (see Table 7.4). Additional significant sources are EAGGF aid, which represented nearly 20% of all aid, and ECHO which provided 7% of the total. Other money came from a variety of budget lines.

Figure 7.2: Sectoral Allocation of EC External Cooperation with NIS
(1990-98, % of total allocable cooperation)

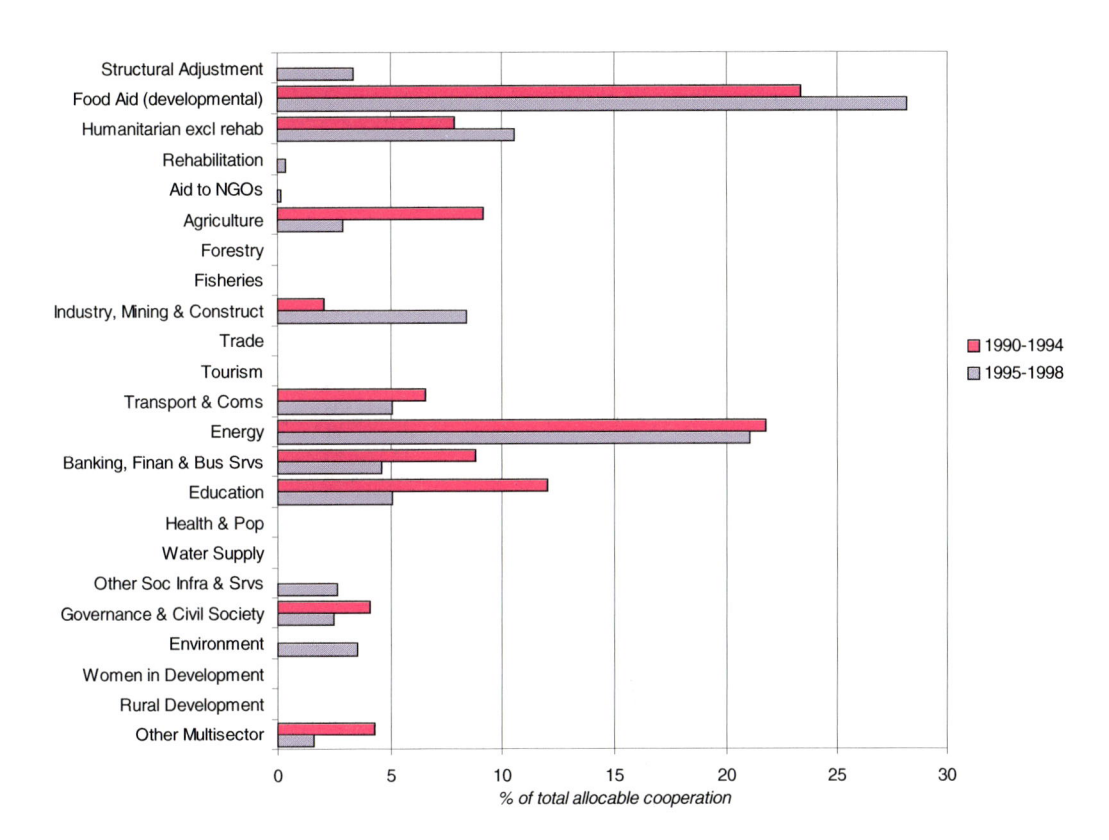

Sector	1990-1994	1995-1998
Structural Adjustment		~3
Food Aid (developmental)	~23	~28
Humanitarian excl rehab	~8	~11
Rehabilitation	~0.5	
Aid to NGOs	~0.5	
Agriculture	~9	~3
Forestry		
Fisheries		
Industry, Mining & Construct	~2	~8
Trade		
Tourism		
Transport & Coms	~6	~5
Energy	~22	~21
Banking, Finan & Bus Srvs	~9	~5
Education	~12	~5
Health & Pop		
Water Supply		
Other Soc Infra & Srvs		~2
Governance & Civil Society	~4	~2
Environment		~3
Women in Development		
Rural Development		
Other Multisector	~4	~2

Source: European Commission/ODI database 1999

Table 7.4: Sources of EC External Cooperation with the NIS
(1990-98 [a], commitments, m euro)

	1990	1991	1992	1993	1994	1995	1996	1997	1998	Total
NIS Commitments:	5	615	679	592	593	821	702	583	1041	**5731**
Tacis Programme	–	397	419	472	470	511	536	485	469	**3759**
Humanitarian Aid through ECHO	–	–	–	53	92	137	54	36	39	**411**
Tajikistan	–	–	–	–	10	16	14	15	17	**72**
Azerbaijan	–	–	–	–	19	29	9	6	5	**69**
Georgia	–	–	–	–	18	27	10	6	6	**67**
Russian Federation	–	–	–	–	10	30	9	4	6	**59**
Armenia	–	–	–	–	19	24	5	2	2	**52**
ex-Soviet Union	–	–	–	51	–	–	–	–	–	**51**
EAGGF	–	207	254	64	29	163	–	–	400	**1117**
ex-Soviet Union	–	207	210	19	12	–	–	–	–	**448**
Regional	–	–	–	–	17	163	–	–	–	**180**
Baltic States	–	–	44	44	–	–	–	–	–	**88**
Macrofinancial assistance[b] (grants)	–	–	–	–	–	15	20	–	18	**53**
NIS Disbursements:	0	209	289	248	377	642	462	449	555	**3231**
Tacis Programme	–	–	32	180	300	374	359	340	382	**1967**
Humanitarian Aid through ECHO	–	–	–	11	40	102	60	49	30	**292**
EAGGF	–	207	254	64	29	163	–	–	–	**717**
Macrofinancial assistance[b] (grants)	–	–	–	–	–	–	–	–	18	**18**

a Commitments to the NIS amounted to 20 m euro (1986–89).
b Balance of Payments grant assistance managed by DG for Economic and Financial Affairs, Directorate for International Matters, financed out of B7-531

Source: European Commission/ODI database 1999

Policy and Objectives

The European Council decided in 1992 that new agreements should be negotiated with the New Independent States, to take account of the new political and economic realities. These agreements, called Partnership and Cooperation Agreements (PCA), replace the Trade and Cooperation Agreement (TCA) which was signed with the Soviet Union in 1989. The first of these PCAs – with Russia – came into force in December 1997, and the first joint steps in its implementation were taken during 1998. PCAs have now been signed with all Tacis cooperation countries except Tajikistan and Mongolia. The agreements have entered into force with most of them.

Each PCA is an agreement between the European Communities and the Member States, on the one hand, and the partner country on the other. They provide a framework for the amicable resolution of disputes. In addition, they offer the possibility to manage trade cooperation and assistance programmes in a way that strengthens overall political and security relationships. In short, the PCA is the reference framework from which the relationship between the European Union and the partner country can grow. It should be stressed that Tacis is the major tool to facilitate cooperation under each Agreement.

The PCAs have a common core. Each establishes a strong and comprehensive political and economic partnership between the EC and the partner country, covering trade in goods and services, political dialogue, investment-related issues, such as intellectual property and company rules, and cooperation ranging from transport to higher education, as well as from agriculture to combating illegal activities. They are designed to play an increasingly important role in expanding trade and investment.

The PCAs incorporate internationally agreed norms regarding human rights and democratic principles as set out in the Helsinki Final Act and the Charter of Paris for a New Europe, *inter alia*. The PCA's furthermore set up mechanisms for regular political dialogue, including on democracy and human rights, in order to assist the partner country in its process of democratisation.

In practical terms, the PCAs mean the following:

- annual meetings between the European Community and the partner country at ministerial, parliamentary and civil servant levels;
- EC companies which invest in a country with a PCA should receive treatment at least as good as any national or third-nation company. Likewise, any national company in a partner country which has invested in EC markets should receive treatment at least as favourable as European companies;
- Elimination of trade quotas.

A new Tacis Regulation is expected to enter into force in 2000. The objective is to concentrate cooperation in six areas:
- support for institutional, legal and administrative reform;
- support to the private sector and assistance for economic development;
- support in addressing the social consequences of transition;
- development of infrastructure networks;
- promotion of environmental protection and management of entergy resources;
- development of the rural economy.

Cooperation Instruments

Regional programmes: To complement its work with individual countries, Tacis aims to find solutions to problems that are of an interstate nature, through actions best undertaken on a multi-country level. The Tacis response to these challenges has taken the form of the so-called Interstate Programme. From a broad approach initially, which extended across enterprise development, financial services, and agriculture, Tacis has increasingly focused its attention on networks in energy, transport (see Box 7.1) and telecoms, plus work on environment, and justice and home affairs.

The future enlargement of the EU will extend EU boundaries up to the frontiers of the Tacis region. This gives added significance to the cross-border and transnational programmes including customs cooperation that Tacis currently operates with EU candidate countries during the preparations for their accession, and to the development of transport and telecommunications infrastructure linking the region to a larger EU. It will also bring further changes to trading and investment patterns, and provide additional urgency to cooperation in the fields of economics, law approximation, environment, migration policy, and justice and home affairs.

> **Box 7.1: Regional transport programmes**
>
> **TRACECA** (Transport Corridor Europe Caucasus Asia) was launched in 1993 to help develop a transport/trade corridor on an east-west axis from Central Asia, across the Caspian Sea, through the Caucasus, and across the Black Sea to Europe. Since then TRACECA has extended its coverage to Mongolia, Ukraine and Moldova.
>
> **INOGATE** (Interstate Oil and Gas Transport to Europe) supports efforts in rehabilitating, rationalising and modernising regional gas transmission systems and oil and supply systems for refined oil products. It also assesses the possible complementary options for the transport of hydrocarbons from the Caspian and Central Asia regions to European and western markets. The aim is to produce a number of large-scale, bankable project proposals so that the necessary investments can take place.

The Tacis Cross-border Cooperation (CBC) Programme funds actions of a cross-border nature between the NIS and the EU, and between the NIS and central European countries. It was introduced primarily in response to the creation of the EU's first border with the NIS, following Finland's accession to the EU in 1995, and the prospect of further EU enlargement in central and eastern Europe as well as the increased importance of the Baltic Sea Region to an enlarged EU. Reinforced cross-border cooperation is designed to ensure stability, where the difference in living standards on either side of the border is extreme, and where cooperation between the communities on either side can lay the foundation for sustainable economic and social development and encourage business development. The development of effective and efficient border crossings, using modern methods, is important to facilitate trade and investment, increase revenue collection for the state, reduce criminal activity, and improve the local environment (several kilometre-long queues of lorries in winter, with their engines running for warmth, is not conducive to local health). Environmental projects are also important, since obsolete and inefficient environmental technology in some industrial sectors has produced waste, which has a harmful effect reaching well beyond border regions.

Nuclear safety: In March 1998, the European Commission adopted a Communication to the Council and to the European Parliament aimed at reinforcing the European Union's efforts to improve nuclear safety in central and eastern European countries and the New Independent States (NIS). The Commission indicated that a reorientation of assistance to the NIS was envisaged, to focus more tightly on improving reactor safety, preferably on those sites seen as more problematic, and to address management of radioactive waste, notably in North West Russia. Nuclear safety would be a high priority on the agenda of the PCAs, with objective and measurable commitments and conditionalities, in particular the PCA with Russia. Meanwhile, assistance to local operators, and on policy and institutional issues, such as regulatory support, safeguards, emergency preparedness and structural reforms, would continue, as would EU efforts to assist Ukraine in the closure of Chernobyl by the year 2000. Furthermore, Tacis will continue to promote the introduction of energy saving and energy efficiency technologies.

During 1998, the Council of Ministers also adopted a new programme of actions in the nuclear sector, the SURE programme, relating to the safe transport of radioactive materials and to safeguards and industrial cooperation to promote safety of nuclear installations in Tacis countries.

Environment: In environment, the overall aim is to promote the integration of environmental considerations through strengthened collaboration between the countries concerned. This is the rationale behind the inclusion of a so-called 'integration obligation' in the current Tacis Regulation, which requires that environmental considerations are taken into account in the design and implementation of Tacis-funded projects. Since the European Ministerial conference on environment in Sofia in 1995, Tacis funding for the environment has increased. Tacis also establishes programmes to bring immediate relief to regions where human health or natural ecosystems are severely jeopardised by environmental hazards, and it works to raise public awareness.

Other programmes in Tacis include: Justice and Home affairs; the small projects programme; The Productivity Initiative Programme; the Managers' Training Programme; the European Senior Service Network; the Joint Venture Programme; the Link Inter European Non-governmental Organisations (LIEN) programme; Tempus (see Box 7.2); Customs; Statistics; City Twinning; Policy Advice Programme; and the Democracy programme.

Box 7.2: Tempus

The Tempus programme of assistance to higher education in the Tacis countries secured a third phase when the Education Council agreed in 1999 to extend it from 2000 to 2006. The aims of Tempus are to promote quality and restructuring of higher education in the NIS and Mongolia and to encourage cooperation with EC universities. Tempus has been the largest technical assistance programme of its type in the former Soviet Union. The programme developed in the face of declining state budgets for university education, a lack of comprehensive education reform policies, low overall efficiency, poor linkages between education, research, and industry, and an educational provision that is no longer in line with national development requirements.

8

A Decade of EC External Cooperation in a Global Context

This book has attempted to describe the nature of European Community external cooperation, its institutional development, and the main trends in its geographical and sectoral allocation. To understand the particular character and role of Community aid, however, it is important to place EC aid in its wider European and global setting. This Chapter assesses the scale of EC aid relative to aid provided by the other major donors.[1]

The totals cited here for aid from EU Member States exclude their contributions to the EC aid programme, unless otherwise specified, to avoid counting this aid twice (under both heads). This does mean, however, that when EU Member States' aid is set against that of donors outside (eg Japan and the United States), the deduction of the EC-contributions element makes their totals appear less than is usually the case in donor tables. Only aid from those countries that were formally in membership of the Union in a particular year is included.[2] To allow comparisons with other donors, *disbursements* of aid are compared, except in the section examining the sectoral spread of aid which uses commitments data.

Global Trends

The overall growth in EC aid described in Chapter 1 must be seen in the context of the general trend in total OECD assistance to developing countries which, in real terms[3], shows steadily increasing disbursements for the period 1984–92, followed by a downward trend (see Figure 8.1). Between 1984 and 1992 total aid increased by 75% in real terms, reaching $76.1bn in 1992. Since the peak in 1992 it has decreased by 29% in real terms to $54.3bn

Between 1984 and 1992 total OECD aid disbursements increased in real terms each year except in 1985 and 1989. The 1989 dip was somewhat larger and was due entirely to a sharp fall in US disbursements in that year. With the exception of 1989, US aid remained largely constant in real terms from 1984–1994 at between $12.5bn and $13.5bn. However, whereas US aid declined from $13.1bn in 1994 to $9.4bn in 1997 (in real terms), the EU Member States[4] increased their assistance from $14.9bn ($17.1bn) in 1984 to $32.5bn ($40.0bn) in 1995, though it subsequently fell back to $23.4bn ($30.0bn) in 1997. Japanese aid increased from $6.6bn in 1984, or about half of that of the USA ($13.2bn) to $12.6bn in 1991, and remained at roughly this level until 1996

---

[1] Unless otherwise indicated, aid is defined as Official Development Assistance (ODA), plus Official Assistance (OA) to Part II countries in transition and more advanced developing countries and territories (see OECD (1999), p. A98).

[2] Since Austria, Finland and Sweden acceded to the EU only in 1995, these countries are not included in the years 1984–94.

[3] Real terms refers to current prices adjusted using GDP deflators (at 1997 base); source: IMF (1998), *International Financial Statistics Yearbook*. IMF Washington DC

[4] The first figure excludes Member State contributions to the EC aid programme, while the second (in parenthesis) includes these amounts.

when it declined to $9.8bn. In 1997 Japanese aid was slightly higher than that for the USA, making it the largest bilateral donor.

A very large portion of the increase in total OECD aid from 1984 up until 1992 is attributable to the rapid growth in EC and Member State aid. Aid flows increased from an annual average of $56.4bn for 1986–91 to $67.3bn for 1992–97. This was very largely due to the growth in European Community and Member State aid, which saw their combined annual average increase by $10.1bn over the two periods. The annual real terms average increase for Japan was $2.8bn, while US flows fell by $1.2bn, and those of other DAC donors by $810m (see also Figure 8.2). The share of OECD aid contributed by the Member States and the EC combined increased from 45% for 1984–91 to 53% for 1992–97. It peaked in 1995 and 1996 at 57% and 58% respectively, mainly due to Austria, Finland and Sweden joining the European Union that year.

In particular, the European Community's aid programme has gained in importance as a channel for development assistance. Its share of total OECD aid increased from 5% in 1984 to 12% in 1997. This contrasts sharply with the US aid programme, which saw its share of total real terms OECD aid fall from 30% in 1984 to 17% in 1997 (see Figure 8.3). Japan's share has varied between 13% and 22% of total OECD aid, but has been roughly steady over longer time periods, standing at 17% for 1986–91 and 18% for 1992–97. Japan contributed 17.4% of all aid in 1997, slightly more than the USA (17.3%).[5]

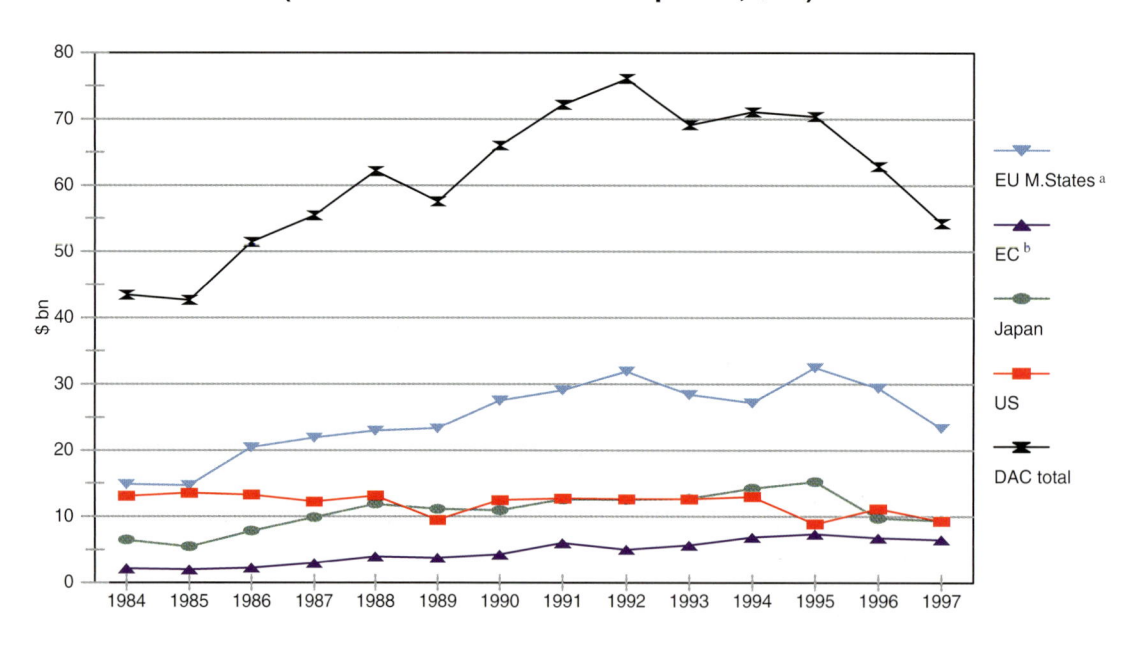

**Figure 8.1: Total Aid by Donor 1984–97
(net disbursements at 1997 prices, $bn)**

[a] Excluding EU Member States' contributions to EC
[b] In this and subsequent figures in Chapter 8, gross disbursements are used in place of net disbursements, as net figures are not available for the entire time period. Data for 1996–98 show gross disbursements to exceed net by about 8%. See also Chapter 1, footnote 2.

Source: 1984–97 data, OECD (1999); EC data, 1986–97, European Commission/ODI database 1999

---

[5] Between 1990 and 1992, US Official Development Assistance excludes debt forgiveness of non-ODA claims, amounting to $3.9bn.

EC External Cooperation Relative to Other Major Donors

When the largest aid donors are ranked by aid volume over the period 1986–97, the EC programme is seen to increase its position from the sixth largest donor to fifth, increasing its share of total aid from 6.6% in 1986–91 to 10.0% in 1992–97 (see Table 8.1). The EC's contribution was larger than that of all but three Member States (France, Germany and Italy) excluding their contributions to the EC during the period 1986–91. It was greater than all but two Member States (France and Germany) between 1992–97. Over the 1984 to 1997 period, the EU Member States have channelled a growing portion of their total aid programme through the European Community, which accounted for 14.7% of total Member State aid in 1984, rising to 27.5% in 1997.

The European Community as a Multilateral Donor[6]

On average about a third of all Official Development Assistance (ODA) was administered by multilateral aid agencies during 1984–97.[7] A third of all multilateral ODA was managed by the European Commission[8] in both 1986–88 and 1995–97 (see Table 8.2), making the Community the largest multilateral donor. The EC maintained its share of total multilateral aid while IDA (World Bank), WFP, and 'Other UN Agencies' saw slight falls. In terms of aid volume, however, all multilaterals increased their aid flows in real terms. Figure 8.4 illustrates a drift downwards in IDA's share of total OECD aid in the 1990s, though it rallied in 1996 and 1997, compared with broad stability in the EC's share. UNDP's share of multilateral aid remained largely static, though it rose in 1996 and 1997, although aid channelled through UN agencies other than UNDP fell somewhat.

Table 8.1: Ranking of Major Aid Donors (share of total aid %)

Rank	Donor	Average (%)	1986–91	Rank	Donor	Average (%)	1992–97
1	United States	20.5		1	Japan	18.5	
2	Japan	17.9		2	United States	17.0	
3	France*	12.7	(11.3)	3	Germany*	14.9	(12.8)
4	Germany*	12	(10.3)	4	France*	13.2	(11.9)
5	Italy*	6.7	(5.8)	5	EC	10.0	
6	EC	6.6		6	United Kingdom*	5.5	(4.3)
7	United Kingdom*	5.3	(4.2)	7	Netherlands*	4.7	(4.0)
8	Canada	4.7		8	Italy*	4.4	(2.8)
9	Netherlands*	4.7	(4.3)	9	Canada	3.6	

* Includes contribution made to EC; figures which exclude contributions are in parentheses.

Source: OECD (1996–98); European Commission/ODI database 1999

---

[6] The European Community is classed as multilateral organisation in DAC reports, though this remains a subject of debate within the Commission.

[7] These figures refer to ODA from DAC countries to multilateral organisations at real prices (year base 1990), and excludes official aid to the CEECs and NIS.

[8] This includes the 7% of European Community external cooperation managed by the European Investment Bank

Figure 8.2: Average Aid
(net disbursements, $m at 1997 prices)

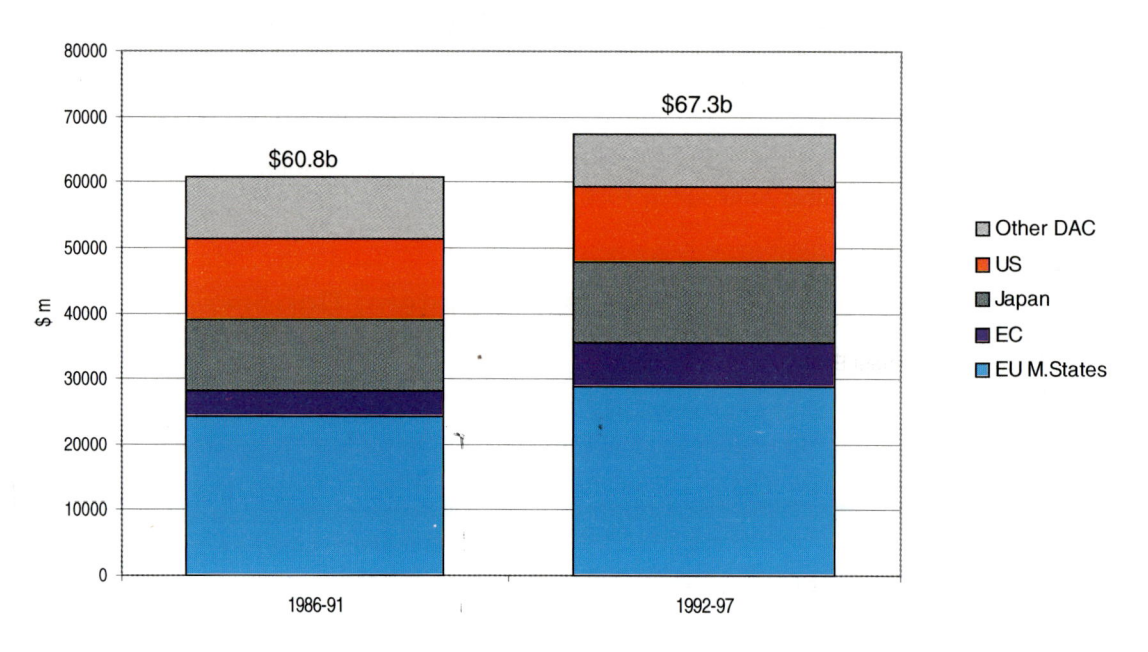

[Stacked bar chart showing 1986-91 total $60.8b and 1992-97 total $67.3b, broken down by Other DAC, US, Japan, EC, EU M.States]

Figure 8.3: Share of Total OECD Aid
(net disbursements)

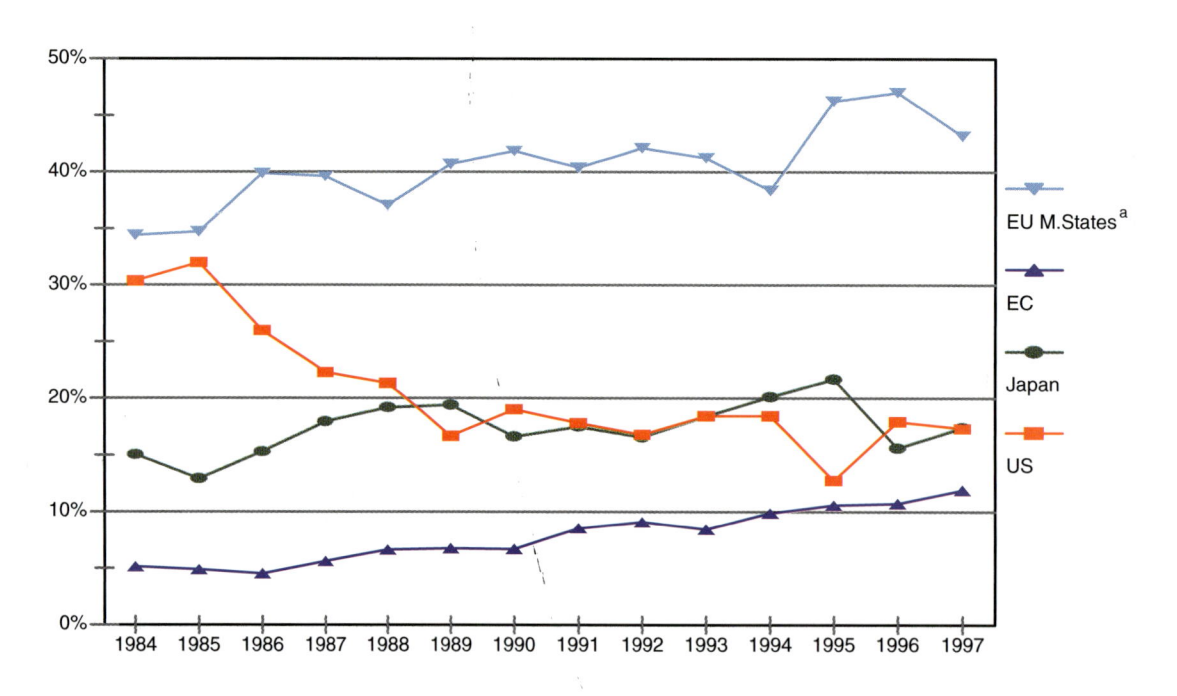

[Line chart showing shares from 1984 to 1997 for EU M.States[a], EC, Japan, US]

[a] Excluding EU Member States' contribution to EC

Sources for 8.2 and 8.3: data for 1984–97, OECD (1996–99); data for EC aid 1986–97, European Commission/ODI database 1999

Table 8.2: Proportion of Total Multilateral ODA (net disbursements, %)

Multilateral Organisations	Average for 1986–88	Average for 1995–97
EC	33.3	33.0
IDA	29.2	26.3
UNDP	6.9	7.2
Asian Development Bank	4.7	5.4
WFP	6.3	5.4
Other UN agencies	6.9	5.0
UNHCR	3.5	4.0
UNICEF	3.1	3.5
African Development Bank	2.8	2.9
IDB	1.5	1.5
UNWRA	1.8	1.4
Other	0.0	4.4
Total	**100**	**100**

a Total for UN excludes those agencies shown individually in Table (UNDP, WFP, UNHCR, UNWRA, and UNICEF)
b Includes capital subscriptions to the African Development Bank

Figure 8.4: Share of Total Multilateral ODA (net disbursements, %)

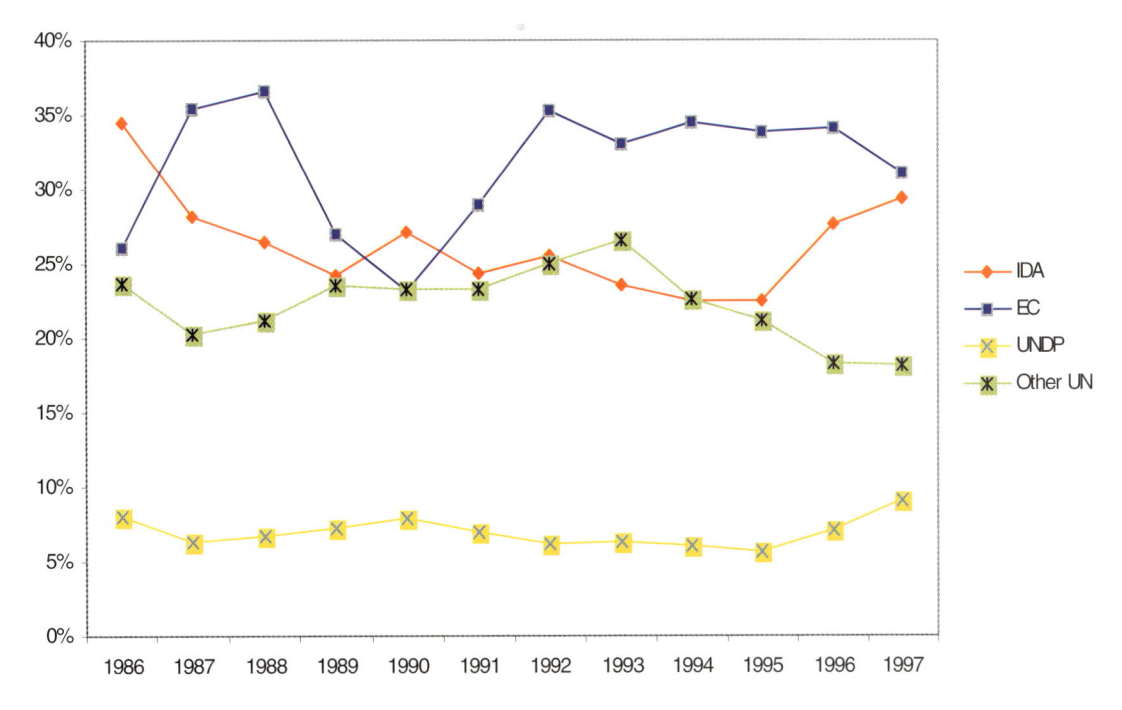

Note: 'Other UN' includes all UN agencies other than UNDP

Source: OECD (1994–99), European Commission/ODI database 1999

The Main Recipients of OECD Aid

Figure 8.5 shows the regional distribution of total aid and the contribution of EC aid relative to that of other donors. Sub-Saharan Africa was by far the largest recipient region, receiving disbursements averaging $16.6bn per annum during the 1986–96 period. More than half (55%) of this was contributed by the EU Member States, while the EC provided 12%, more than any other single donor including Japan (9%) and the USA (10%).

In the case of the four next largest recipient regions, EC aid constituted the smallest share among the major donors indicated, with only 3%–6% of the total. Japan was the largest donor of aid to Oceania and Far East Asia by a large margin, providing close to half the aid, while the US predominated in the Middle East, North Africa and Southern Europe, contributing 39% of total aid; this is a direct result of the dominance of Israel and Egypt in the US aid programme. The EU Member States, on the other hand, occupied first place collectively as donors to Latin America and Caribbean (43% of total regional aid) and to South and Central Asia (35%).

The recipients of Official Aid, mainly the Central and East European countries and the New Independent States of the former Soviet Union, received an average of $4.2bn per year during the 1986–96 period. As a result of major political changes in these countries and the desire to assist economic reform, aid to the CEECs and NIS increased substantially from 1990 onwards. Table 8.3 shows that during 1993–96 the CEECs and NIS received $7.5bn a year, 63% of which was provided by the EU Member States and the Community together. EC aid alone contributed 16.1% of total aid to the region, more than Japan (2.5%) but less than the US (16.6%). All regions, received more aid in the period 1993–96 than in the previous period, in current prices.

A closer look at the evolution of aid flows reveals that, although all donors increased their total aid between 1986–89 and 1993–96, some reduced their assistance to particular regions. Table 8.3 indicates, for instance, that US aid to South and Central Asia decreased $326m, falling from 11.1% to 6.4 % of total US aid. The Oceania and Far East Asia region also saw a reduction in aid from the US between 1986–89 and 1993–96 of $160 m.

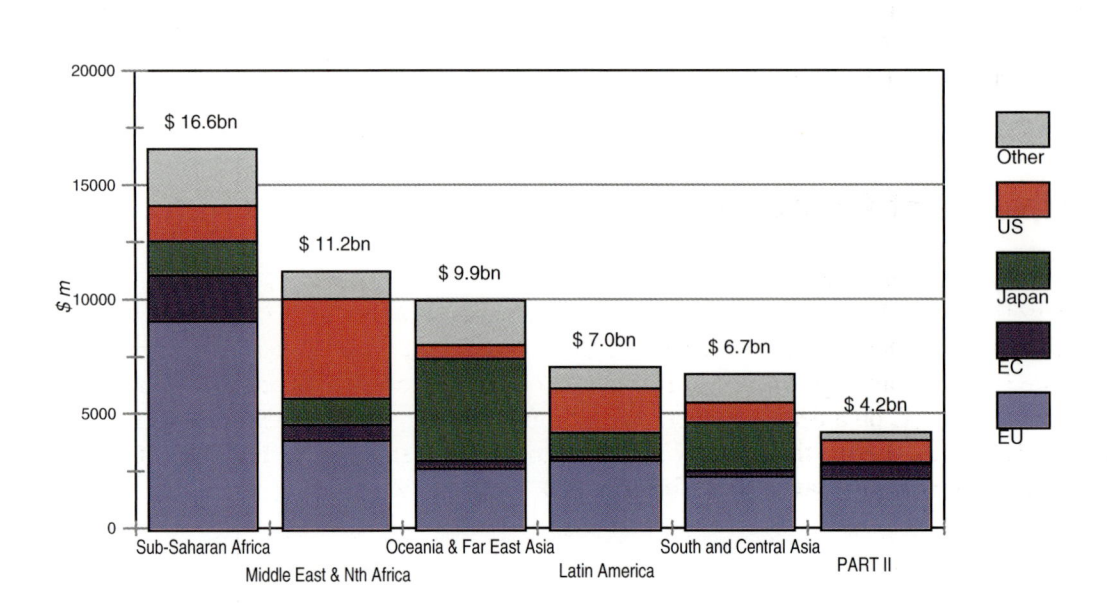

**Figure 8.5: Regional Distribution of Aid
(annual average 1986–96 net disbursements $m)**

Note: The CEECs and NIS received the vast majority of aid to Part II countries.
Source: Development Cooperation, OECD, DAC, 1984–97, European Commission/ODI database 1999

Table 8.3: Regional Distribution of Aid by Major Donors
(average annual net disbursements, $m and %)

Disbursements $m	EU[a] 1986-9	EU[a] 1993-6	EC 1986-9	EC 1993-6	Japan 1986-9	Japan 1993-6	USA 1986-9	USA 1993-6	Total OECD[b] 1986-9	Total OECD[b] 1993-6
Sub-Saharan Africa	7335	10210	1395	2344	1162	1543	1353	1821	14048	17788
South & Central Asia	2314	2141	127	452	1663	2538	1023	697	6212	6951
Oceania & Far East Asia	2408	3265	177	598	3794	5158	708	548	8836	11644
Mid East, Nth Africa, Sth Europe	2093	5243	292	1085	582	1669	3866	4068	7591	13473
Latin America & Caribbean	1768	3884	166	268	598	1408	1840	1877	5355	8348
Part II CEECs/NIS	–	3498	2	1210	–	310	–	1791	–	7496
Total[c]	15545	28241	2531	6457	7972	12626	9208	10803	43743	65701

Share of total donor's aid (%)	EU[a] 1986-9	EU[a] 1993-6	EC 1986-9	EC 1993-6	Japan 1986-9	Japan 1993-6	USA 1986-9	USA 1993-6	Total OECD[b] 1986-9	Total OECD[b] 1993-6
Sub-Saharan Africa	47.2	36.2	55.1	36.3	14.6	12.2	14.7	16.9	32.1	27.1
South & Central Asia	14.9	17.6	5.0	7.0	20.9	20.1	11.1	6.4	14.2	10.6
Oceania & Far East Asia	15.5	11.6	7.0	9.3	47.6	40.9	7.7	5.1	20.2	17.7
Mid East, Nth Africa, Sth Europe	13.5	18.6	11.45	16.8	7.3	13.2	42.0	37.7	17.4	20.5
Latin America & Caribbean	11.4	13.8	6.6	4.2	7.5	11.2	20.0	17.4	12.2	12.7
Part II CEECs/NIS	–	12.4	0.1	18.7	–	2.5	–	16.6	–	11.4

[a] Excluding contributions made to EC
[b] Including regional aid from other DAC countries
[c] Includes unallocable aid

Source: Development Cooperation, OECD, DAC, 1987–97; European Commission/ODI database 1999 for EC Aid 1986–98

The EC increased its annual net disbursement to Sub-Saharan Africa by $949m between 1986–89 and 1993–96, yet the proportion of EC aid to this region actually decreased by 18.8%. Most of this change was taken up by the Part II countries (mainly CEEC and NIS) which saw an increase of 18.6% in total EC aid. The EU member states followed a similar pattern with the proportion of EU aid to sub-Saharan Africa decreasing whilst Part II CEECs and NIS countries experienced a rise in the proportion of total EU aid.

Recipients of Aid by Level of Income

Table 8.4 shows the proportion of EC and OECD Official Development Assistance disbursed to countries classified by level of income. In 1986–87 some 60% of all EC ODA went to the poorest countries (Least Developed Countries (LLDCs) and Other Low Income Countries (OLICs)), compared with an average of 54% for all OECD bilateral donors. This represented a substantial decrease for the EC on a decade earlier, down from over 78%, though a slight rise for other OECD donors. In the late 1990s, the share of EC ODA to the poorest countries fell again, to 52%, while other OECD donors also saw a slight fall (from 54.4% to 53.8%).

Lower middle-income countries, on the other hand, received a larger share of EC aid in 1986–87 (35%) compared with 1976–77 (19%) and a slightly larger share again in 1996–97 (40%). In 1996–97, therefore, lower middle-income countries received nearly 8% more EC ODA than least developed countries. The share of OECD aid to lower middle-income countries remained roughly constant over all three time periods. High income countries receive a lower share of EC ODA, virtually zero in 1996–97, than they do from other DAC donors (3.5% in 1996–97). However, this picture covers ODA only, and it must be remembered that the EC provides very large sums of Official Assistance to Part II countries in transition (mainly CEECs and NIS) which are not reflected here.

Table 8.4: Share of Bilateral OECD and EC ODA to Recipients by Level of Income (% and gross disbursements)

Level of Income	Bilateral OECD ODA				European Community ODA		
	1976-77	1986-87	1996-97		1976-77	1986-87	1996-97
LLDC	24.2	31.2	24.6	LLDC	52.8	33.3	32.4
OLIC	27.6	23.2	29.2	OLIC	25.6	26.6	19.9
LMIC	37.3	35.6	35.7	LMIC	19.4	35.7	40.0
UMIC	4.6	5.4	6.9	UMIC	1.3	4.1	4.9
HICS	6.2	4.6	3.5	HICS	0.8	0.3	0.3

Source: OECD (1996-98); EC data, European Commission/ODI database 1999

Sectoral Distribution of EC and other OECD ODA[9]

A comparative analysis of the sectoral breakdown of EC and bilateral DAC ODA for 1994–96 suggests differences in the priority attached to particular sectors (see Figure 8.6). Table 8.5 shows that the share of EC aid through three instruments, programme aid, food aid and humanitarian aid, stood at 38.5%, or five times the 7.1% averaged by other DAC donors. The greatest difference appears to be in developmental food aid, where the EC committed some 9% of total ODA. The comparable figure for OECD donors is not available, since it is included within the Programme Aid category, but given that their total commitments under this category were 5.6%, it is clearly far lower than for the EC. The others sectors which receive a significantly larger share of Community aid than that allocated by OECD donors in general are trade, banking and tourism, and industry, mining and construction.

As a result of high commitments from the EC programme to programme aid, food aid and humanitarian aid, allocations to other sectors tend to be lower than the OECD average. Those sectors which receive a significantly smaller share of EC ODA than OECD ODA include education, health and population, other social infrastructure, transport and communication, and energy.

---

[9] Data refer to Official Development Assistance (ODA) rather than total aid, as DAC data refer only to ODA.

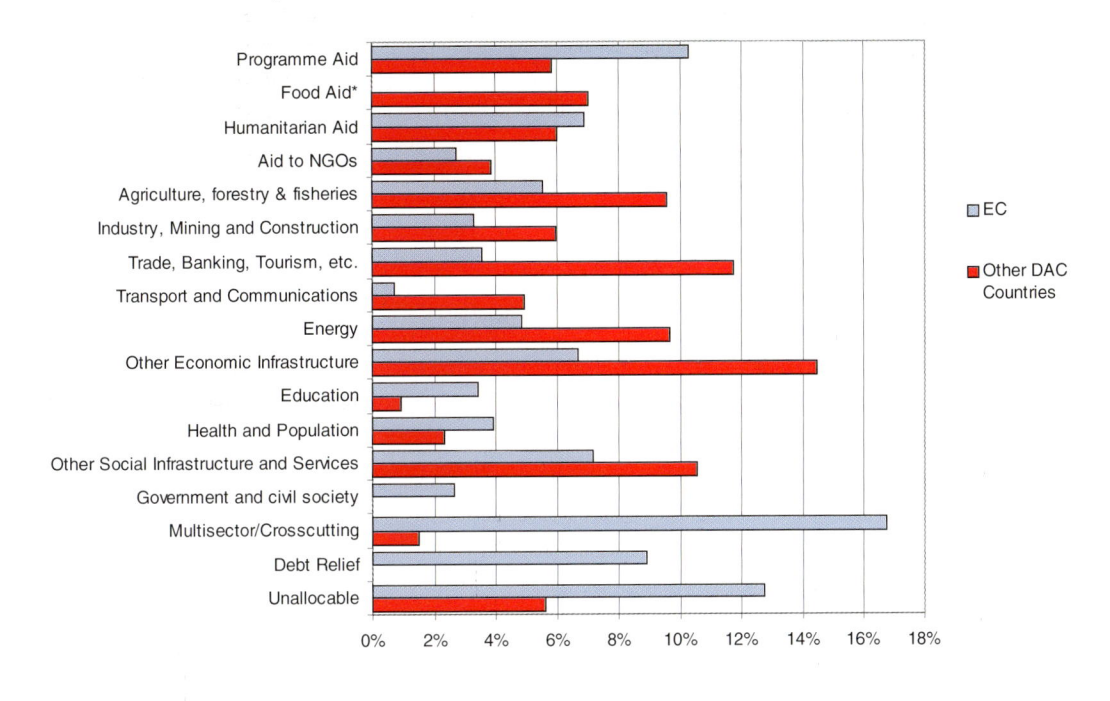

Figure 8.6: Total OECD[a] ODA and EC ODA by Sector (commitments, % of allocable ODA, 1994-96)

Note: Multi-sector/cross-cutting activities include activities such as multi-sector environmental interventions, multi-sector women in development interventions, and certain rural and urban development interventions.

[a] Total OECD ODA excludes EC ODA

Table 8.5: Total OECD ODA and EC ODA by Sector ($ m, commitments) and EC ODA as % of Total Bilateral ODA 1994-96

	EC ODA	Total OECD ODA	Total	EC ODA as % of total
Programme Aid	941	2144	3085	30.5
Food Aid*	669	–	669	–
Humanitarian Aid	1261	436	1697	74.3
Aid to NGOs	200	–	200	–
Agriculture, forestry & fisheries	539	4133	4672	11.5
Industry, Mining and Construction	289	904	1193	24.2
Trade, Banking, Tourism, etc.	262	334	596	43.9
Transport and Communications	505	5647	6152	8.2
Energy	360	3747	4108	8.8
Other Economic Infrastructure	54	1916	1970	2.8
Education	266	4610	4875	5.4
Health and Population	256	2328	2584	9.9
Other Social Infrastructure and Services	429	3717	4145	10.3
Government and civil society	210	1497	1708	12.3
Multisector/Crosscutting	515	2326	2841	18.1
Debt Relief	–	2802	2802	–
Unallocable	783	2195	2978	26.3
Total	**7539**	**38735**	**46275**	**16.3**

* The latest OECD DAC data include developmental food aid under the programme aid category. DAC data do not identify Aid to NGOs as a separate category in OECD DAC (1999) document.

Sources: OECD (1995-99); EC data 1986-1997, European Commission/ODI database 1999

Appendix 1

The Major Recipients of European Community External Cooperation (commitments, m euro)

	Country	Total	1986	1987	1988	1989	1990	1991	1992	1993	1994	1995	1996	1997	1998
1	Egypt	2479	71	45	66	185	101	285	167	114	216	189	210	297	533
2	Ethiopia	2033	6	140	214	116	96	183	190	149	201	117	57	142	419
3	Yugoslavia (ex)	1936	–	0	1	1	31	20	210	439	314	269	327	124	200
4	Poland	1785	–	2	–	3	182	197	200	225	209	174	204	193	197
5	Russian Federation	1662	–	–	9	–	1	218	111	161	170	201	163	108	521
6	India	1228	70	179	37	114	70	98	41	176	43	103	126	113	57
7	Ivory Coast	1183	28	56	168	130	172	95	112	76	141	76	85	7	38
8	West Bank/Gaza	1141	57	27	28	35	36	144	53	94	113	129	170	139	116
9	Tunisia	1130	115	1	93	56	76	50	86	130	39	78	139	205	62
10	Mozambique	1031	10	92	75	66	57	80	136	121	123	88	45	36	101
11	Morocco	996	0	0	13	130	43	10	58	13	158	47	52	246	226
12	Romania	989	–	0	0	5	13	135	152	140	100	67	126	94	157
13	South Africa	963	7	19	30	25	31	58	81	91	103	125	134	131	130
14	Bangladesh	935	1	20	41	89	77	145	74	67	75	98	86	63	100
15	Cameroon	902	21	38	112	79	70	115	120	55	109	69	37	17	60
16	Hungary	867	–	–	–	–	90	115	102	100	85	92	101	89	94
17	Sudan	842	66	49	107	60	62	156	69	42	63	33	6	24	105
18	Tanzania	811	10	130	46	28	38	30	128	97	119	40	-5	44	107
19	Algeria	801	61	25	4	34	20	82	76	58	13	13	218	85	114
20	Malawi	778	41	58	47	29	31	48	42	68	60	96	82	38	136
21	Jordan	766	14	4	45	10	27	175	57	74	62	60	111	74	54
22	Bulgaria	762	–	–	–	–	25	107	88	90	86	83	64	69	151
23	Zambia	761	4	58	27	5	28	36	194	77	71	64	29	1	167
24	Uganda	760	2	65	32	34	59	83	95	73	112	68	26	27	85
25	Kenya	751	0	77	151	65	22	67	56	42	102	63	57	23	26
26	Guinea	732	–	108	130	21	0	29	115	57	35	91	5	82	60
27	Nigeria	700	0	35	218	100	61	137	178	33	30	-16	-19	-27	-31
28	Mali	693	1	39	91	75	5	47	36	65	101	49	35	27	122
29	Turkey	675	–	12	21	0	0	180	1	3	2	47	129	144	137
30	Senegal	671	56	176	37	3	39	4	114	71	52	38	17	9	55
31	Albania	667	–	–	–	–	–	10	154	150	56	89	55	99	54
32	Angola	644	0	48	26	19	33	34	55	48	95	138	53	59	37
33	Burkina Faso	618	1	3	66	51	28	58	29	82	49	127	30	13	80
34	Ghana	596	18	43	47	18	6	78	25	90	71	35	60	50	54
35	Rwanda	581	1	55	26	43	22	44	62	55	112	33	76	29	24
36	Zimbabwe	579	5	47	33	65	13	29	78	86	150	32	22	-4	23
37	Madagascar	579	15	75	48	14	11	33	48	10	136	24	18	47	101
38	Mauritania	557	0	74	62	10	6	68	50	48	16	139	11	19	53
39	Papua New Guinea	547	17	56	75	7	31	71	21	45	74	109	11	4	24
40	Bosnia & Herzogovina	537	–	–	–	–	–	–	–	–	–	–	159	225	153
41	Soviet Union (former)	523	–	–	10	–	5	213	213	71	12	–	0	–	–
42	Peru	489	17	6	29	14	29	37	32	45	60	58	67	46	49
43	Democratic Republic of Congo (Zaire)	477	67	96	28	42	7	43	-8	49	7	53	63	30	0
44	Niger	468	19	66	104	6	7	21	16	46	89	9	18	36	30
45	China	459	5	12	29	49	23	21	8	19	38	61	75	59	62
46	Ukraine	438	–	–	–	–	–	29	48	43	54	36	89	51	88
47	Jamaica	421	19	14	26	21	1	18	29	78	14	33	80	73	15
48	Lebanon	418	1	7	6	27	9	9	12	42	8	15	80	194	8
49	Nicaragua	409	3	9	12	17	25	23	27	25	56	61	65	32	55
50	Czech Republic	404	–	–	–	–	–	–	60	60	110	55	73	47
51	Bolivia	396	13	24	12	31	26	21	42	34	7	35	41	74	35
52	Haiti	391	7	1	7	25	14	21	14	12	60	92	83	33	21
53	Chad	377	7	66	27	59	7	7	49	22	29	12	26	9	58

54	Regional Med & Mid East	376	1	0	1	1	1	3	64	60	71	165	0	8	–
55	Somalia	372	1	30	22	78	14	25	13	50	49	3	61	9	16
56	Pakistan	367	0	27	1	34	22	34	78	29	26	7	5	26	76
57	Burundi	351	6	38	56	53	7	39	61	19	76	15	-2	-17	-1
58	Namibia	324	0	1	4	8	31	12	12	100	31	39	29	3	54
59	Philippines	324	19	2	14	22	30	6	51	49	27	52	20	29	5
60	Guatemala	320	0	20	11	3	4	18	15	29	55	34	53	37	42
61	Benin	307	4	42	55	15	16	27	14	65	29	17	-5	11	17
62	Botswana	290	3	27	25	52	1	9	14	29	19	56	55	0	0
63	Viet Nam	287	1	0	0	3	5	15	27	50	27	18	31	71	37
64	Afghanistan	286	1	0	7	2	5	4	19	24	37	38	61	38	51
65	Lithuania	274	–	–	–	–	–	–	20	25	39	42	53	50	44
66	Central African Republic	273	1	37	38	37	7	10	8	21	20	62	0	1	31
67	Cambodia	267	0	0	3	0	3	3	23	15	68	37	19	31	65
68	Lesotho	265	17	12	21	14	2	39	12	21	36	16	14	1	57
69	Rwanda/Bur Emergency	259	–	–	–	–	–	–	–	–	177	82	–	–	–
70	Sierra Leone	256	7	20	7	2	10	23	65	34	30	14	22	6	17
71	Dominican Republic	256	0	1	0	2	3	4	51	76	19	38	32	3	26
72	Slovak Republic	256	–	–	–	–	–	–	–	40	40	45	5	46	81
73	Slovenia	254	–	–	–	–	–	–	9	58	24	70	55	22	16
74	Iraq	244	–	–	–	–	–	116	3	22	23	30	33	3	15
75	Brazil	239	1	1	5	13	6	13	24	18	30	27	39	30	34
76	El Salvador	237	4	18	1	8	4	14	55	44	17	22	13	28	8
77	Czechoslovakia (ex)	233	–	–	–	–	34	99	100	–	–	–	0	0	–
78	Liberia	221	–	28	0	3	13	20	10	39	44	3	-11	28	44
79	Togo	215	12	2	34	86	11	17	36	4	8	-15	2	-2	18
80	Latvia	208	–	–	–	–	–	–	15	18	30	33	37	43	33
81	Cyprus	207	4	2		4	0	37	7	1	21	12	19	58	42
82	Mauritius	203	23	34	16	1	3	3	14	20	34	9	15	2	29
83	Trinidad & Tobago	198	–	0	1	29	9	40	10	17	27	6	54	-3	10
84	Georgia	197	–	–	–	–	–	5	9	–	26	32	58	22	45
85	Azerbaijan	193	–	–	–	–	–	0	13	0	27	33	50	22	47
86	Indonesia	190	10	3	3	0	27	13	33	6	10	66	4	8	7
87	Thailand	188	7	1	13	55	10	8	13	9	12	11	9	14	26
88	Chile	173	5	5	5	13	12	19	25	20	13	18	9	27	2
89	Estonia	165	–	–	–	–	–	–	10	12	23	21	62	5	29
90	Colombia	165	5	1	5	3	16	10	23	17	11	15	23	17	19
91	Syria	160	18	0		3	1	1	22	21	16	14	18	42	3
92	Armenia	157	–	–	–	–	–	2	10	9	20	28	50	8	30
93	Macedonia	156	–	–	–	–	–	–	–	–	–	–	25	33	98
94	Korea DPR (North Korea)	147	–	–	–	–	–	–	–	–	–	–	1	83	63
95	Ecuador	145	0	12	4	5	7	13	3	13	21	21	14	18	13
96	Guinea Bissau	142	1	28	9	4	5	2	26	22	10	4	22	3	5
97	Congo	142	20	0	68	1	5	2	16	5	10	7	4	1	1
98	Cape Verde	141	–	1	24	12	3	3	14	14	20	10	6	11	23
99	Gabon	136	0	17	2	3	1	0	6	13	42	9	11	6	25
100	Honduras	136	3	15	0	5	4	3	11	2	16	31	10	21	15
101	Cuba	135	–	–	–	4	8	5	7	14	22	31	17	13	15
102	Guyana	128	–	2	17	10	4	1	5	50	4	26	0	0	8
103	Eritrea	124	–	–	–	–	–	–	–	32	48	34	7	2	2
104	Swaziland	120	4	13	22	11	1	0	19	15	7	13	8	1	7
105	Tajikistan	113	–	–	–	–	–	–	–	–	14	24	23	30	22
106	Yemen	106	0	–	–	6	3	7	2	15	2	4	3	38	26
107	Baltic States	104	–	–	–	–	–	15	44	44	0	–	–	–	–
108	Paraguay	102	–	1	0	3	0	14	1	5	17	5	21	9	26
109	Kazakhstan	102	–	–	–	–	–	8	21	14	20	17	2	20	0
110	Laos	101	6	0	7	5	1	1	4	16	17	15	14	6	10
111	St Vincent and the Grenadines	101	0	4	9	4	0	0	0	3	15	31	14	0	20
112	Nepal	96	0	3	0	4	1	1	3	3	18	30	22	4	8
113	St Lucia	94	8	1	7	1	0	0	0	1	11	24	28	0	13
114	Mexico	93	6	0	1	9	3	8	9	7	13	7	10	7	14
115	Uzbekistan	89	–	–	–	–	–	2	19	–	15	8	22	0	24

116	Sri Lanka	87	0	1	1	10	15	7	9	2	4	10	11	7	8
117	Comoros	86	2	7	10	11	2	9	7	11	10	6	0	2	9
118	Venezuela	84	–	1	0	1	0	1	2	13	3	22	13	16	12
119	Solomon Islands	83	1	26	13	0	8	11	4	4	12	2	0	2	1
120	Kyrgyz Rep.	75	–	–	–	–	–	1	9	10	–	8	15	22	11
121	Fiji	74	6	1	5	27	8	5	2	3	10	4	2	1	0
122	GDR (ex)	71	–	–	–	36	35	–	–	0	–	–	–	–	–
123	Netherlands Antilles	66	–	0	6	6	15	0	8	6	6	1	10	2	7
124	Djibouti	65	1	1	15	4	7	2	13	2	6	0	6	3	6
125	Dominica	64	4	4	0	2	1	1	2	3	6	12	15	0	14
126	Argentina	63	1	3	3	1	2	3	4	3	6	18	8	6	5
127	Belarus	63	0	0	0	0	0	9	15	9	11	12	1	1	6
128	Barbados	62	–	1	2	6	4	3	0	13	12	-8	24	0	4
129	Suriname	61	–	0	1	12	5	1	2	8	19	10	1	1	0
130	Western Samoa	59	0	8	10	2	8	4	3	1	4	3	0	0	18
131	Malta	58	–	3	11	0	18	9	-1	14	-2	3	1	3	0
132	Bahamas	57	10	9	4	0	1	0	0	4	0	3	24	1	0
133	Uruguay	54	1	0	1	1	1	3	3	2	4	14	10	13	1
134	New Caledonia	53	0	–	3	7	5	1	0	20	9	1	0	3	4
135	Equatorial Guinea	52	8	1	4	7	5	8	7	1	2	2	1	0	6
136	Belize	52	1	4	6	2	1	2	9	5	10	-1	5	1	7
137	French Polynesia	51	–	6	13	3	3	0	0	15	6	1	2	2	0
138	Portugal	50	44	–	–	–	–	–	–	6	–	–	0	–	–
139	Vanuatu	46	2	12	7	3	0	5	1	0	7	0	1	1	8
140	Moldova	44	–	–	–	–	–	1	9	–	13	8	0	14	0
141	Panama	44	–	0	1	–	4	0	1	7	1	21	3	4	4
142	Grenada	44	4	4	1	3	2	4	6	2	7	4	7	0	0
143	Sao Tome and Principe	44	4	6	2	1	2	1	7	3	1	12	3	1	1
144	Costa Rica	42	0	0	–	1	7	1	2	11	2	5	11	1	1
145	Bhutan	38	–	–	4	0	4	6	6	1	0	–	7	10	0
146	Turkmenistan	31	–	–	–	–	–	1	9	–	8	3	0	10	0
147	Tonga	31	1	3	1	4	7	1	1	2	2	0	5	5	0
148	Regional Caribbean	29	–	–	–	–	–	–	–	–	–	–	25	0	4
149	Seychelles	25	0	1	0	6	2	2	0	1	3	4	0	1	4
150	Mongolia	24	–	–	–	–	–	–	2	4	1	1	7	0	9
151	Gambia	24	–	–	6	1	0	5	0	0	0	1	1	3	6
152	Myanmar (Burma)	24	0	0	0	–	–	0	0	–	3	–	4	3	13
153	Aruba	23	–	–	2	0	4	4	0	6	6	1	1	0	0
154	Mayotte	20	–	0	0	4	0	2	1	0	0	7	2	0	3
155	Iran	19	–	–	–	–	5	2	2	5	3	–	0	4	0
156	Hong Kong	18	–	–	–	5	3	–	3	2	2	1	3	–	0
157	Serbia & Montenegro	18	–	–	–	–	–	–	–	–	–	–	0	18	0
158	Croatia	17	–	–	–	–	–	–	–	–	–	–	1	12	4
159	Kiribati	16	1	2	1	0	0	6	1	1	1	3	0	0	1
160	Montserrat	16	0	–	–	–	0	6	0	0	8	0	0	1	0
161	Antigua & Barbuda	15	–	–	0	3	0	0	3	0	2	4	0	1	0
162	Virgin Islands	14	–	–	1	6	1	0	1	1	2	2	1	0	0
163	St Kitts and Nevis	13	–	3	0	3	0	0	0	0	1	6	0	0	0
164	Cayman Islands	10	–	–	2	–	4	0	1	0	0	0	–	5	0
165	Dominique	9	–	4	0	–	–	0	3	0	0	1	–	–	–
166	Falkland Islands	8	–	–	0	–	1	0	1	3	0	3	0	–	–
167	Anguilla	7	–	–	3	0	2	0	2	0	1	0	0	0	0
168	Turks & Caicos	7	–	–	–	2	0	0	–	0	1	4	0	0	0
169	Wallis & Futuna	7	–	–	–	1	2	0	0	–	3	0	0	0	0
170	Greece	5	0	–	4	1	–	–	–	–	–	–	0	–	–
171	Malaysia	5	–	–	–	1	0	0	0	1	0	0	0	1	0
172	Tuvalu	5	–	1	0	0	0	0	2	1	0	0	0	0	0
173	Maldives	3	–	0	–	1	–	0	0	–	0	1	0	–	0
174	Singapore	3	–	–	–	–	0	0	3	–	–	0	0	0	0
175	Caribbean	3	–	–	–	–	–	–	–	–	–	–	0	–	3
176	Macao	3	–	–	–	–	–	–	–	–	0	1	1	0	1
177	St Helena	3	–	–	–	–	1	0	0	1	0	0	0	0	0

178	France	2	–	–	–	–	–	–	–	–	–	–	2	0	–
179	Tibet	1	–	–	–	–	–	–	–	–	–	–	1	–	–
180	Belgium	1	–	–	–	–	–	–	–	–	–	–	1	–	–
181	St Maurice	1	0	–	–	0	0	0	–	0	0	0	–	–	–
182	St Pierre & Miquelon	1	–	–	–	–	–	–	–	–	–	–	0	0	1
183	Germany	1	–	–	–	–	–	–	–	–	–	–	1	–	–
184	United Arab Emirates	1	–	0	–	0	–	–	–	0	1	0	–	–	–
185	United Kingdom	1	–	–	–	–	–	–	–	–	–	–	1	–	–
186	Denmark	1	–	–	–	–	–	–	–	–	–	–	1	–	–
187	Switzerland	0	–	–	–	–	–	–	–	–	–	–	0	–	–
188	Netherlands	0	–	–	–	–	–	–	–	–	–	–	0	–	–
189	Italy	0	–	–	–	–	–	–	–	–	–	–	0	–	–
190	Austria	0	–	–	–	–	–	–	–	–	–	–	0	–	–
191	Kuwait	0	–	–	–	–	–	–	–	0	–	–	–	–	–
192	Qatar	0	–	–	–	–	–	–	0	–	–	–	–	–	–
193	Oman	0	–	–	–	–	–	–	0	–	–	–	0	–	0
194	Brunei	0	–	–	–	–	–	0	–	–	–	–	0	–	–
195	Korea Rep. (South Korea)	0	–	–	–	–	–	–	–	–	–	–	–	0	0
196	Finland	0	–	–	–	–	–	–	–	–	–	–	0	–	–
197	Bermuda	0	–	–	–	–	–	–	–	–	0	–	–	–	–
198	Reunion	0	–	–	–	–	–	–	0	–	–	–	–	–	–
199	Spain	0	–	–	–	–	–	–	–	–	–	–	0	–	–
200	Saudi Arabia	0	–	–	–	–	–	–	–	–	–	0	–	–	–
201	Martinique	0	–	–	–	–	–	–	–	–	–	–	–	–	0

Appendix 2

Distribution of EC External Cooperation by DAC Region 1970–1997
(average annual disbursements, $m and share of total EC aid, %)

	Average annual disbursements $m				Share of total EC aid, %			
	1970–71	1980–81	1990–91	1996-97	1970-71	1980–81	1990–91	1996–97
sub-Saharan Africa	148	751	2200	2033	73.1	60.4	48.8	30.4
Asia	18	256	320	763	9.1	20.6	7.1	11.4
Latin America & Caribbean	12	67	346	640	5.9	5.4	7.7	9.6
Middle East & Southern Europe	12	65	397	901	5.9	5.2	8.8	13.5
North of Sahara	10	85	424	384	5.0	6.8	9.4	5.7
Oceania	2	20	63	61	1.0	1.6	1.4	0.9
Part III CEECs & NIS	–	–	559	1349	–	–	12.4	20.2
Unallocable	n.a	n.a	197	552	n.a	n.a	4.4	8.3
Total	203	1244	6863	6683	100.0	100.0	100.0	100.0
OECD average, $m	7602	27617	73256	57256				
EC share of OECD total, %	2.7	4.5	9.3	11.7				

Note:
This appendix has used the OECD DAC regional classification, and permits a comparison between ODI data for 1996–97 period with that of published by OECD DAC.

Source: Data for 1991-92 and 1996-97, European Commission/ODI database 1997; other data, *Development Cooperation*, OECD, DAC, 1999

Appendix 3

EC External Cooperation by DAC Region 1986–98 (disbursements in m euro and $m)

1.1 Disbursements (m euro)

	1986	1987	1988	1989	1990	1991	1992	1993	1994	1995	1996	1997	1998	Total
sub-Saharan Africa	925	1050	1398	1639	1586	1880	2475	1774	2281	1909	1645	1669	1711	21942
South & Central Asia	92	91	89	187	165	153	191	213	284	493	455	480	438	3331
Other Asia & Oceania	110	187	166	130	147	164	213	159	153	288	258	311	304	2589
Middle East, North Africa, Southern Europe	311	164	249	342	288	1043	638	912	718	856	1022	1237	1319	9099
Latin America and the Caribbean	126	117	137	260	265	320	310	386	415	567	557	567	617	4645
Part II CEECs/NIS	3	0	0	6	357	526	620	683	1168	1023	1034	1071	1958	8448
Unallocable	103	356	604	238	77	240	273	403	488	373	362	485	364	4366
TOTAL	1669	1964	2644	2801	2886	4326	4720	4529	5507	5510	5334	5821	6710	54420

1.2 Disbursements ($m)

	1986	1987	1988	1989	1990	1991	1992	1993	1994	1995	1996	1997	1998	Total
Sub-Saharan Africa	910	1212	1653	1805	2014	2323	3203	2078	2715	2495	2089	1892	1914	26304
South & Central Asia	91	105	105	205	210	189	248	249	338	644	578	544	489	3996
Other Asia & Oceania	108	216	196	143	187	203	275	186	182	377	327	352	339	3092
Middle East, North Africa, Southern Europe	306	189	295	377	366	1290	826	1068	854	1119	1298	1402	1475	10864
Latin America and the Caribbean	124	135	163	286	336	396	402	452	493	742	706	643	690	5568
Part II CEECs/NIS	2	0	0	7	454	650	802	801	1390	1336	1312	1213	2190	10158
Unallocable	102	410	714	263	98	297	353	472	581	488	460	549	407	5193
TOTAL	1642	2268	3126	3087	3664	5348	6110	5305	6554	7200	6770	6596	7505	65174

Notes:
i) This appendix uses the OECD DAC regional categorisation and therefore allows for the direct comparison of EC aid flows with those of other OECD members; see DAC 1997.
ii) The euro:$ exchange rates used were provided by the OECD DAC for 1986-98: 0.9842; 1.1545; 1.1825; 1.1018; 1.2695; 1.2361; 1.2943; 1.1714; 1.1902; 1.3068; 1.2594; 1.1333; 1.1184.
iii) In converting the European Community regional categorisation to one that is consistent with DAC usage, the portion recorded as ACP unallocable within the EC programme has been added to the totals for sub-Saharan Africa, Other Asia & Oceania, and Latin America & the Caribbean in proportion to allocable aid to the EC regional categories of sub-Saharan Africa, the Caribbean and the Pacific.
iv) The portion which is unallocable is significantly higher when the DAC categorisation is used than in the rest of the report when the EC geographical categories are used. This is because DAC regions are not directly compatible with the EC regions on which the database is built.

Source: European Commission/ODI database 1999

Appendix 4

Recipients of EC External Cooperation Grouped by EC Region and by Level of Income

EC Region	Part I: Developing Countries and Territories (ODA)					Part II: Countries & Territories in Transition (OA)
	LLDCs	Other LICs	LMICs	UMICs	HICs	
Africa	Angola, Benin, Burkina Faso, Burundi, Cape Verde, Central African Republic, Chad, Comoros, Democratic Republic of Congo, Djibouti, Equatorial Guinea, Eritrea, Ethiopia, Gambia, Guinea, Guinea Bissau, Lesotho, Liberia, Madagascar, Malawi, Mali, Mauritania, Mozambique, Niger, Rwanda, Sao Tome, Sierra Leone, Somalia, Sudan, Tanzania, Togo, Uganda, Zambia	Cameroon, Côte d'Ivoire, Ghana, Kenya, Nigeria, Senegal, Zimbabwe, Congo Republic, Guyana	Botswana, Namibia, Swaziland	Gabon, Mauritius, Mayotte, Seychelles, South Africa (since 1997)		
Caribbean	Haiti		Belize, Dominica, Dominican Republic, Grenada, Jamaica, St Vincent-Grenadine, Suriname	Anguilla, Antigua and Barbuda, Barbados, Montserrat, St Helena, St Kitts Nevis, St Lucia, Trinidad and Tobago, Turks and Caicos Islands	Aruba, Netherlands Antilles, Virgin Islands	Bahamas, Cayman Islands,
Pacific	Kiribati, Solomon Islands, Tuvalu, Vanuatu, Western Samoa		Fiji, Papua New Guinea, Tonga, Wallis and Futuna		French Polynesia, New Caledonia	
Med & Middle East	Yemen		Iran, Iraq, Jordan, Lebanon, Palestinian Administered Areas, Syria, Algeria, Egypt, Morocco, Tunisia, Turkey	Bahrain, Oman, Saudi Arabia, Libya, Malta		Cyprus, Israel, Kuwait, Qatar, United Arab Emirates
Asia	Afghanistan, Bangladesh, Bhutan, Maldives, Nepal, Cambodia, Laos, Myanmar	China, India, Pakistan, Sri Lanka, Vietnam	Democratic Rep of Korea, Indonesia, Philippines, Thailand	Malaysia	Rep of Korea, Macao	Hong Kong (China), Chinese Taipei, Singapore
Latin America		Honduras, Nicaragua	Costa Rica, Cuba, El Salvador, Guatemala, Panama, Bolivia, Columbia, Ecuador, Paraguay, Peru, Venezuela	Mexico, Argentina, Brazil, Chile, Uruguay		
CEECs		Albania, Bosnia/Herzegovina	Federal Republic of Yugoslavia, Macedonia	Croatia, Slovenia		Bulgaria, Czech Republic, Estonia, Hungary, Latvia, Lithuania, Poland, Romania, Slovak Republic
NIS		Armenia, Azerbaijan, Georgia, Kyrgyzstan, Mongolia, Tajikistan	Kazakhstan, Moldova, Turkmenistan, Uzbekistan			Belarus, Russian Federation, Ukraine

Appendix 5

Major European Community External Cooperation Budget Lines
(arranged in descending order of size as at 1998, commitments in m euro)

Chapter	Post	Description
More than 500m euro		
B7-50	B7–5000, B7–5010, B7–5020, B7–5030	CEECs
B7-41	B7–4100	MEDA
100m – 500m euro		
B7-20	B7–2000, B7–2010, B7–2020, B7–2040	Food Aid
B7-21	B7–2100, B7–2120, B7–2140, B7–2150, B7–2170, B7–2190	Humanitarian Aid
B7-52	B7–5200, B7–5210	NIS
B7-30	B7–3000, B7–3010	Asia
B7-54	B7–5400, B7–5410, B7–5430, B7–5440, B7–5450	ex-Yugoslavia
B7-31	B7–3100, B7–3110, B7–3120	Latin America
B7-60	B7–6000, B7–6001, B7–6008	NGOs
B7-32	B7–3200, B7–3210	South Africa
50m – 100m euro		
B7-70	B7–7000, B7–7001, B7–7010, B7–7020, B7–7021, B7–7030, B7–7040, B7–7050, B7–7060, B7–7070, B7–7080, B7–7090	Democracy/ human rights
B7-42	B7–4200, B7–4210, B7–4220	Middle East
B7-62	B7–6200, B7–6201 (environment and tropical forests) B7–6210, B7–6211 (Drugs/ drug addiction and AIDS)	Environment/health
B7-53	B7–5310, B7–5340, B7–5350, B7–5360	Exceptional aid and nuclear security CEECs/NIS
Less than 50m euro		
B7-40	B7–4010, B7–4011, B7–4020, B7–4032, B7–4034, B7–4050, B7–4051	Mediterranean
B7-51	B7–5100	EBRD
B7-64	B7–6410 (Rehabilitation/ reconstruction) B7–6430 (Decentralised cooperation)	Specific actions
B7-66	B7–6600, B7–6601, B7–6602, B7–6610, B7–6620, B7–6630	Other specific actions
B7-87	B7-8700, B7-8710, B7-8720	External chapters: commerical relations
B7-81	B7–8100, B7–8110	External chapters: Environment
B7-63	B7–6310	Demography
B7-65	B7–6510, B7–6595	Evaluation
B7-61	B7–6100, B7–6110, B7–6140	Training
B7-82	B7–8200, B7–8210	External chapters: UN/FAO
B7-71	B7–7100	Other specific actions
B7-83	B7–8300	External chapters: Education
B7-84	B7–8400	External aspects of transport policy
B7-95	B7–9500	Support for external policies